Carlos Pires
10/28/06

THE MISSING GOSPELS

PRAISE FOR
THE MISSING GOSPELS

Darrell Bock has written a timely and valuable study for anyone curious about the question of lost or missing gospels. Cutting his way through a great deal of hype and misinformation, he provides a solid, scholarly grounding to the early history and development of the gospel traditions. In the process, he makes nonsense of theories that Gnostic texts in any sense represented the suppressed core of Christian truth, concealed by a sinister institutional church. A breath of sanity!

> — PHILIP JENKINS
> Professor of History and Religious
> Studies, Pennsylvania State
> University

This is not another lame Christian paperback whose chief purpose will be to steady a wobbly table. No! This is first-rate scholarship translated into clear, readable prose. It is classic Bock.

> — JAY SMITH
> Assistant Professor of New
> Testament Studies, Dallas
> Theological Seminary

A necessary book that corrects many still fashionable but even more questionable hypotheses about the origin of the Gospels, the Nag Hammadi texts, and the development of Christian theology in the first two centuries AD.

> — PROF. DR. MARTIN HENGEL
> Professor Emeritus of New
> Testament and Ancient Judaism,
> University of Tübingen, Germany

Every generation has its hawkers of wondrous new discoveries that amazingly everyone else has missed, but which, thanks to a few enlightened individuals, will dramatically rewrite history. But the vast majority of these headline-grabbing fancies evaporate under more sober scrutiny. Darrell Bock's careful book shows why recent sensationalist claims based on the Gnostic gospels are no different.

> — RIKK E. WATTS
> Associate Professor of New
> Testament Studies, Regent
> College, Vancouver, BC

Darrell Bock follows up here his informed critique of the recent frenzy about *The Da Vinci Code* with an equally informed and readable discussion of the variety of beliefs and writings of early Christianity. Those who don't want their prejudices disturbed will want to avoid this book. Those with an open mind and readiness to learn from scholarship . . . read with profit.

— LARRY HURTADO
Professor of New Testament
Language, Literature, and
Theology, University of
Edinburgh, Scotland

Jesus and the origins of Christianity are the subjects of extensive media coverage and everyday conversations—a New Testament scholar's dream! Yet Jesus is demoted from God to guide, and the early church is said to have been hopelessly divided, even confused, as to whom Jesus was. In his superb book, Darrell Bock patiently, and accessibly, sifts through all the relevant issues and offers much-needed guidance to those who want to discern fact from fiction. If you read only one book on this issue, this is it!

— ANDREAS J. KÖSTENBERGER, PhD
Editor, *Journal of the Evangelical Theological Society*, Professor of
New Testament and Greek,
Southeastern Baptist Theological
Seminary, Wake Forest, NC

Darrell Bock has produced a much needed antidote to the sensationalist claims made by those touting the discovery of "lost" gospels. He demolishes the frequently encountered argument that these Gnostic gospels represent the original Christianity and that orthodoxy is only a late development that suppressed earlier viewpoints. Bock's presentation is not a matter of faith against scholarship, but of better scholarship against inferior scholarship. In a nontechnical and accessible way, he provides solid evidence that reveals how inflated and ill-founded these current hypotheses are. This book deserves to be read widely and needs to be put in the hands of unsuspecting readers who are being hoodwinked by what some highly recognized scholars are saying.

— DONALD A. HAGNER
George Eldon Ladd Professor of
New Testament, Fuller Theological
Seminary, Pasadena, CA

Darrell Bock provides an informed and scholarly critique of the new perspective on Gnosticism and the recently discovered texts from Nag Hammadi. Although he rightly highlights the new scholarship's shortcomings, he also has the grace and wisdom to underscore the notable contributions that the new perspective has made to our understanding of early Christianity. Bock's insight into the relevant literatures from antiquity, moreover, is particularly well demonstrated by his claim that most of the "alternative texts" (e.g., the Nag Hammadi tractates) are less countercultural than "the traditional teaching" (e.g., the New Testament and early patristic writings); indeed, if the implications of that insight alone are given the attention they deserve, Bock's study could have a salutary impact not only on scholarly debate but also on contemporary Christian theology, ethics, and political practice.

— TODD KLUTZ
Senior Lecturer in New Testament
Studies, University of Manchester,
England

Who were the Gnostics, and what did they teach? And was second-century Christianity a mass of contradictory teachings, none of which can claim to truly represent the minds of Jesus and His first followers? Darrell Bock guides the reader clearly through the maze, providing a helpful summary of Gnostic theologies, arguing for the wide spread of the "orthodox" traditional teaching about Jesus, and showing that attempts to rubbish its claims to authenticity and to relativize its significance are not successful. Theological students, in particular, will be grateful for this careful assessment of early alternative forms of Christianity, based as it is on detailed assessment of the new sources that have come to light over the past half-century or so.

— I. HOWARD MARSHALL
Professor Emeritus in New
Testament, University of
Aberdeen, Scotland

A welcome alternative to sensational hype and fictional novels. Here is a clear and readable account on just what these "missing gospels" are and their real relationship to Christianity.

— CRAIG A. BLAISING
Executive Vice President and
Provost, Southwestern Baptist
Theological Seminary, Fort
Worth, TX

Darrell Bock is what theologians should be, accessible. This book tackles a complicated subject matter in an accessible way. The New Testament is simply summarized: Jesus calls us into an intimate union and relationship with Him; then Jesus sends us into the world. The world to which we are sent is different than the one that confronted our parents. With Postmodernism the dominant ideology, Dr. Phil the ever present counselor, Hollywood dabbling in theology and the occult, and Gnosticism making a comeback, we need to tread carefully and learn wisely. Bock's treatment of the texts found at Nag Hammadi, the Gnostic gospels, the claims of Walter Bauer and the "new school" of theological thought, and facts surrounding the sources of Christianity is fair, clear, thorough, and . . . accessible. Having read it, I am better equipped to engage a confused and drifting culture, and I'm protected against becoming a confused drifter myself.

— PETE BRISCOE
Senior Pastor, Bent Tree Bible
Fellowship, Dallas/Fort Worth, TX

In his *Breaking the Da Vinci Code*, Darrell Bock has already exposed the allegedly factual portion of that novel's story of Christian origins for the fiction it really is. But what *are* we to make of the various "Gnostic" Gospels that never "made it" into the Christian canon? Are there sound historical and theological reasons for judging them to be later, inferior, and even distorted versions of the original traditions emanating from Jesus? Or was it all a political power play so that "history" is just the perspective of the "winners"? In this volume, Bock answers all these questions, conclusively demonstrating the real nature of Gnostic "Christianity," which often doesn't even support the *avant-garde* convictions of its modern proponents the way they make it out to do. A must-read for anyone caught up in the debate!

— CRAIG L. BLOMBERG
Distinguished Professor of New
Testament, Denver Seminary

The Missing Gospels provides a meaty overview of the so-called "Gnostic" works, as compared with the real message of the earliest Christian writings. This volume will be a unique resource for those who wish to respond to the "new school" with accuracy and confidence.

— FREDERICA MATHEWES-GREEN
National Public Radio's *Morning
Edition* Commentator

Darrell Bock has provided an antidote to the misleading and sensationalist claims about alternative early Christianities. His work is informed, fair, and convincing and offers a good introduction to the literature and thinking of both traditional and alternative early Christianities. This work needs to be placed both in the hands of students and in the libraries of churches.

— KLYNE SNODGRASS
Paul W. Brandel Professor of New
Testament Studies, North Park
Theological Seminary, Chicago, IL

Darrell Bock's new book provides a much needed critical review of the non-New Testament gospels that have gained a great deal of attention in recent years. Although most of these writings and the dubious theories that go with them have received trenchant criticism in scholarly literature, no work has yet appeared that makes sense of all of this for the laity and beginning students of Bible and Christian origins. *The Missing Gospels* is just the book that has been needed. Here at last, non-experts have a reliable guide!

— CRAIG A. EVANS
Payzant Distinguished Professor,
Acadia Divinity College, Nova
Scotia, Canada

The challenge today to traditional orthodox belief as the center of the Christian message is not from the voices who contend that the Gospels are not reliable or that the Apostle Paul invented Christianity, but that the orthodox faith was but one voice in a virtual cacophony of voices—voices that differed on who Jesus was, what salvation was, and who God was. Bock's book patiently examines the resurgence of such voices, demonstrates that the evidence cannot support the modern resurgence, and offers in their place a supporting voice for the historical reliability of the orthodox faith as the faith once and for all delivered to the saints.

— SCOT MCKNIGHT
Karl A. Olsson Professor in
Religious Studies, North Park
University, Chicago, IL

THE MISSING GOSPELS

Unearthing the Truth Behind
Alternative Christianities

DARRELL L. BOCK, PHD

NELSON BOOKS
A Division of Thomas Nelson Publishers
Since 1798

www.thomasnelson.com

Published in Nashville, Tennessee, by Thomas Nelson, Inc.

Nelson Books titles may be purchased in bulk for educational, business, fund-raising, or sales promotional use. For information, please e-mail SpecialMarkets@ThomasNelson.com.

Scripture taken from the NET Bible®, copyright © 1996–2006 by Biblical Studies Press L.L.C. from http://www.bible.org. All rights reserved. Used by permission.

Maccabees quotations noted RSV are from the REVISED STANDARD VERSION of the Bible. Copyright © 1946, 1952, 1971, 1973 by the Division of Christian Education of the National Council of the Churches of Christ in the U.S.A. Used by permission.

Text quoted from *The Apostolic Fathers: Greek Texts and Translations*, ed. Michael Holmes, 1999, is used by permission of Baker Academic, a division of Baker Publishing Group.

Texts quoted from the Coptic Nag Hammadi Library are used with kind permission of Koninklijke Brill, originally published in *The Coptic Gnostic Library: A Complete Edition of the Nag Hammadi Codices*, Vol.1–5, edited by James M. Robinson.

Library of Congress Cataloging-in-Publication Data

Bock, Darrell L.
    The missing Gospels : unearthing the truth behind alternative Christianities / Darrell L. Bock.
      p. cm.
    Includes bibliographical references (p. 222).
    ISBN 0-7852-1294-9 (hardcover)
      1. Nag Hammadi codices—Theology. 2. Gnosticism—Relations—Christianity. 3. Christianity and other religions—Gnosticism. 4. Theology, Doctrinal—History—Early church, ca. 30–600. I. Title.
BT1391.B63 2006
270.1—dc22   2006001318

Printed in the United States of America

06 07 08 09 10 QW 5 4 3 2 1

An Invitation to You

The human intellect demands accuracy
while the soul craves meaning.
History ministers to both with stories.

— Joyce Appleby, Lynn Hunt, and Margaret Jacob
Telling the Truth About History
(New York: W. W. Norton, 1994), 262

Explorers of the past are never quite free. The past is their
tyrant. It forbids them to know anything which it has not
itself, consciously or otherwise, yielded to them.

— Marc Bloch
The Historian's Craft
(New York: Random House-Vintage Books, 1953), 59

Words are weapons, often the most dangerous
types of weapons . . .
In the end we assure ourselves, the truth will prevail.
But what about in the meantime?

— Conyers Read
at the Presidential Address for
the American Historical Society, 1949,
cited in *That Noble Dream* by Peter Noviak
(Cambridge: Cambridge University Press, 1998), 318

History springs from the human fascination with self-
discovery, from the persistent concern about the nature
of existence and people's engagement with it.

— Appleby, Hunt, and Jacob
Telling the Truth About History, 306

CONTENTS

CONTENTS

PREFACE

For more than ten years I have wanted to write this book for a popular audience. When I first encountered the work of Walter Bauer, the new school, and a host of new gospels, I was teaching doctoral courses in New Testament studies at Dallas Theological Seminary. His work struck me as intriguing and provocative. As works about the new gospels continued to pour forth for the religion sections at bookstores like Barnes and Noble and Borders, I decided at some point I would like to address the issues that the recovery of many new gospels raise. I would do this not primarily for those who study this material as a vocation, but for those who were hearing about it.

In the last decade, the ideas represented in these newly discovered materials, many of them coming out of "new" gospels, have shown up in religion sections of newspapers, magazine articles, and TV documentaries. Revolutionary kinds of questions about Christianity have been raised, aimed especially at nonspecialists. What was one to do with all of these missing and newly discovered texts, including the gospels that have such distinct portraits of Jesus? How radically have these texts changed or should they change our view of Christianity? I wanted to write a work that gave people a solid taste of this material and did not merely talk about pieces of it. I wanted to examine the hype about the mysteries surrounding the missing gospels. I also wanted to consider the accompanying claims that in this faith's earliest days all we had was a kaleidoscope of alternative Christianities and that there was no such thing as orthodoxy.

This meant producing a book that walks into the sometimes strange conceptual world of the first two centuries of what has been called the common era (CE) or what is more popularly known as AD 1–200. That was the time when Christianity was founded and explosively grew across the Greco-Roman world, transforming it and our history in the process. My goal is to introduce this new gospel material, along with the debate surrounding it, and compare it to material we have long possessed. I hope to solve the mystery of these formerly missing but now newly discovered gospels. I also pay attention to related works from the period. I hope to show and explain their relationship to Christianity as well as to alternative expressions of this faith.

The book is not always easy reading. These works treat the topic of Creation, the existence of an array of spiritual beings, and what makes humanity long for and seek after God against a foreign conceptual background. Nonetheless, I believe reading these new materials and understanding the debate about them will repay your effort and free you to make your own judgments about this material. At least that is my hope.

—DARRELL L. BOCK
Tübingen, Germany
August 1, 2005

ACKNOWLEDGMENTS

I need to thank several people who made this work possible. First of all, I thank my wife, Sally. She often saw me reading works like the *Hypostasis of the Archons*, one of my favorite titles for an ancient book, and one you will also read about here. Her support has been wonderful. She and her sister read through a draft to help make sure the discussion was accessible. I also want to thank the administration and New Testament department at Dallas Theological Seminary for a year's sabbatical in 2004–2005 so I could do final research and write this work. Special thanks go to Brooke Meyer, my administrative assistant, and Brittany Burnette, my research assistant in Dallas. My daughter, Elisa Laird, gave her editorial eye to a very rough initial draft, as did ministry colleagues Carl Anderson and Keith Heilman. My special thanks go to Ed Yamauchi for agreeing to write the Foreword and to Brian Hampton and Paula Major at Thomas Nelson for excellent editorial work.

My appreciation goes to the German government for granting me an Alexander von Humboldt Stiftung (scholarship) in support of my research at the University of Tübingen in Germany. The stay allowed me to appreciate how European scholarship handled the issues I write about, something I also have endeavored to indicate by noting key points in both English and German works. I also should thank the University at Tübingen and Professor Doctor Herman Lichtenberger, Frau Lehmann, and Frau Schuh, who took care of housing for Sally and me and made us feel so welcome. The postgraduate seminar at the university, hosted by Scott Caulley, allowed me to test some of my ideas in peer review. In particular, John Marshall became a constructive conversation partner on this topic even though he views matters very differently from the way I do.

Above all, I express my gratitude to Professor Doctor Martin Hengel and his wife, Frau Hengel. Their support over three sabbatical stays in Tübingen has made this our second home. His keen interest in this project and his exhortation to realize the importance of the second century for Christian history are precious gifts that will stay with Sally and me forever. This has been a *Zusammenarbeit* (a working together) in the best sense of that term. I dedicate this work to them, for their support represents what the collegial spirit of the Humboldt scholarship program is designed to foster—mutual engagement and cross-cultural communication for important topics of research in the sciences and humanities. The public square deserves to have access to the results of such work; it should not be the private domain of scholars.

FOREWORD

The phenomenal sale (forty million plus copies) of Dan Brown's novel *The Da Vinci Code* has aroused great public interest in the possibility that the (Catholic) Church has engaged in a conspiracy to conceal the "fact" that Jesus was married to Mary Magdalene, who Brown alleges was portrayed in Da Vinci's painting of the Last Supper. Brown claims that his thesis is based in part on the Gnostic Gospels, discovered at Nag Hammadi in Egypt in 1945. This allegation of a conspiracy theory has shaken the faith of not only a few Catholics, but also of uninformed Protestants. While Brown's mystery novel may be easily dismissed as fictional fantasy, as by Darrell L. Bock's *Breaking the Da Vinci Code* and several other refutations, the more serious challenges that Brown has raised about what Bart Ehrman has called "Lost Scriptures" and "Lost Christianities" must be addressed.

Some scholars assert that the selection of books in the New Testament was rather arbitrary and that the emergence of orthodox or "traditional" Christianity was based not on its merit but on the politics of the winning side. Now that we have additional gospels, which reveal as never before the beliefs of the Gnostics themselves, we are in a better position to judge and to choose what to believe and value about early Christianity.

This new way of looking at the foundations of Christianity

has been popularized by articulate and prolific scholars such as Elaine Pagels of Princeton University, Karen King of Harvard University, and Bart Ehrman of the University of North Carolina in highly readable books and on television specials on Mary Magdalene, *The Da Vinci Code*, and more.

While evangelicals are quite familiar with the New Testament, for the most part, they are not familiar with the apocryphal books that were not included in the Canon or with the development of early church history, in particular with the important heresy of Gnosticism.

Darrell L. Bock's study addresses all of these questions with comprehensiveness and lucidity, setting out the primary textual evidence, which has often been quoted selectively. He judiciously evaluates not only the new views but also helpfully contrasts them with the core "traditional" views that were developed out of the New Testament by successive generations of church fathers. Readers may thus judge for themselves the validity of the new claims for favoring Gnostic and other views, which were rejected by the early church as heretical, but which have recently become fashionable in our generation.

—Dr. Edwin M. Yamauchi
Professor of History
Miami University
Oxford, OH

INTRODUCTION

DO NEW DISCOVERIES MEAN CHRISTIANITY NEEDS A MAKEOVER?

New Discoveries at Nag Hammadi

This book is about the discovery of new documents, buzz, the writing of history for a popular audience, and an old faith. The year 2005 marked the sixtieth anniversary of one of the major discoveries of our time, a library of ancient texts found at Nag Hammadi in Egypt. This discovery has unleashed a host of popular works about how this library of fifty-two Coptic language texts should change the way we look at Jesus and Christianity because they included several "new" gospels and dialogue texts involving Jesus. Using catchy titles with such words as *alternative* or *lost* Christianities or *missing, secret, lost,* or *Gnostic* gospels, these modern works argue for a makeover of Christianity.

Here is the argument they make:

These documents, and others like them, show that all of us, from historians and theologians to believers, really have misunderstood the faith that has changed lives and inspired centuries of art and architecture and, yes, even war. The documents represent a historical exposé of our faith's origins and reveal the diversity of early Christian views. They open the possibility for new vistas and new ways of thinking about religion that breathe life into an old faith suffering a kind of religious arthritis. And the beauty of it all is that these new vistas are really the views of other ancients whose perspectives have been buried in sand for centuries.

These are the claims we shall examine.

THE BUZZ IN POPULAR RELIGIOUS WRITING THAT CALLS FOR A MAKEOVER OF CHRISTIANITY

These works involve professors from well-known universities, bringing into the public square what scholars and archaeologists claim to have known for a long time. No longer reserved for classes of a few dozen students in ancient religion, these new truths and their associated claims are now successfully being marketed to the masses. The claim from these writers is that this information can liberate you from an old, tiresome, constraining, and narrow faith. They claim that you can see the world afresh. Discoveries can be fun, even exhilarating. So, they ask, why not learn something new and join in the new world of religion?

What has this buzz and its reception been like? In 1979, Elaine Pagels of Princeton University published *The Gnostic Gospels*. Her work won the National Book Award and the National Book Critics Circle Award. On the book's back cover is this claim:

> . . . to illuminate the world of the first Christians and to examine the different ways in which both Gnostics and the ortho-dox constructed God, Christ, and the church. Did Jesus really rise from the dead? Was there only one God, and could He be both Father *and* Mother? Whose version of Christianity came

down to us and why did it prevail? Brilliant, provocative, and stunning in its implications, *The Gnostic Gospels* is a radical yet accessible reconsideration of the origins of the Christian faith.

In 2003, Bart Ehrman of the University of North Carolina published *Lost Christianities: The Battles for Scripture and the Faiths We Never Knew* with Oxford University Press. The inside jacket summary of the book reads as follows:

> The early Christian church was a chaos of contending beliefs. Some groups of Christians claimed that there was not one God but two or twelve or thirty. Some believed that the world had not been created by God but by a lesser, ignorant deity. Certain sects maintained that Jesus was human but not divine, while others said he was divine but not human. In *Lost Christianities*, Bart D. Ehrman offers a fascinating look at these early forms of Christianity and shows how they came to be suppressed, reformed, or forgotten . . . Modern archaeological work has recovered a number of key texts, and as Ehrman shows, these spectacular discoveries reveal religious diversity that says much about the ways in which history gets written by the winners.

In the same year, Pagels released a follow-up work on this topic, *Beyond Belief: The Secret Gospel of Thomas*. This *New York Times* bestseller highlighted the value of what others have called "The Fifth Gospel," a second-century work whose origins are obscure but claims to reflect 114 sayings of Jesus. This gospel has received the bulk of the attention since Nag Hammadi. On the inside jacket of *Beyond Belief* is an important claim about the origin of orthodox Christianity. Orthodoxy is called "emergent" in its earliest years because it was not yet clear that it was *the* Christian faith. So *Beyond Belief* argues this "emergent" faith outmaneuvered its opponents, namely, "To stabilize the emerging Christian church in times of devastating persecution, the church fathers constructed the canon, creed, and hierarchy—and in the process, suppressed many of its spiritual resources." So orthodox Christianity is really the product of a late second-century church father, Irenaeus, and those who followed him.

In 2005, Marvin Meyer, professor of Bible and Christian studies at Chapman University in California, published *The Gnostic Gospels of Jesus: The Definitive Collection of Mystical Gospels and Secret Books About Jesus of Nazareth*. The January–April 2005 catalog announcement reads, "These texts, especially when taken together, present an image of Jesus as the ultimate wisdom teacher, a kind of mysterious Jewish Zen master who scandalized listeners by his radical egalitarianism, regarding women, slaves, the poor, the marginalized as having equal status and by his insistence on truly living the message." Meyer is introduced as "the expert whom Dr. Elaine Pagels herself regards as the master of the original texts." The new vision of Jesus involves a teacher of wisdom that not only spans the continents and religion but also has a full social agenda; Jesus can be our guide, but he is not our God.

The hype over Nag Hammadi is not isolated to scholars. We can look to articles in magazines like *Time* and *Newsweek*. Hardly a Christmas or Easter season goes by without such an article, and within many of those pieces "not a discouraging word" about the new ideas is even raised. I know. I was interviewed and so were other disagreeing colleagues for one of these recent December pieces. Not one of the counterpoints from any of the dissenters made it into the article. Balanced journalism has also lost its way in this new wave. These many works are no accident. There is a concerted effort to change our history and the way we look at our religious and cultural roots.

Works of fiction play on such ideas. Dan Brown's widely read *The Da Vinci Code* alluded heavily to such theories in weaving the "historical" skeleton for his novel. Brown claimed in public interviews that this skeleton reflected the scholars' new view of history. He argued that the historical roots of his novel needed public discussion. Brown was right. A closer look at such theories is needed.

THIS BOOK: A FRESH LOOK AT THE BUZZ

There is a concerted effort to persuade every layer of our culture that there is new wine (new historical truth) present that requires new wineskins (a new view) for Christianity and the culture influenced by it. Some questions, however, should accompany such rhetoric. Is this buzz the thin veneer of a glitzy PR blitz that has captured our culture as avant-garde (Henry 1992)? Have these claims connected not because their portrait of history is cutting edge and fundamentally accurate but because they successfully yet anachronistically have tapped into the spirit of our twenty-first-century culture? Is there truth in such claims or even *some* truth in them? Our goal is to answer such questions by examining the range of teaching in these newly touted texts, not to cull out what fits nicely with our culture. In addition, we will work through the debate that these texts have engendered to sense whether a case exists for a historical makeover of early Christianity.

In short, this is a comprehensive look at the key texts that have helped or could help to define what Christianity was and is. My role will be that of a tour guide: to set enough context to help you understand the works.

The Book's Outline

To set the stage for our examination, we will review the current discussion. In the few chapters on the modern period, we have to consider where this "new" perspective came from and what caused it. In the historical overview (Chapters 2–5), I will name key scholars and summarize their work. Most of them will not be familiar names, but they have driven the debate. As your tour guide, I will point out the arguments on each side and offer commentary, assessing what has taken place.

Many strange names appear in the key ancient evidence: Gnostics, Judaizers, Docetists, Valentinians, and Marcionites. There are also key figures: Jesus, Paul, Peter, John, Clement of Rome, Justin Martyr, Marcion, Valentinus, Ignatius, Polycarp, Irenaeus, Tertullian, and Hippolytus. For such figures, you might need a scorecard to keep up with them. So I begin with a chronological outline of where these works fit.

I shall also have to discuss historical method, the modern debates about this history, and the studies, ideas, and arguments that fuel this debate. I leave a "paper trail" in the parenthetical notes, so you can go further and read the detailed discussions firsthand, making your own assessments. I will give special attention to the movement often called Gnosticism because as the classical scholar A. D. Nock noted, it is "the central issue today in the study of early Christianity" (Stewart 1972, 2:940). That this is so for the first two centuries will become clear in our early chapters. After we map out the ancient and modern territories, we look at specific passages to assess what they actually taught in certain key areas, putting you in a position to make your own call about these texts.

This study concentrates on the period before Irenaeus, that controversial church father of the late second century. The new school claims that Irenaeus "won" and was the key architect of orthodoxy. The claim is that this orthodoxy (or the claim of a defined, legitimate Christianity) emerged even more clearly in the third and fourth centuries. So the new school argues that the Christianity we know has roots that do not really go back to the time of Jesus or even to the apostles in a way that precludes other alternative views of Christianity.

There is no doubt that Irenaeus is a major figure for the church, but it is possible to see what Christianity, including orthodox Christianity, looked like before him. Throughout this book, all the passages we examine from the "orthodox" side precede Irenaeus and his supposed organization of themes for the orthodox view. By looking at the texts, we can test the claims of the two views. Was orthodoxy something that emerged out of the earliest period (the traditional view)? Or were there merely competing and alternative Christianities with no real orthodoxy present in that early period (the alternative or new school view)?

The missing gospel texts and other types of works closely related to them receive special attention. These include key gospels: *of Thomas, of Philip, of the Savior, of Truth,* and *of Mary Magdalene.* They also include other significant works tied to the alternative tradition(s): *Apocryphon of John, Dialogue of the Savior,* and *Apocryphon of James.*

For comparative purposes, the following topics are examined: (1) God and creation, (2) the person of Jesus as human and divine, (3) the saving of man (spirit, soul, and/or body), and (4) the point of Jesus' life and death. In each case, the contents of the missing gospels on these themes are presented alongside the better-known texts of Christianity. We will explore whether there are lines of connection to see which views are tied to the oldest texts or traditions.

Let's examine the debate. Where do these texts fit into the early church's history? That is Chapter 1. Chapters 2 through 5 discuss the modern debate. Then we look at the texts and topics in Chapters 6 through 13, the book's core. Read on, and unearth what the missing gospels—and the buzz about alternative Christianities—are all about.

• ONE •

MAKING A SCORECARD:
THE PERIODS AND PLAYERS
OF EARLY CHRISTIANITY

This chapter assumes you have little or no knowledge of early Christianity, especially the time period of the second and third centuries. Here, I introduce the three periods of early Christianity, noting the Jewish origins from which Christianity arose—the apostolic period, the period of the apostolic fathers and the rise of alternative texts, and the period of the apologists and more alternatives.

CHRISTIANITY AND THE PROMISE OF ISRAEL'S GOD

The starting point for early Christianity was as a Jewish movement that appealed to the promise of God in the Scripture of Israel. In the beginning, there were Jesus and the apostles, claiming Jesus Christ fulfilled God's promise.

All the writings we have from the works of the first century to the works of the apologists show an intense concern, whether positive or negative, with issues raised by the Scripture of the Jews (Mitros 1968, 448–50). The apologists were defenders of Christianity against Greco-Roman religion, Judaism, and threatening movements that also claimed the name of Christ.

Their work emerged in the mid-second century and continued to discuss how Jesus fulfilled the original Jewish promise.

Scholars debate when the promise was first uttered. Was it found in Genesis 3:15 when God said the seed of man would crush the head of the serpent? Was it in Genesis 12:1–3, in His promise that the seed of Abraham would be a source of blessing to all the world? Was it in texts like Isaiah 9, where a messianic-delivering figure is described? Was it in Daniel 7:13–14, where the Son of man rides the clouds with divine authority? Was it in a composite of all of these? In the first century, was there one unified expectation, or was there a promise described in diverse ways with diverse forms of expectation in Judaism?

For us, the key fact is that in the first century, most Jews had some form of hope that one day God would send a deliverer for His people and for the world, even though these Jews saw the fulfillment of that promise in differing detail or highlighted in different texts. That large parts of Israel's faith were driven by such a promise in the first century is one of the few things about which virtually all scholars agree. This root in scriptural hope is the seed of Christian faith. God would send a deliverer one day according to the promise of the Hebrew Scripture.

Much of Christianity in the first two centuries claims that Jesus was and is the fulfillment of that promise. This root in the Scripture of Israel—its promise and its portrait of God—is part of what became a source of contention when Marcion in the mid-second century rejected the God of Israel as identified with the God that Christians worship. It also became a point of contention when others calling themselves Christians—but whom many scholars today call Gnostics—suggested that the God who created the Earth and the true transcendent God were not the same figure. But we are jumping ahead in our story.

As we shall see in Chapter 4, some today argue that the

roots of Christianity are not found in this promise of deliverance because Jesus was merely about wisdom and pointing to a way of life pleasing to God. It was the later church, some say—not Jesus—that transformed this wise teacher into a figure of worship, promise, and divinity. Strangely enough, in many ways, the core of the modern debate about Christianity is centered on how connected the earliest Christianity was to the theology of Judaism, God's promise, and Israel's portrait of God. We shall keep an eye on this connection since it is a central piece to our puzzle.

THE PERIODS OF EARLY CHRISTIANITY: PUTTING THE NEWLY DISCOVERED GOSPELS IN CONTEXT

These periods are standard in early church history, but the new school claims these categories obscure the real diversity of the earliest forms of Christianity. The claim is, if you make the rules and define the categories the way you want, you get to win the game before it starts. Because the issue of Christianity's roots is in question, you should note that the descriptions presented here are *not* claims that these divisions reflect the full picture of what was taking place in the first two centuries of Christianity. These descriptions can obscure the diversity that was at work in the early centuries of Christianity. The divisions used here merely provide a time structure for these lesser-known figures and movements of early Christian history, showing where and when people fit in our historical tour.

Period 1: Jesus and the Apostolic Period
This first period covers roughly the last seventy years of the first century. It is generally acknowledged that Jesus ministered

in the late twenties or early thirties of the first century. Those who were closest to Him, the apostles, ministered throughout the first century. That period is called the apostolic era. Although scholars debate the exact dates of the composition of the four Gospels and those of the newly discovered gospels, there is widespread acceptance that the gospels of Matthew, Mark, Luke, and John fit into this period with John, written in the nineties, being the last of the four.

We have little explicit evidence for alternative groups from this early period. We lack materials directly from these groups, with the possible exception of the *Gospel of Thomas,* but we have hints of opposition and dissent from the traditional materials of the first century. To reconstruct the dissent, let's look at a few brief remarks in those traditional texts.

One alleged leader of an alternative movement from this period is Simon Magus. The church fathers I shall mention shortly tend to lay the entire blame at his feet for the movements that they contest. Simon Magus is noted in Acts 8, where he is described as a magician. Acts has no remarks about him founding a heretical movement. The source of this claim is unknown, and the credibility of the claim that heresy originated with Simon is very problematic (Yamauchi 1983, 60). Beyschlag's detailed study (1974, 218) places the rise of this tradition about Simon as the father of heresy in the first half of the second century.

Another set of opponents surfaces in 1 Timothy 1:20. Here Hymenaeus and Alexander "shipwrecked" their faith. In 1 Timothy 1:3–7, they are included in a discussion of people teaching a different doctrine that includes myths and endless genealogies, promoting speculation rather than faith. First Timothy 4:1–3 warns of those in the last days who will teach against marriage. Some later Gnostic movements did teach against marriage, but so did some traditional movements, reflecting a concern by some with spiritual interests about sexuality. In 2 Timothy 2:17–18, Hymenaeus is mentioned again with Philetus as teaching that the decisive resurrection of believers has already occurred. What these epistles describe as a different doctrine many regard as potentially similar to things that appear in even more detail in some of the newly discovered works that have been called Gnostic. This is all we can say from the earliest material, which is not very much (Hengel 1997, 190–92). In other words, these remarks do not evidence the presence of Gnosticism, but the presence of elements that showed up later in Gnosticism. At best, they reflect what has been called *incipient Gnosticism.*

What do appear in our earliest sources are ideas that the writers of the Epistles challenged rather than named. For example, 1 Corinthians 15 (written mid-fifties) indicates that some denied a resurrection from the dead for the body. Scholars debate whether the views Paul challenged were a reflection of some type of Gnostic denial of the resurrection of the flesh or simply a reflection of the general Greco-Roman belief that denied a physical life after death. First John (written early nineties) shows that some did not believe Jesus came in the flesh. People who divided between a sent Christ and a physical Jesus are called *docetists* because they believed that Jesus only "appeared" to be in the flesh.

Passages like these let us know that there was diversity in early belief. The questions they raise include these: How was this diversity perceived? Did diversity reflect competing orthodoxies, mere alternatives, or the naming of the presence of a heretical view? And on what basis was such a judgment to be made? Was it on politically competing points of view where one side simply won? Or were there appeals to teaching that could credibly claim to have association with Jesus or the apostles? These questions will drive our tour.

Where the newly discovered gospels fit. Dating is one key issue tied to the newly discovered gospels. Most of the gospels we have recently discovered are dated in the second or third century (see suggested dates in the following: Rebell 1992; Ehrman 2003; Klauck 2003; Lapham 2003; White 2004). But a few, such as the *Gospel of Thomas,* are sometimes placed earlier, in the apostolic period or with roots that may go back to that period. This is why some have talked about the importance of this gospel. For example, White (2004, 304) argues that the earliest layers of *Thomas* date from 60–70 with roots in some material that goes back to Jesus, while later layers are from the late first or early second century. Ehrman (2003, xii) places it in the early second century but with parts that may go back to Jesus. On the other hand, Klauck (2003, 108) dates the work outside this period, between 120 and 140. Snodgrass (1989–90) argues that there is much evidence of dependence of *Thomas* on Luke and the synoptic tradition, for several of *Thomas*'s sayings appeal to rarely used words and editorial tendencies in these other works (sayings 10, 16, 31, 33, 39, 47, 53, 65–66, 72, 76*b*, 79, 104). Perrin (2002) sees a relationship between Tatian's *Diatessaron* from circa AD 170 and *Thomas.* This suggests the gospel has roots in a late tradition, not an early one. Hedrick (1989–90) has shown it is likely that some material for *Thomas* comes from sources other than the synoptic Gospels, so the material has to be assessed one saying at a time. In sum, it is possible that a portion of the material in *Thomas* reflects tradition circulating among the churches that could belong to this early period, but these must be examined on a saying-by-saying basis (Klauck 2003, 108). Nevertheless, the gospel itself is likely later rather than earlier.

The sayings that parallel those in Matthew, Mark, and Luke help us see the later date for *Thomas.* Klauck (2003, 108) notes that roughly 50 percent of *Thomas* has no contact with anything expressed in the New Testament. In his view, the other half is split between texts that resemble things in Matthew, Mark, and Luke and independent sayings that claim to be revelatory and have a "more strongly gnostic character" (Klauck 2003, 108). The debate about *Thomas* includes what and how much of this material goes back to Jesus and how much of it is a reflection of later Gnostic concerns. Most of *Thomas* does not go back to Jesus, but a few pieces could.

The debate has a few other keys. So we cover the age of Gnosticism in Chapter 3. *Thomas* and the Jesus tradition receive attention in Chapter 4. Making headway on these topics requires treating another issue, historical method and judgment, also considered in Chapter 4.

A review of the newly discovered material, including the missing gospels, indicates that the bulk of it comes from the second and third centuries. On this, almost all scholars are agreed. Three corollaries tied to this fact are important:

1. Many of these works reflect the period in which they were written and have no coherent links to the period to which their title points. The issues these works discuss appear later in the history of the church and not in the earliest period. This is one way we can see that these works are later than the earliest period. For example, the *Gospel of Peter* is not from Peter nor does it give teaching preserved by those familiar with his teaching; it is simply a name given to lend authority to a work written much later. Almost every scholar agrees with this view of this gospel. This situation stands in contrast to Mark or Luke in that neither writer of these gospels was an apostle, yet many accept that Mark and Luke had access to the apostles and were aware of what they taught. For Mark, the contact point was Peter (Taylor 1966, 1–8, 26), while Luke likely had contact with several of the apostles and traveled with Paul (Fitzmyer 1981, 40). Roots of portions of other gospels, like *Thomas*, are more debated

and difficult to assess. A question exists whether *Thomas* has early roots.

Newly discovered but later works still have value for us as historical documents. They describe what some people associating themselves with Christianity believed at the time these documents circulated, even though these texts have little value in illuminating the earliest Christianity. Nag Hammadi is an important find even if it contains documents whose dates of composition are post–first century. We learn what was going on in this later period from people who held these alternative views. Diversity of views existed among groups associating themselves with Christianity in the apostolic period as the disputes already noted in 1 and 2 Timothy show. The debates are about what those views were, how widespread they were, and whether these alternatives were regarded as orthodox or not.

2. We possess only a portion of the writings that existed in the first century. The nature of all historical records is that the surviving collection is partial, and this is especially true of ancient history. The problem is what to make of this lack of evidence. This gap creates room for debate and contributes to the existence of various modern views on the question.

3. This leads to the subtlety of a third corollary sometimes offered for the late nature of these materials in the extant manuscript record—the claims that these texts were suppressed and/or destroyed. We lack such texts because the other side removed them from the scene long ago, so the evidence we have does not really reflect what was. Now we know such suppression and destruction took place in the third century and beyond. We also know it happened with all kinds of Christian texts during the persecutions of Christians in the earliest centuries. Nevertheless, this position is really an argument from silence. The claim is that if we had a fully documented record, surely early or more materials like these alternative gospels

would exist. There is no way to evaluate such a hypothetical claim. Proponents of this scenario hold that it is remarkable anything like *Thomas* has survived while they also acknowledge it is unlikely that this work comes from the apostle Thomas.

But what about a couple of other options? Might we lack such materials because they were simply lost, as most ancient works are, rather than suppressed? Or might we have no clear early record of such movements because they did not yet exist? The problem is that any of these three scenarios (loss by suppression, simple loss, or absence because such movements did not yet exist) can explain the evidence we have. The presence of various potentially plausible options also leads to the debate. An overview of the issues surrounding the missing gospels is necessary before looking at the gospels themselves so we can understand where they fit and why there is controversy about them.

Period 2: The Apostolic Fathers and the Rise of Alternative Works

This period covers a few generations after the apostles. The apostolic fathers were men who had contact with the apostles or fit in the period just after them. Generally speaking, their works belong in the first half of the second century (Holmes 1999). They include the Letter of Clement of Rome, known as *1 Clement*, written at the end of the first century; *2 Clement* (a sermon, not by the same Clement but by an unknown preacher); the seven letters of Ignatius, bishop of Antioch in Syria (*Ephesians, Magnesians, Trallians, Romans, Philadelphians, Smyrneans,* and *To Polycarp*); one letter from Polycarp, bishop of Smyrna in Asia Minor, to the Philippians; the *Martyrdom of Polycarp*; an ethical tract known as *Didache*; the letter of *Barnabas* (but not the apostle of the New Testament; also called *Pseudo Barnabas*); the *Shepherd of Hermas*, a collection of parables and visions; the *Epistle of Diogenes*; and the *Fragments of Papias*, mostly preserved for us by the fourth-century church historian Eusebius. We will pay careful attention to these works because they tell us what many Christians believed in the early second century.

Alongside the works of the apostolic fathers come other works in this period. Many reflect alternative views. At it's latest possible dating, *Thomas* belongs in the early to mid-second century. Among the most widespread alternative forms of Christianity belonging to the explicit textual evidence from this period is what modern scholars have called Gnosticism. It took on a variety of forms, as we shall see in Chapter 3. Here belong names like Carpocrates (appears ca. 120), Saturninus (ca. 120), Basilides (ca. 120), and Valentinus (ca. 140). Other alternatives also existed, such as the movement founded by Marcion (ca. 140), who died in 160. His movement was distinct from those seen as Gnostic. Key sources of this period include *Gospel of Peter, Gospel of the Hebrews, Gospel of the Ebionites, Gospel of the Egyptians, Gospel of the Nazareans, Infancy Gospel of Thomas,* and *Papyrus Egerton 2* (Ehrman 2003, xi–xii). Chapters 6 to 13 will give us a glimpse of what such sources teach and where they fit in more detail.

Period 3: The Apologists and More Alternatives

This period moves beyond the time frame our tour shall consider. It covers the mid-second century into the period of the formation of the church creeds like Nicaea in 325 and beyond. It has been adequately covered in works for a long time, with a classic study being that of Hilgenfeld on the history of heresy in early Christianity. Hilgenfeld traces the evidence we have from the church fathers, especially from Justin Martyr, Irenaeus, and Hippolytus with his contemporaries, Tertullian and Clement of Alexandria (Hilgenfeld 1884). We stop with the mention of

Epiphanius in the fourth century because he wrote an encyclopedic work on heresy, known as the *Medicine Chest* (*Panarion*). However, one key figure predates Irenaeus and sits at the edge between periods two and three. He is Justin Martyr, who was the first early church writer to take up explicitly a comprehensive defense of the faith. We place him here because his work came in this period. Justin wrote what is called his *1 Apology* circa 155. It was one of two apologies (or defenses of the faith) he wrote. He also debated Judaism in the work *Against Trypho*.

A work of defense in Greek is called an *apology*. One who writes such a defense is an apologist. This explains part of the name of this grouping. (It does not mean the writers are sorry or apologizing for anything as the word *apology* in English can suggest.) Apologists spent their time making the case that Christianity was superior to paganism, Judaism, or Greek philosophy. However, they also challenged the claims of some associating themselves with Christianity to be genuine or orthodox Christians. The new school often calls this group of writers *heresiologists* because they sought to identify and refute heresy.

The presence of alternatives already clearly emerging in the period of the apostolic fathers concerned the apologists. Yet other movements existed during this period: Ebionites (a Jewish-Christian movement), Encratites (an ascetic movement that advocated chastity and no marriage), and Montanists (a group claiming to have access to new revelation).

This proliferation of alternatives caused the apologists to write detailed assessments of these movements, showing that the name *heresiologist* reflects the thrust of their work. These writings developed full arguments that formed what became the details of orthodox faith. Other famous apologists followed Justin Martyr. Among the most prominent are Irenaeus (writing in the second half of the second century) and Tertullian (late second and early third centuries), followed in importance by the group of

Clement of Alexandria (last third of the second century), Origen (early third century), and Hippolytus (very late second and early third centuries). Later apologists of significance include Eusebius (third and fourth centuries) and Epiphanius (fourth century). The issue here is whether "orthodoxy" emerged in these later writings or was already present in root form earlier. Was it Irenaeus and those like him who produced orthodoxy, as the new school claims, or was it orthodoxy that produced Irenaeus and the apologists?

Summary of the Periods

The ancient players and movements fit into three basic periods. The scorecard, summarized in the charts provided here, includes likely geographical regions where we know them [for a similar chart of the last two periods, see Smith (2004, 124)]. Geography will become important later in our tour. The scorecard includes dates for the apologists. The lists in each of these three periods have no intended order.

AD 30–100
Apostolic Period

Jesus (Judea, Galilee)	Matthew	Simon Magus (Samaria)	Clement of Rome
Peter (Jerusalem, Galilee, Antioch, Galatia, Rome)	Mark	Hymenaeus (Ephesus)	Docetists
John (Asia Minor, Ephesus)	Luke	Alexander (Ephesus)	Gnostics?
Paul (Antioch, Asia Minor, Greece, Rome)	Hebrews	Philetus (Ephesus)	Encratites?
James (Jerusalem)	1 Peter	*Gospel of Thomas?* (i.e., date uncertain)	
Q (shared church source of Jesus' teaching; Matthew and Luke likely used)	1 John	*1 Clement*	

AD 100–150
Period of the Apostolic Fathers and the Rise of Alternative Works

Clement of Rome (a bridge between the periods)	Gospel of Thomas (period of date held by most scholars)	Gospel of the Egyptians
2 Clement	Carpocrates (Alexandria in Egypt)	Gospel of the Nazareans
Ignatius (Antioch)	Saturninus (Antioch in Syria)	Infancy Gospel of Thomas
Polycarp (Smyrna in Asia Minor)	Basilides (Alexandria in Egypt)	Gospel of Mary Magdalene?
Didache	Marcion (Sinope in Pontus of Asia Minor, Rome)	Papyrus Egerton 2
(Pseudo) Barnabas	Valentinus (Alexandria of Egypt, Rome)	Gnostics
Shepherd of Hermas	Gospel of Peter	Encratites
Diognetus	Gospel of the Hebrews	
Papias	Gospel of the Ebionites	

AD 150–400
Period of the Apologists and More Alternatives

Justin Martyr (100–165; Samaria, Asia Minor, Rome)	Eusebius (260–340; Caesarea)	Tripartite Tractate	Apocryphon of James	Teachings of Silvanus
Irenaeus (130–200; Lyon)	Epiphanius (315–403; Palestine, Egypt, Salamis)	Pistis Sophia	Interpretation of Knowledge	Gnostics
Hippolytus (170–235; Rome)	Gospel of Philip	Sophia of Jesus Christ	Apocalypse of Peter	Theodotus
Tertullian (155–220; Carthage)	Gospel of Mary Magdalene	Gospel of Truth	Dialogue of the Savior	Ebionites
Clement (150–215; Alexandria)	Gospel of the Savior	Gospel of Bartholomew	Hypostasis of the Archons	Encratites
Origen (185–254; Alexandria, Caesarea)	Letter to Rheginos (= Treatise on the Resurrection)	Apocryphon of John	Second Treatise of the Great Seth	Montanists

This overview shows that some significant claims of the new school do reflect history. They include (1) evidence for a diversity of views claiming the name Christian in the early centuries, (2) the fact that our sources reflect only partially what was available from the early period, and (3) the suggestion that the new discoveries have helped us be more careful about how we view this history.

But are the new school's most important claims historical? Several ancient factors contribute to the modern debate: (1) the difference between when a work is written and the age of the views that work reflects (Could it incorporate older tradition, and if so, where did that come from?), (2) the significance of the incomplete nature of our collection of sources, as well as (3) the nature of the content of the works themselves and what they teach, including the range of what they taught. Most important, what evidence is there for the connection of the teaching in any of these works to the earliest era?

Before we leave this orientation to the ancient context, we must discuss the major alternative present in so many of our new sources, namely, Gnosticism.

STUDY QUESTIONS

1) *What does the new school argue?*

2) *What role does Irenaeus play according to the new school, and why concentrate on texts before Irenaeus to study this historical issue?*

3) *What role did Israel's promise play in the development of Christianity?*

4) *What are the three periods of early Christian history, and what allows them to be distinguished from each other?*

5) *What claims of the new school have merit, and what ancient factors turn the discussion into a debate?*

· TWO ·

DISCUSSION OF A KEY ALTERNATIVE VIEW: ABOUT GNOSTICISM AND ITS DEFINITION

The second question of background involves the most important alternative Christian expression in the second century: Gnosticism. This movement is complex and subject to much recent historical debate. How should one define this movement, given the variety of views associated with it and the debate over its date of origin? Does it go back to the first century? This discussion will also raise initial questions about the similarities and differences between Gnosticism and Christianity based on both movements' origins.

THOSE IN THE KNOW: ON THE TERM *GNOSTICISM* AND THE PROBLEMS ASSOCIATED WITH THE TERM

At the most basic level, the terms *Gnostic* and *Gnosticism* refer to a belief that is rooted in special knowledge. Those in the know are called Gnostics. The term *Gnosticism* is not ancient. The Protestant Henry More coined the term in 1669 as a polemical name for heresy. More used it to complain about Catholic theology (Layton 1995, 348–49). It is likely the name came from Irenaeus's complaint circa AD 180 about the views he was writing against in his work known as *Against Heresies*. This work also had the title of *Exposé and Overthrow of What Is Falsely Called "Knowledge."* A Greek word for knowledge is *gnosis*. Gnosticism in its broadest sense is about a religious view based on a claim about knowledge.

Indeed, the Greek term for knowledge (*gnosis*) was widely used in a positive and a negative sense in the first century. For example, 1 Corinthians 8:1 uses the word positively and negatively in the same verse. There Paul says, "We know that 'we all have knowledge.' Knowledge puffs up, but love builds up." So knowledge is something possessed by those who claim to know Jesus, but the danger is that knowledge will lead to arrogance.

Nock, in his solid article "Gnosticism," shows the variety of this general usage for knowledge in the first two centuries (Stewart 1972, 2:944–45). This general use of the term was applied to all types of religious experiences and claims. Then Gnosticism developed a more technical, historical use, applied by both secular and church historians to the views that Irenaeus and others challenged. But a specific definition of this ancient Gnosticism was not developed to the satisfaction of scholars. The problem became so great that a famous conference in 1966 in Messina gathered experts to try to reach an agreed upon definition, but the attempt failed. In 1996 Michael Williams wrote a book published by Princeton University Press called *Rethinking "Gnosticism": An Argument for Dismantling a Dubious Category.*

The first issue was the wide variety of views within the ancient works called *Gnostic*. It has been difficult to pin down the features that make a work Gnostic and the features that make it simply something different from what we know today as orthodox Christianity but not necessarily Gnostic.

A second problem was that Gnosticism became a catchword, almost a slogan, for calling something heretical, so specifying what it might apply to was important. In the view of some, doing this stains the term. At least that is the argument of Karen King from Harvard in her *What Is Gnosticism?* (King 2003a, 7). She writes, "Gnosticism as a category served several important intellectual aims, defining the boundaries of normative Christianity—especially with reference to Judaism—and aiding colonialism by contrasting Gnosticism as an Oriental heresy with authentic Western religion. Moreover, it offered a single category to refer to a vast range of ideas, literary works, individuals, and groups."

A third problem was the new finds at Nag Hammadi. Those works were seen to fit into this category (whatever Gnosticism might be exactly) but displayed a significant difference among themselves. Not only that, but there were other works in the collection that did not fit into existing definitions.

King prefers to neutralize the comparative discussion and suggests the term's inadequacy. She says it this way: "the variety of phenomena classified as 'Gnostic' simply will not support a single, monolithic definition, and in fact, *none of the primary materials fits the standard typological definition*" (King 2003a, 226, emphasis hers).

By a "typological definition," King refers to a description of Gnosticism that names several common or typical traits within such works that identify them as Gnostic. The key here is identifying traits that are widely enough distributed throughout the various texts to indicate Gnosticism's presence. There also is the issue of determining how many of these traits are needed to point to its presence.

Most current definitions of Gnosticism either claim that there is one main trait or that a few of them are necessary. Other scholars argue that any work that has several of a list of five to eleven features counts. King's argument is that we simply need to realize that a single label does not fit the variety of views extant within Christianity, and so it is misleading to make any connection between these varieties. Again King summarizes, "Because none of the texts contains all the listed characteristics, typological phenomenology [or definition by a listing of traits] raises the question of how many elements of the ideal type any particular case has to evince in order to qualify as an example of Gnosticism" (King 2003a, 226, bracketed explanation mine).

This claim so focuses on the varieties among these texts that it obscures the fact that these texts reflect a set of religious ideas within the same family of concerns. While King asks what single characteristic counts to make a work Gnostic and argues, probably correctly, that there is no single, "magical" trait that guarantees a Gnostic presence, most working in the area argue that the issue is not which one thing counts, but what does the whole work reflect? Does a given work use several of the possible traits of evidence for a "Gnostic" view? Most scholars argue that Gnostic works share a common general outlook on the world that we can describe and define.

A DEFINITION OF *GNOSTICISM*

In order to understand the alternative gospels cited in the coming chapters, let's survey the characteristics that suggest a work is Gnostic. An expert in the field offers us a useful definition.

Kurt Rudolph

Kurt Rudolph was professor of the history of religion at the University of Marburg, Germany. He is widely acknowledged as a leading student of this period. His list has five traits (Rudolph 1983, 57–59).

1. Dualism comes first. Dualism means that there is both in the creation and in man a mix of good and evil that is distinguishable even as the two qualities exist side by side. Included in this dualism usually is the distinction between the good and largely transcendent unknowable God and the God who created the world. The knowable God who is a projection into the creation is the Creator, while the unknowable God is over everything but is too transcendent to be directly involved with the creation. The true God and the Creator God of Genesis are not the same being.

2. Next there is cosmogony. Here in the creation, there is a contrast of spheres, often called light versus darkness, soul and/or spirit versus matter and/or flesh, and knowledge versus ignorance or forgetfulness. Point one addressed dualism in God; here it is dualism in the creation. On the one hand, light, soul, spirit, and knowledge represent what is good; on the other, darkness, matter, flesh, and ignorance or forgetfulness reflect evil. So evil was in the creation from the start. The positive features in man are often characterized as a "divine spark" within him. Thus, the cosmogony is dualistic. Some scholars use a shorthand description of this creation and call it "anti-cosmic dualism," which rejects the physical material world as evil and inferior.

3. Soteriology (or salvation) is next. Salvation and redemption are understood primarily in terms of knowledge about creation's dualistic nature. Salvation of the nonmaterial spirit or soul within a person is what matters, not a salvation of the creation or of the flesh. In fact, the flesh is not redeemable. There is no resurrection of the body from the dead.

4. Eschatology (or the teaching about the last things) means that one understands where existence is headed, namely, the redemption of the soul and the recovery of the creation into the "fullness" or "pleroma" that is where good dwells. What matters is that one (*a*) understands the value of the spiritual

above other elements of existence, (*b*) establishes a sense of connection with the spiritual, and (*c*) has a sense of separateness from the evil physical world of matter and flesh.

5. Although we know little about this area, there are the cult and the community, that is, the worship and the people who nurtured such views. This involves their rites of worship, for we know that they had practices beyond baptism. Rudolph fills out this definition in the portion of his book called *Gnosis*, citing a series of texts to make the point under each heading (1983, 59–272; also Klauck 2000, 461–99; Markschies 2003, 16–17, has eight elements in his definition that basically subdivide Rudolph's categories; Pearson 1990, 7–8, has eleven elements, but elements six through eleven are not as key as Yamauchi 1997, 72–73, notes).

Rudolph's list shows that Gnosticism was quite complex but operated as a comprehensive faith covering the key issues of God, the creation, man, salvation, and the resolution of the creation. In fact, A. D. Nock, a well-known classical scholar of the mid-twentieth century, noted that Gnosticism addressed three principal human concerns: "a preoccupation with the problem of evil, a sense of alienation and recoil from man's environment, and a desire for a special and intimate knowledge of the secrets of the universe" (Stewart 1972, 2:940). Gnostics shared these concerns with the larger ancient world to which they belonged but gave unique answers to these themes. Rudolph's definition also shows that although one detail cannot encapsulate what Gnosticism is, a variety of these kinds of traits identifies its presence. These key ancient ideas appear in many of the texts we shall encounter.

A Key Observation

One point can be made from this definition. An essential aspect of Gnosticism was its view of deity, namely, the distinction between and relationship of the transcendent God to the Creator

God. This is important because this view of God produced the orthodox reaction against those texts.

On the other hand, we need to be reminded that not every "alternative" text from the first two centuries is Gnostic. Adolf Harnack (1851–1930), a famous professor of church history at Leipzig, Giessen, Marburg, and Berlin in the late nineteenth and early twentieth centuries, is known for his description of Gnosticism as an "acute secularizing or hellenising of Christianity," a view that argues that Gnosticism was a derivative of Christianity. This is the classical view of the historical relationship between Christianity and Gnosticism (Harnack 1893, 1:227). Recent finds and the new school have challenged this derivative link. But those who critique Harnack often ignore his entire statement (e.g., Klauck 2000, 556), which reads the "acute secularizing or hellenising of Christianity, *with the rejection of the Old Testament*" (emphasis added). The splitting up of God and the resulting view of the creation along with the rejection of the Old Testament are clues to understanding the debate over orthodoxy.

The age and possible roots of Gnosticism, yet another highly contentious area, is the final issue about the ancient context to survey. Almost everyone in the field regards it as unresolved. The next chapter differentiates what we know from what is debated. This distinction will force us also to consider how historical method works and what to look for when we study history.

STUDY QUESTIONS

1) *What three factors make defining Gnosticism difficult?*

2) *What five traits are often associated with Gnosticism?*

3) *What is it in Harnack's observation about Gnosticism that is often ignored, and why is its perspective important?*

· THREE ·

DATING THE ORIGIN
OF GNOSTICISM

It is one thing to define Gnosticism but quite another to discuss its date and origin. Did Gnostic views predate Christianity? Did they emerge in reaction to Christianity? Was Gnosticism influenced by Greek philosophy and/or by Judaism? In other words, where does Gnosticism fit on the map of history?

WHY GNOSTICISM'S ORIGINS
ARE DIFFICULT TO TRACE:
SYNCRETISM, PHILOSOPHY, AND LACK
OF STRUCTURE LEAD TO VARIETY

The scope and variety of Gnostic works reflect a kind of syncretism. Syncretism is bringing together views from various sources and combining them into one. Hans-Josef Klauck, professor of New Testament at the University of Chicago, has discussed this variety of influences in his work on the religious context of early Christianity (Klauck 2000, 458–61). Gnosticism drew from Greek philosophy, especially middle Platonism and Neoplatonism, for its dualism; reacted to Jewish traditions of creation and the end (often called *apocalypticism*) for its views of creation, wisdom, and redemption; and drew from Christianity its appeal to the impact of Jesus and the significance of the Christ figure.

In fact, most discussions of Gnosticism move too quickly past the role of Greek philosophy in the movement, a key to understanding Gnosticism's origin. The classics scholar A. D. Nock (Stewart 1972, 2:949) calls Gnosticism "Platonism run wild." The idea involves a soul weighed down by and in bondage to a body. Plato alluded to a dualism in the world (*Polit.* 296E) and spoke of a *Demiurge* (*Timaeus* 36 b–c). The most important world was the world of ideas, while matter was less important. In his famous painting in the Vatican called the *School of Athens*, Raphael portrays Plato, the idealist, pointing up to the sky, indicating the superiority of ideas, while Aristotle, the realist, points to the ground because of his differing view of what is important. Some middle Platonists of the second century BC had taken this in a negative direction, arguing that "if the gods exist they do not care for men" (Grant 1970, 107 of Carneades the skeptic, and 111). Other Platonists held that knowledge was a divine gift sent to men. Grant (p. 127) speaks of the syncretistic forces at work in Gnosticism of the second century. Langerbeck (1967) faults twentieth-century work on Gnosticism for understating, ignoring, or misrepresenting Greek philosophy's role. This point is notable because the new school bases its work to a great degree on studies that Langerbeck criticizes.

The key point is that *Gnosticism was not a singular connected movement but more a way of seeing the world that produced a myriad of viewpoints on the themes tied to its definition.* However, in this varied form it was never a clear alternative to the earliest expression of Christianity until a variety of Gnostic schools began to emerge, which each tried distinctly to organize Gnostic thinking.

Yet—and this is crucial—there was never a "Gnostic church," only a conglomeration of disconnected schools that disagreed with each other as well as with the traditional Christians. These Gnostic groups operated initially more like Greek philosophical schools than they did like communities similar to a church (Langerbeck 1967, 30). Nock notes that Gnosticism in this period was "broken up and unorganized" (Stewart 1972, 2:957–58). In the earliest three centuries, the Gnostic groups also lacked any semblance of organization between communities as the church possessed. This difference explains in part why we lack within the Gnostic materials any detailed discussion of their community practices, a fact that stands in contrast to other early Christian material where praise and community practice dominate the contents.

In other words, there was never a Gnostic *code*; there were Gnostic *codes*. The more organized form of response emerged in the middle part of the second century, according to the textual sources we have. This variation also reflects Gnosticism's "parasitic" quality. Each expression of Gnosticism took ideas from a variety of sources and combined them in unique ways so that a variety of combinations resulted. Untangling these strands by working backward from sources to the origin is a little like trying to unwind DNA. Several views about the roots of Gnostic ideas have emerged, and almost all who work in the area recognize this morphing quality of Gnosticism. Thus, determining its date and origin is difficult.

GNOSTICISM: GREATEST OF THE SECOND-CENTURY ALTERNATIVE OPTIONS

Another reason for this difficulty lies in the sources themselves. Klauck expresses succinctly what all who study Gnosticism know about these sources:

The fundamental problem, however, is connected with the sources available to scholars. We have no literary testimonies to a developed gnosis that can be dated *indubitably* to the first century CE [CE = Common Era or AD] or even earlier. The *unambiguous* attestation of gnosis by means of quotations by non-gnostic authors of the original documents begins, at the earliest, at the start of the second century CE; this fact would speak in favor of the Church history hypothesis [i.e., that the church belief was first and the alternative of Gnosticism followed]. The only loophole remaining to other models is opened by the words "indubitably" and "unambiguous," which have been used above. It is possible that the literary testimonies have a longer prehistory, and that these, taken together with many hints in early texts, permit us to postulate an earlier date for the beginnings of gnosis. (Klauck 2000, 458, emphasis his, bracketed explanations added)

So we are back to how the sources are read. This is a primary reason why we must look at texts.

One observation remains. Our current evidence suggests that the Gnostic movement is not as old as early Christianity. The only question is whether the loophole Klauck mentions is large enough to squeeze Gnosticism through it. Of all the alternatives from within Christianity in the earliest centuries, only Gnosticism or ideas related to it seem to have created great concern or offered real alternatives with potential staying power. Its creative treatment of the doctrines of God and Jesus along with claims to special revelation gave Gnosticism a seeming power, especially given that its teaching was more in line with common Greco-Roman thinking.

This raises the question of what else was in the period besides Gnosticism and traditional views. Why did Gnosticism have a staying power that other alternatives did not? Our ancient sources help us here. Besides traditional views, the sources show that there were three alternatives, with the greatest being Gnosticism.

The three major alternatives were the Gnostic movements, the movement of Marcion, and Montanism. Marcion was a figure of the mid-second century. He rejected the Old Testament and spoke of a good God and an evil God, but was not Gnostic, lacking many of the other elements that point to Gnosticism. His movement quickly died. Marcion's rejection of so much material already received by most of the church as authoritative made his effort short-lived. Montanism arose in the same period and focused mostly on an appeal to ongoing special revelation, but it lacked a dualistic view of God and creation and so was not Gnostic. It had a longer life and met with traditional resistance not so much because it taught divergent views but because it consistently added claims of revelation on top of the church's older teaching. These additional claims, detached from the apostolic roots of the tradition, made traditionalists nervous.

H. E. W. Turner's *The Pattern of Christian Truth* records his Oxford University Bampton Lectures from 1954. In it he described the difference between these three movements as "Heresy Considered as Dilution—Gnosticism; Heresy as Truncation—Marcion; Heresy as Distortion—Montanism" (Turner 1954, 97–148). He also noted that Gnosticism added to Christian faith, while Marcion subtracted from it (p. 118). This difference becomes apparent in how each used the Old Testament and appealed to the creation accounts. Gnosticism brought in outside elements and "diluted" Christianity while Marcion simply took fragments of the Old Testament's teaching and portions of Luke and Paul, throwing away the rest.

Of these three movements, Gnosticism was the most powerful and widely received. In other words, Gnosticism emerged as the only credible alternative. This is why our tour has had to stop and give it a closer look.

FOUR VIEWS OF GNOSTICISM'S AGE AND ROOTS

What views exist about the origins and date of Gnosticism? Smith (2004, 18–43) offers a more complete discussion, but here are the major options:

1. A formerly popular view of the so-called history of religions school is that Gnosticism is independent and pre-Christian. Yamauchi (1983) has evaluated the evidence in English while careful German analyses come from Carsten Colpe (1961) and Karl Prümm (1972). This view represented the dominating perspective in the first two-thirds of the twentieth century. Scholars such as Richard Reitzenstein, Hans Jonas, Rudolf Bultmann, and Walter Bauer believed that there was evidence of Gnosticism being older than Christianity and teaching a "redeemer myth." (We will take a closer look at Bauer in Chapter 5, for his views generated the new school.) Bultmann argued that Christianity made use of this independent Gnostic redeemer myth, so that Christianity reacted to Gnosticism rather than preceded it. However, as Colpe in particular showed, the evidence used for this view came from later Gnostic sources, centuries after the time of Jesus. Bultmann's view of the age of Gnosticism is now discredited.

2. Gnosticism is independent and existed alongside the emergence of Christianity. This is the view of Kurt Rudolph, who sees gnosis also interacting at the same time with a wide array of philosophical influences and with Judaism (1983, 275–94). Greek philosophy is evident in Gnosticism's dualism and in some of its views on matter. Judaism is reflected in its

concern with creation, the nature of God, and its detailed attention to the book of Genesis.

This view also goes back to the history of religions school and Wilhelm Bousset (Klauck 2000, 456), but Bousset's view has always been controversial. Reviewing Bousset's work in 1908, Adolf Harnack considered it "utterly antiquated, a weird collection of fossils, a junk room and a rubbish heap" (Rudolph 1975, 232, 237). Harnack complained that Bousset's use of sources evaluated and valued things backward so that later Mandean sources (fifth century) were more important than earlier Marcionite ones (second century), and later figures such as Athenagoras (late second century) were more important than Justin Martyr (mid-second century). (The Mandeans were a syncretistic, Gnostic movement whose roots may go back to Western Palestine but who ended up in Mesopotamia). The problem has always been garnering clear, early evidence for this movement's existence (Hengel 1997).

Another counterargument comes from Langerbeck (1967, 27–28). He notes that the kind of dualism present in Gnosticism is distinct from first century Greek philosophy but does reflect currents that later existed. If he is right, then a gnosis contemporaneous to the founding of Christianity is unlikely. Which of the two remaining views is more likely is even less clear.

3. That Gnosticism emerged in reaction to Christianity has been powerfully argued by Simone Petrément in *A Separate God* (1984) and was the view of Harnack (Harnack 1893, 223–66) and Nock (Stewart 1972, 2:956–57). Until the last century, it was the classic view of development rooted in accepting the work of the church fathers. Working through Gnostic themes and figures in detail, Petrément's book is almost five hundred pages. It shows the difficulty of arguing that Gnosticism existed alongside Christianity and makes the case that Gnosticism was a reaction to Christianity. Her complaint about other options is that

they are "based on hypotheses, hypotheses that *unnecessarily* multiply obscurities in the history of the Gnostics and absurdities in their doctrines" (Petrément 1984, 486, emphasis hers). The strongest points for Petrément are that (*a*) Christian expression and reaction to it dominate the Gnostic materials and (*b*) the handling of Judaism in Gnosticism is so negative that it is hard to believe the movement originated in Judaism, which is the remaining alternative.

4. Gnosticism was a Jewish reaction to Judaism. The idea that Gnosticism originally involved a strong rejection of Judaism and later reacted to Christianity has grown in popularity. Among those holding this view are Carl Smith (2004), Ed Yamauchi (1983), R. McL. Wilson (1968), who taught at the University of St. Andrews in Scotland, and Alan Segal (1977), a Jewish scholar from Barnard College, Columbia University. Most versions of this view place Gnosticism's origin in one of two time frames between the late first century and early second century although Pearson (2004, 98–99) takes it back to a time contemporaneous with early Christianity and coming out of Egypt.

The roots of the movement saw the world as evil in light of recent devastating Jewish losses. One of three settings is posited. The movement was (*a*) a reaction to the devastating fall of Jerusalem in AD 70 (e.g., Wilson 1968, 27), (*b*) a later reaction to the fall's impact in the early second century (Segal 1977, 109–20, 206, 265), or (*c*) a reaction to a devastating persecution by the Roman emperor Trajan after a Jewish revolt that took place in Egypt in 116–17 (Smith 2004, 72–112). What speaks for this view is the intense negative engagement with Jewish concerns and Scripture about God, creation, and evil, including the early chapters of Genesis.

Evidence against the early version of Pearson is that first-century Jewish writers Philo and Josephus have no discussion of such views existing in Judaism. Furthermore, the rabbinic tradition reveals no traces of an early origin for such ideas in Judaism. The difficulty with the view in general is that Gnosticism is so negative toward traditional Judaism and its view of God that one wonders whether Jews could be the originators. However, one needs only to think how today's harshest critics of Christianity often are those who come out of a conservative Christian background. Such an intense rejection becomes humanly possible, especially in the face of disappointment over the way in which Jews had been treated. The idea that Gnosticism could be rooted in the harsh reaction of some ancient Jews to their difficult history is plausible.

It seems that one of these last two views is the most likely origin for developed Gnostic views. Gnostic systems of belief emerging late from Judaism or in reaction to Christianity best explain the date of our sources and the traits evidenced in them. In fact, this likely origin best explains why all of a sudden in the second century such views seemed to be popping up in our sources. Once Gnosticism was finally in the air, it was spreading and morphing with variation.

However, our survey also indicates that individual Gnostic-like elements were floating around before there was full-blown Gnosticism. This is why many who speak of a later origin for Gnosticism will also speak of Gnostic "tendencies" in material, including the New Testament, which come before the time of full-blown Gnosticism. This likelihood complicates our historical discussion because the potential for similarity of expression from diverse sources, philosophical and religious, is rich in the first century. But with this observation comes another very important point. *The diversity that predates the development of full-blown Gnosticism is likely to have been fairly random because what emerged later from the Gnostic and Gnostic-like sources that we have is a lack of connection and cohesion in such movements.* By the first third of the second century, these Gnostic movements existed in great diversity. What about the diversity in Christianity? Were the dynamics of diversity the same as in Gnosticism? Such questions raise the issue of how we make historical judgments, our next topic.

STUDY QUESTIONS

1) *Why speak of Gnostic codes?*
2) *Name three major alternative views of the second century.*
3) *What are the four views of the origin of Gnosticism, and which of them is the most likely?*

· FOUR ·

EARLY CHRISTIANITY'S DIVERSITY AND HISTORICAL JUDGMENTS

Was the reality of diversity in the second century also present in the first century? Was not diversity so great for the earliest forms of what is now called Christianity that speaking about orthodox Christianity in the earliest period is an anachronism? The new school asks those basic questions. Is not such a variety reflected in what we now call the New Testament? Does not that variety mean that there was not Christianity but a diversity of first-century Christian movements, each having a right to the name by following Jesus in its own way? Our tour examines such questions.

Some variety in earliest Christianity did exist. A reading of the New Testament shows different writers with different concerns and emphases. We must remember that when we examine these works in a historical way, we appeal to them not primarily because they are a part of the Bible, but because they are among our earliest witnesses to Christian faith. The most basic historical question is whether there was something shared at the core of these traditional writings.

Two Key Dynamics:
Tradition and Linked Communities

Was there a common set of dynamics in these expressions of traditional Christianity that kept such groups united across ethnic and geographical lines even as they experienced persecution? Was there something about what they believed and the way they worshipped that gives evidence of this underlying connection? These are *historical* questions even though we are studying *theological* belief. In many ways, this book seeks to answer them in light of claims that all there was in the beginning was variety with everyone claiming to be associated with Jesus.

An observation about the nature of the early Christian movement might give us a preliminary answer. Two distinct dynamics in the earliest pre-Irenaean traditional Christianity and in alternative Gnosticism point to the differing social and historical perspectives of the two movements. The importance of instruction by tradition and a missionary link between communities are two dynamics that Gnosticism seems to have lacked.

First, tradition-oriented Christians *from the earliest days* appealed to what had been passed on orally to them as teaching. They did not simply appeal to the texts that we now call the New Testament. In fact, they very rarely did this explicitly until the middle of the second century. The new school points this out, and this observation is mostly correct. However, the new school has exaggerated the point. It is as if the writings of what became the New Testament were almost irrelevant or, more important, as if the ideas presented in the New Testament were not the conceptual points of appeal early on.

The new school is right in saying that it was about three centuries before the full collection of books that became the New Testament were used as a matter of course to explain and defend

Christian understanding. So what was done before those texts had their functional role? How was teaching presented and defended before there was a version of the Bible that included a New Testament? What dynamic drove the teaching?

By the end of the second century, the four Gospels and most of the Pauline works were handled as authoritative, but knowing this does not help us with most of the first two centuries. *We have to look at sources from this period to see how the traditional Christians presented and defended their beliefs before they appealed to the New Testament.*

We will examine these strands of passed-on tradition when we get to the texts. They are important pieces of material. They consist of short confessional statements and pieces of structured teaching, and they reflect a Jewish mode of instruction. This material is found within our oldest sources, pointing back to an age that predates the early traditional written materials we have. The ideas expressed within the written material also point to the level of veneration for Jesus that was in these early sources. These ideas and the person they pointed to linked distinct communities together. In addition, these communities interacted with each other, something the early Gnostic movements seemed to lack.

Second, the very missionary nature of the earliest church linked these communities together and gave them a basic identity as the message was taken from one place to another. It allowed them to refer to themselves as the Way or later as the Church with its members described as the saints or brothers and sisters. In the earliest period, these believers in Jesus did not call themselves Christians. That term appears only three times in the New Testament. Rather, they were members of the Way, a movement emerging from Judaism that still hoped in promises of the God of Israel. These roots explain the consistent appeal to the Law, Psalms, and Prophets of Israel.

Neither of these dynamics—an appeal to tradition or to a linking of community in the context of promises from the God of Israel's Scripture—surfaces in the Gnostic alternatives. Gnostics appealed to new revelation and special spiritual knowledge that did not come with a parallel appeal to the role of oral or written tradition being passed down.

GROUND BENEATH OUR FEET: FOUR WAYS THAT SOURCES WORK

Ancient sources give us the hard evidence about these differences in ancient practice. Langerbeck (1967, 26) says that sources "give us ground beneath our feet," translated from the German, "gibt uns Boden unter die Füße." They are the starting point from which to work with ancient ideas. That is why we will work directly with the ancient texts.

Sources raise the question of historical method. How do we attempt to reconstruct what happened in the past? The theories that are at the center of the debate and discussion are spun out from facts, observations, and deductions made from sources, their ideas, and their social-historical context. Modern theories generated from ancient sources reflect a variety of hypotheses depending on how the sources are dated and the contexts into which the sources are placed. However, there is a difference between (1) what the source says, which we try to determine more directly *by interpreting* the source itself; (2) when ideas presented in the source were actually expressed, which we can determine *by dating* the source; (3) whether what that source says is true, which we discuss *by assessing* the source; and (4) when the ideas expressed emerged, which requires that we try to get behind the source in a less direct manner *by working with the history of the ideas* it expresses. To understand date and origin, we have to work backward from the source to the origins of the ideas the source expresses because often ideas are older than a particular source in which the ideas appear. Virtually every step in this process can be debated—and often is!

Sometimes during our tour, we shall work back from the second century into the first. The premise being that the credible alternatives that *might have* existed in the first century are likely to have left some significant trace in the second century. In other words, the movement's potential early roots might speak for its later widespread existence. This is especially necessary because we lack alternative-view sources for the first century; our collection of sources is incomplete. Yet the premise for an earlier origin for Gnostic or alternative ideas will have to be tested by sources. Such work is never easy and takes patience. It also often leads to debate.

There is one rule of historical work that can never be ignored, however. Historical work—to really be historical—can never leave "time and space," a phrase that Martin Hengel, professor of New Testament at the University of Tübingen, used often with me in our discussions about historical method. His complaint about many of the recent works is that the debate has become a discussion of ideas detached from the sources and the ancient context. The result of this detachment is the spinning of theories that are historical fantasies, no matter how brilliantly creative or rhetorically powerful the argument for them is. I hope to show that he is right, by carefully working backward in time for the ideas expressed in second-century sources.

The last two of the four factors presented on page 35 produce the most historical debate. They are: whether a source is accurate and where and how far back a source's ideas go. These judgments are harder to pin down. The process of historical debate, whether about the emergence of Gnosticism or the nature of early Christianity, involves making assessments of this mixture of evidentiary facts and judgments. In sum, everyone interprets the evidence. The issue is, which reading does the best with the most factors one is treating? Even though historical study is not always airtight, we are always on better ground if we actually look at the sources.

AN EXAMPLE OF HISTORICAL ANALYSIS: TESTING THE *GOSPEL OF THOMAS* AND NEW SCHOOL CLAIMS ABOUT JESUS

I do not want our discussion to be too abstract. So let's return to an issue I alluded to when we discussed the dates of our sources in Chapter 1. It provides a good example of using sources with care. The debate about the *Gospel of Thomas*'s date leads to the new school's more subtle claim of what *Thomas* as a whole represents—a potential early source whose roots coincide with the appearance of the four Gospels. It reflects an alternative Jesus, who only gave wise sayings and was not worshipped. Is this *Thomas*'s Jesus, and is *Thomas* early enough to warrant embracing?

Let's examine the argument for *Thomas*'s portrayal of an alternative Jesus, which appears in two forms. The first approach simply appeals to *Thomas*'s contrast with the Gospels. The second approach ties the argument to a claimed parallel between *Thomas* and Q, a source of Jesus' teaching that many New Testament scholars accept. Elaine Pagels represents the contrast argument. Bart Ehrman makes the second claim about Q.

Elaine Pagels says it this way:

> Many Christians today who read the *Gospel of Thomas* assume
> at first that it is simply wrong, and deservedly called heretical.
> Yet what Christians have disparagingly called Gnostic and
> heretical sometimes turns out to be forms of Christian teaching

37

that are merely unfamiliar to us—unfamiliar precisely because of the active and successful opposition of Christians such as John. (2003, 75)

She contrasts *Thomas* and John's gospel as follows:

Now we can see how John's message contrasts with that of Thomas. Thomas's Jesus directs each disciple to discover the light within ("within a person of light there is light" [*Thomas* 24]); but John's Jesus declares instead that "I am the light of the world" [John 8:12*b*] and that "whoever does not come to me walks in darkness" [John 8:12*b*]. In Thomas, Jesus reveals to the disciples that "you are from the kingdom, and to it you shall return" [*Thomas* 49] and teaches them to say for themselves that "we come from the light" [*Thomas* 50]; but John's Jesus speaks as the one who comes "from above" and so has rightful priority over everyone else: "*You are from below; I am from above . . . The one who comes from above is above all*" [John 8:23; 3:31 in a comment by John]. (2003, 68 emphasis hers)

Remember, this claim often adds the idea that *Thomas* is early or, at least, almost as early as John, so the contrastive portraits of *Thomas* and John are equally old.

So does *Thomas* teach a nonexalted Jesus? A close look at sources shows that Pagels has overplayed the contrast. Yes, *Thomas* is a sayings-only source, but does it present Jesus only as a teacher of the way to wisdom, a nonexalted Jesus? What is to be done with *Thomas* 77? It reads, "Jesus said, 'It is I who am the light which is above them all. It is I who am the all. From me did the all come forth, and unto me did the all extend. Split a piece of wood, and I am there. Lift up the stone, and you will find me there'" (Robinson 2000, 2:83). Does this not suggest a higher view for a unique Jesus than Pagels presents? This omission indicates that the source's teaching may be more complex than the new school suggests. Even if *Thomas* is early and has only sayings, it does not present a Jesus who only teaches about wisdom. In other words, the fact that *Thomas* has only teaching need not indicate that Jesus be viewed as a teacher only. The content of the sources, not their form, is key. All the evidence needs attention.

What is important here for the new school is that *Thomas* is not like the four Gospels because it is merely a collection of 114 sayings attributed to Jesus. *Thomas* lacks the Gospels' theological narrative.

The other claim is that *Thomas* is more like the document Q, in which there also is not much discussion about who Jesus is. To understand Ehrman's point, let's first look at some scholars' view of Q.

Many scholars regard Q as sayings-only material shared by Matthew and Luke, so that makes Q earlier than either of these two gospels. Q, like much of *Thomas,* is mostly a wisdomlike portrait of Jesus' teaching. So the new school, in a second argument for *Thomas's* importance, suggests the existence of an alternative form of Christianity corroborated by Q. This alternative perceived Jesus only as a revealer. The argument is that Q and *Thomas* are sayings-only sources because teaching about the way to God was all that made Jesus significant. The key to this second argument is that both of these sayings-only sources are early, serving as evidence for the early date of the alternative approach to Jesus. The form and content of Jesus' teaching in these sources show how early on many understood Jesus. If this were so, then it is an important element of evidence.

To analyze the argument, we'll consider two questions: (1) What can we say about Q? and (2) How does the new school connect Q and *Thomas*? It is quite possible that something like Q as a text or collection of oral tradition existed in

the church's collection of accounts about Jesus. It is a recon-
structed source, now lost. This source was one way that information was passed on about Him. The evidence for this now
lost source consists in the amount of overlap in some two hundred verses of Matthew and Luke and the corresponding belief
that Matthew and Luke did not use each other (see Matt.
3:7–10 and Luke 3:7–9, which almost match verbally across
more than sixty words). Where did such agreement come from
if not from a shared oral or written source? Luke 1:1–4 tells us
Luke was aware of sources. So their presence is compatible
with things the Gospels say. If Q existed as a source for
Matthew and Luke, then it would date to the middle of the first
century. This would make it an important source in understanding the history of the passing on of teaching tied to Jesus.
While we can acknowledge Q's existence, we know nothing of
Q's nature, size, and import beyond its use in Matthew and
Luke. We lack this source except for what remains of it in the
Gospels. It is also claimed that Q does not discuss the Cross,
Jesus' resurrection, or the importance of Jesus' person.

To connect Q and *Thomas*, the new school argues the two
are alike not only in form but also in perspective. *Thomas* has
no discussion of the Cross and does not stress the importance
of Jesus' resurrection, just like the old but now lost Q. The
claim is that two early texts point to an alternative Jesus by not
telling his story as the four Gospels do.

Ehrman, in comparing the *Gospel of Thomas* with the sayings source Q, makes the second claim this way:

> Many people today have trouble accepting a literal belief in
> Jesus' resurrection or traditional understandings of his death
> as atonement, but call themselves Christians because they try
> to follow Jesus' teachings. Maybe there were early Christians
> who agreed with them, and maybe the author of Q was one of

them. If so, the view lost out, and the document was buried. In part, it was buried in the later gospels of Matthew and Luke, which transformed and thereby negated Q's message by incorporating it into an account of Jesus' death and resurrection. One more form of Christianity lost to view until rediscovered in modern times. (2003, 58)

Note how Ehrman's argument works. We go from a series of maybes to what is a seeming historical reality. He ignores numerous other likely possibilities that can be raised about Q. Nowhere does he consider that within the church a collection of Jesus' sayings like Q existed that was merely intended to collect His practical teachings without seeking to articulate a full theology of what the church believed (Hurtado 2003, 241). If that were so, then the Q material was not lost, transformed, or negated by the traditionalists who used it. Q was merely incorporated into the larger Gospels so that its role as an isolated collection was no longer necessary. In Ehrman's framing of the evidence, there is a rush to judgment. Q becomes the earliest, seemingly historical, witness for lost Christianity. *Thomas* is joined to it, mostly on the basis of parallel form, giving two pieces of evidence for this "lost" faith.

However, we have just challenged the description of *Thomas* as evidence for a Jesus who only teaches by showing that *Thomas* has a trace of the exalted Jesus. What is more, Q also has a trace of evidence for the exalted Jesus. The presence of the temptation accounts in Q suggests a high view of Jesus because Jesus is called God's Son by a heavenly enemy (Matt. 4:1–11; Luke 4:1–13). Q also has evidence of a belief in the Cross in its discipleship teaching (Matt. 10:38 = Luke 14:27). *Again, the new school omits key evidence.* This is why we shall have to take a close look at the *Thomas* material as we continue our tour.

Thus, these texts are different in form from the Gospels, but they are not as contrastive in their perspective as some in the new school claim. Nor does the form of their content, as sayings collections, point necessarily to their view of who Jesus is. To suggest this conclusion is to confuse form *with* content. The new school's claim ignores content in *Thomas* and *Q* that gives evidence of an exalted or suffering Jesus.

This example provides an essential lesson about sources. Their content needs careful and close attention. Selective use of evidence should be avoided. Now in fairness, it must be said that each side in this debate has failed in using sources well. A careful look at Gnostic sources, for example, will show that the church fathers' charge that all Gnostics were immoral is wrong. This charge does not stand up in some of the Gnostic Nag Hammadi texts where there are numerous calls to live morally while other of these texts do seem indifferent to moral behavior. The church fathers' charge seems exaggerated and may well reflect the polemical context of their writings.

Summarizing the lesson from our examples, historians seek to work with all the evidence and must avoid being too selective with the materials. All the key evidence within the sources for each side of the debate should be presented for assessment.

Summary

Finding historical context is not easy work. In fact, historical study itself is difficult, patient business. It is about sources, settings, and assessments.

We have surveyed the three periods of early Christian history and given careful consideration to the most common alternative Christianity, the Gnostic-Christian option. We have considered the debate about the term among scholars and the diversity within those groups.

We begin to see the likelihood that Gnosticism is more recent than the earliest Christianity, something that the very structure of the growth of the movements suggests from within their own documents.

We also see that the groups claiming to be Christian in the period were diverse. This diversity will need a closer examination involving the texts themselves. Considering historical method and looking at an example involving the new school, we have discovered why we must carefully scrutinize our sources.

One preliminary step remains: examining the modern thesis that drives the new school's approach. It is the work by Walter Bauer (1964), *Orthodoxy and Heresy in Earliest Christianity*. Originally published in 1934, it was coolly received, but when Bauer's study was reissued in a second edition in 1964, it became more influential. The story surrounding this work also raises questions.

STUDY QUESTIONS

1) *What major differences existed in the dynamics of early traditional and alternative Gnostic communities?*

2) *What four different issues must be distinguished in working with historical sources?*

3) *Do Thomas and Q teach that Jesus is only a teacher of wisdom?*

4) *In dealing with sources, what are the key points from our examples?*

FIVE

THE CLAIMS OF WALTER BAUER AND THE ROOTS OF THE NEW SCHOOL

Ｎew theories are fun. They have the feel of a new product, a new way of looking at things, and a way of grabbing attention. Sometimes that attention is fleeting; sometimes it lasts. New historical theories usually do not make headlines, but they can have an impact like a successful sales campaign. This is especially the case when the new way fits the spirit of the age.

The Danish classical scholar M. P. Nilsson (1960, 346) in 1947 wrote a letter to classicist A. D. Nock in which he complained about the impact of new theories that try to wipe away the labor of past generations. He said, "These young scholars would imply that, in the light of more recent research, the work of an older generation is fit only for the waste paper basket, but this is not true. The putting of the questions, the results achieved, the terminology of an older generation are more enduring than a younger generation is willing to admit." While Nilsson did affirm that there is value in the new approaches, his complaint was that these theories seldom rewrite the history books as much as they claim.

The story of the new school of early church interpretation fits this category. The theory is fairly new, claiming to rewrite early church history and how it is written. However, the results of that claim are a reach, even in the midst of the approach's valuable insights.

In 1934, the German New Testament scholar and early church historian Walter Bauer released a work titled *Rechtgläubigkeit und Ketzerei im ältesten Christentum* for an academic series on historical theology. Such works seldom make a splash in the public square, but this work was an exception.

The title, when translated into English, is clear about its subject: *Orthodoxy and Heresy in Earliest Christianity*. Bauer sought to challenge the consensus of his day about the relationship between orthodoxy and heresy in Christianity's earliest centuries. The old view was that heresy came after orthodoxy, which was rooted in the Christian movement's start. The old view emerged from the study of our best sources at the time, the church fathers' writings about heresy.

Bauer's challenge (1964, xxi) began with this rhetorical question:

> If we follow such a procedure, and simply agree with the judgment of the anti-heretical fathers for the post–New Testament period, do we all too quickly become dependent on the vote of but *one* party—that party which perhaps as much through favorable circumstances as by its own merit eventually was thrust into the foreground, and which possibly has at its disposal today the more powerful, and thus the more prevalent voice, only because the chorus of others has been muted? Must not the historian, like the judge, preside over parties and maintain as a primary principle the dictum *audiatur et altera pars* [let the other side be heard]?

Here are the roots of a mantra heard in much of the recent buzz about the new gospels. That saying goes, "History is written by the winners." Like a triumphant chorus, the mantra never asks whether the winners won for a reason other than "favorable circumstances." The impression is that historical accident more than substantive discourse produced victory. The victory is usually defined as dictated by a favorable social situation. The winners simply gained the most power, suppressing the losers. In addition, there is the matter of fairness, letting both sides have a voice. All of this sounds reasonable enough. Indeed, as principles, they are good ones. The issue is not these principles but their execution.

WALTER BAUER'S THEORY ON ORTHODOXY AND HERESY IN EARLY CHRISTIANITY

Bauer's theory is the base for current material. If there is any doubt, listen to comments from some of these recent works.

Helmut Koester taught as professor of New Testament at Harvard University. He is the figure most responsible for promoting Bauer's ideas in recent decades. He was aware that Bauer's ideas needed refinement but still lauded the work. He wrote in 1965, "Walter Bauer . . . demonstrated convincingly in a brilliant monograph of 1934 that Christian groups labeled heretical actually predominated in the first two or three centuries, both geographically and theologically. Recent discoveries, especially those at Nag Hammadi in Upper Egypt, have made it even clearer that Bauer was essentially right and that a thorough and extensive revaluation of early Christian history is called for" (Koester 1965, 114).

Elaine Pagels (1979, xxxi) says, "Bauer recognized that the early Christian movement was itself far more diverse than orthodox sources chose to indicate." She then goes on to mention but dismiss substantive criticism of Bauer: "Certainly, Bauer's suggestion that, in certain Christian groups, those later called 'heretics' formed the majority, goes beyond the gnostics' own claims: They typically characterized themselves as 'the few' in relation to 'the many' (*hoi polloi*). But Bauer . . . opened up new ways of thinking about Gnosticism."

Pagels's remarks are accurate, but let's consider what she says. In effect, she says that although the evidence *from the voices of the unheard* does not agree with Bauer, he still has opened up new ways of thinking about these groups. It is almost as if history be damned; what counts are the new ideas.

Bart Ehrman (2003, 172–80) also offers praise. Ehrman says of Bauer (1877–1960), "His most controversial and influential work was a study of theological conflicts in the early church. *Orthodoxy and Heresy in Earliest Christianity* (1934) was arguably the most important book on the history of early Christianity to appear in the twentieth century" (p. 173). Ehrman summarizes the assessment of Bauer this way:

> Specific details of Bauer's demonstration were immediately seen as problematic. Bauer was charged, with good reason, with attacking orthodox sources with inquisitorial zeal and exploiting to a nearly absurd extent the argument from silence. Moreover, in terms of his specific claims, each of the regions that he examined has been subjected to further scrutiny, *not always to the advantage of his conclusions.* Probably most scholars today think that Bauer underestimated the extent of proto-orthodoxy [Ehrman's term for orthodoxy in the early period] and overestimated the influence of the Roman church on the course of the conflicts. (p. 176, emphasis and bracketed explanation added)

This summary is exceedingly fair to the post-Bauer discussion, but it raises a serious question. If the two central Bauerian positions are flawed, why does his overall thesis stand? When does this schizophrenic handling of historical evidence lead to a conclusion that Bauer had it wrong?

ASSESSING BAUER'S THEORY

His Contributions in Terms of Method

What are we to make of this schizophrenic handling of Bauer's work? On the one hand, this work has been epoch-making with regard to method. Bauer's study has reconfigured how historians talk about the historical evidence from this period. Bauer's appeal to listen to both sides of the historical material and to consider how the alternative views expressed their own beliefs was a much-needed word. Nag Hammadi discoveries reinforced this point.

Two methodological emphases of Bauer have stood the test.

1. In their desire to refute these views, the church fathers overstated their own case and sometimes were inaccurate about what was taking place, especially when it came to treating all heresies as coming from a singular root, whether it was back to Simon Magus or calling most of these movements Gnostic (Wisse 1971; Beyschlag 1974). Scholarly consensus exists on this point (Harrington 1980).

This observation about the fathers should not be exaggerated. A check of Irenaeus against the sources of views he challenged reveals that he described those views accurately. Many of the details of views noted in other fathers also stand corroborated. The implications are important. The new and secret gospels, now paraded as fresh discoveries, were in fact well-known centuries ago. What the blurbs and endorsements claim is new and exciting information is not so fresh after all.

Nonetheless, Bauer's questioning produced a more careful assessment of the fathers. His call to view the sources from the church fathers in light of their polemics and to listen to proponents from both sides describe and present their views was a necessary historical corrective.

2. The examination of evidence by geographical region was an important insight. Ideas move across time and space in different directions at different speeds. Sometimes they reflect a variety of cultural factors, with some of those factors being unique to a given region.

These lasting observations make Bauer's work significant. However, *one must distinguish Bauer's* method *from his* thesis. *The content and value of Bauer's claims are not synonymous with his methodological breakthroughs.*

Bauer's Content: His Two Main Theses

Bauer had two main content ideas.

1. There were originally varieties of Christianities, not a fixed orthodoxy. Thus, in the beginning there were Christianities, existing side by side with no one option having a superior claim on apostolic roots. He claimed that hard evidence suggested this conclusion. In his regional survey, especially at Edessa of ancient Syria (located now in modern Turkey) and Alexandria in Egypt, Bauer argued that what became known as heresy was the faith's original form. Other regions such as Asia Minor and Macedonia give evidence that such heretical views were at least a more prevalent minority than the church sources suggest. So Bauer's key point is that orthodoxy is a construct of the later church. Between the fourth and sixth centuries a later orthodoxy was projected back into this earlier period. Bauer's implication is that what Christianity has been and what it originally was are so different that we should rethink (or make over) the faith.

2. What allowed for the development of orthodoxy was the Roman church's successful control over other areas in the late second century. Thus, for example, Rome threw its weight

around in Corinth, even though Corinth had more diversity than orthodoxy.

Eventually, Rome won across most of Christendom, so orthodoxy won. Bauer claimed that this victory distorted the earliest history, and subsequent writers, embracing his thesis, formed the new school with its push to reassess this history.

An Assessment of Bauer's Content Theses

What have critics said about Bauer's content theses? We start with the second claim.

Did Rome control? Is the orthodox church Rome's work? Subsequent critique has discredited this thesis. In fact, the German church historian Hans-Dietrich Altendorf (1969, 64) described this feature of Bauer's work as playing with the argument from silence so that the result was the "constructive fantasy of the author" (*konstruktive Phantasie des Verfassers*). Later he spoke of an "elegantly worked-out fiction" (*elegant ausgearbeitete Fiktion*) to describe Bauer's view of how Rome directed Corinth.

A closer look at Bauer's argument helps us. If Rome is the center of orthodoxy, then Bauer must show two things: (1) that orthodoxy really did not exist elsewhere and (2) that Roman communication in *1 Clement* (ca. AD 95) to Corinth was not merely an attempt to persuade but was a ruling imposed on Corinth. However, neither of these is the case (Norris 1976, 36–41).

On the first point, we know that Antioch and Asia Minor were strongholds for what became orthodox views in this early period (Robinson 1988). Ephesus was an especially important center as well as Jerusalem, which Bauer completely ignored. There were several key, orthodox locales for the early church besides Rome. But perhaps Rome still threw her weight around.

Six further points argue against the Roman control thesis.

1. Norris notes (1976, 38–39) that the idea of a city having a single bishop, which some consider integral to Roman powers and claims, emerged first in Jerusalem and Syria, not Rome. Ignatius and Polycarp represent the evidence here from Syria, while James oversaw the church in Jerusalem very early on.

2. This same Ignatius can speak of a separation between competing groups that points to a sense of orthodoxy versus heresy. As just noted, Ignatius was not from Rome.

3. Some of the most important witnesses we have of "orthodox" materials come from books written for Asia Minor. This is the locale for the Johannine materials (John's gospel, his three epistles, and Revelation). Many of Asia Minor's communities received Paul's letters. It was a vital center outside of Rome.

4. Marcion developed his system assuming the authority of certain works shared with orthodoxy, especially Luke and the Pauline epistles.

5. The earliest liturgical texts we possess come from Syria.

6. Pliny the Younger wrote to Trajan about a Christian community in Bythnia that worshipped Jesus, a practice that reflects orthodox belief there (*Epistles* 10.96–97).

So early expressions of orthodoxy were not as geographically isolated as Bauer argued. As Turner noted (1954, 59) in his critique of Bauer's ideas, Asia Minor as a region is "less promising" for Bauer's views than Edessa or Alexandria, which Turner had just finished critiquing at this point in his lecture. After surveying Asia Minor, Turner stated, "Nothing here supports the more daring features of Bauer's reconstruction" (p. 63).

The failure of the idea that Rome was prevalent in influence is important. If Rome did not drive the move to define orthodoxy more precisely in this earliest period, then the sense of orthodoxy may have been more widely distributed than Bauer argued. This may well explain orthodoxy's "success." It may be that it was widely distributed because of the nature of its roots, but more on that later. That there was much contact from other churches with Rome is not surprising because it was the culture's dominant city (Turner 1954, 72), but this falls far short of ecclesiastical control. In fact, Turner notes (p. 74) occasions when Polycarp and Polycrates opposed efforts by Rome to step into their affairs. In his major study of Rome in the first two centuries, Lampe explained an element of orthodoxy's success there. It was simply the majority belief among the many options; it was more attractive to the masses (Lampe 1989, 323). So one of Bauer's two content pillars is made of sand.

Does a regional survey show that the earliest origin and majority presence are with alternative views? Bauer's first point that alternatives dominated in many regions requires a region-by-region overview to be fully developed. I cannot do that here because each would be a major study. I have already noted that Antioch and Jerusalem are problematic for Bauer's claims. For western Asia Minor, Thomas Robinson (1988) made a detailed study of Bauer's claims and found his conclusions wanting, as does Arland Hultgren (1994, 47–54). Both conclude that the heretics were neither early nor strong (Robinson 1988, 199; Hultgren 1994, 47). Michael Desjardins (1991, 73) calls Robinson's study "another row of nails to the coffin enclosing Bauer's thesis." Robinson's critique on Asia Minor and Ephesus is sound.

What can be said of Alexandria in Egypt? Bauer's claim was that Gnostic-like views were prevalent there before orthodoxy (Bauer 1964, 44–60). Five points make this argument problematic: (1) To make his case, Bauer must make certain assumptions about the second-century work of *(Pseudo) Barnabas* not being orthodox but Gnostic. Most reject that description of this work. (2) Bauer must also ignore that Clement of Alexandria and Irenaeus independently spoke of the second-century alternative group known as the Valentinians arising after orthodoxy (on the first point, Pearson 2004, 90; on the second, McCue 1979, 124–30). (3) Pearson (2004, 95–99) adds reference to the presence of the orthodox *Teachings of Silvanus* from the region. This work has traits of the Jewish writer Philo and leads in a conceptual direction to Clement, Origen, and Athanasius, fathers of the late second and early to mid-third centuries. (4) Pearson notes that *(Pseudo) Barnabas* is our earliest Christian source from the region. It reflects an apocalyptic concern with the end of history that is like Judaism and strands of Christianity with Jewish Christian roots reaching back to Stephen (pp. 92–93). Pearson argues there were varieties of Christianity in Alexandria that also reflected interaction with that city's strong Jewish presence. The next and last point is the most noteworthy. (5) Colin Roberts examined the evidence from the earliest papyri remains in Egypt outside of Alexandria. He found that of the fourteen pieces of papyri from the second century, only two pieces reflected a Gnostic context, and those two potential sources are debated as even being Gnostic since they are from the *Gospel of Thomas* (Roberts 1977, 12–14; Pearson and Goehring 1986, 133; Hultgren 1994, 11–12). Löhr has suggested that Roberts's work cannot prove the prevalence of orthodoxy, but he also argues that Roberts does not provide very much comfort for Bauer's thesis (Löhr 1996, 33–34). In fact, this evidence runs counter to what one would expect from Bauer's portrait. For example, Pearson, probably the world's leading expert for this region, is persuaded by Roberts's arguments. This suggests that with regard to Alexandria, Bauer erred. An alternative strand was not dominant there.

This leaves Edessa, the one case where Bauer's claim might hold. The problem, however, is that we have very little material from Edessa. Turner (1954, 40–45) summarizes, "The evidence is too scanty and in many respects too flimsy to support any theory so trenchant and clear-cut as Bauer supposes" (p. 45). Turner does acknowledge, "It is, however, clear that apart from the highly individual character of Syrian Christianity as a whole, heretical or at least sub-orthodox influences counted for more at Edessa than in other Churches nearer to the centre of Mediterranean Christianity" (p. 45). Edessa, Turner argues, gave evidence of a "penumbra" between orthodoxy and heresy (p. 46). A *penumbra* is a boundary or something that exists on the fringe of something.

Bauer's claims for diversity lack support. Of all the regions he surveyed, only Edessa may be correct. That locale hardly represents the center or hub of Christian development. For all that Bauer claimed with his book and all he gained in clarifying method, Bauer failed to show the extensive, early nature of alternative views.

SUMMARY AND CONCLUSION ABOUT BAUER

What this means should not slip past us, given the recent hype. New school claims are exaggerated. Evidence for an extensive array of *alternatives that were the majority* is simply not there.

This critique of Bauer does not show that there was a lack of diversity. The documents we have from the first and second centuries point to a wide diversity among those claiming the name of Christian. How should one assess that diversity? What kinds of things did the earliest Christians believe? How did they themselves assess their differences?

Hultgren (1994, 7–18) notes four logical options for the potential relationships between what he calls normative and alternative teachings of earliest Christianity. (1) Normative came first. This is what has been called the traditional view. (2) Mostly alternatives came first. This reflects Bauer's view, which we have already shown is flawed. (3) There were both fixed and flexible elements, which is the view of Turner in his 1954 lectures. Turner, however, did not really spell out this claim, so it is largely vague and undefined. (4) The views existed side by side with none having a claim to original authority. This option reflects the views of Robinson and Koester, leaders of the new school (Robinson and Koester 1971; Robinson 1982; Koester 1990).

With view 2 exposed as incorrect, a more recent, new school alternative is view 4. On the other hand, view 3 is a modification of view 1. The issue's increasing nuance is reflected in these last two views. The nuanced options 3 and 4 are a positive legacy of Bauer's work. However, can we sort out the remaining options? What do the ancient texts tell us? One thing we can say for sure, the base of the new school's claims in its earliest, most radical form (view 2) cannot stand.

STUDY QUESTIONS

1) *What were Bauer's two contributions to the study of the early church?*

2) *What were the two elements of Bauer's thesis?*

3) *How is his thesis to be assessed?*

· SIX ·

THE NATURE OF GOD AND CREATION, PART 1

INTRODUCTION TO HOW TEXTS WILL BE HANDLED

Our tour begins in the first two centuries with discussions about God and Creation. Many of the works are unfamiliar to a modern audience, so the first time I reference a work, I include a summary of its background and literary character. For these summaries, I use standard discussions of the materials' origins and dates. Since dates and places of origin are sometimes debated, I have noted the accepted range of dates and locales.

We will rely on the standard translations and introductions for the Nag Hammadi works from *The Coptic Gnostic Library* (Robinson 2000). Easy access to translation in English appears in *The Nag Hammadi Library in English* (Robinson 1990). There are some minor differences between these two, but in such cases I have consistently followed *The Coptic Gnostic Library*. Three peculiarities of this collection need attention.

First, these translations were not standardized in terms of form and the treatment of titles. Some translators capitalized titles, while others did not. Sometimes, for example, *Savior* will appear, and in other discussions, it will be *savior*.

Second, for the longer translations, the volume and page numbers are noted. This extensive collection of texts is now a five-volume paperback edition rather than its original four-teen volumes. The pagination starts over with each of the four-teen volumes now placed in the five-volume collection. To check a reference, one must check the specific volume for the work cited.

Third, this work is a diglot version: the Coptic language ver-sion is on one page, and the English translation is on the other. Some long citation page references skip a page in the noting because the English translation is being cited.

The Apostolic Father citations come without page numbers from the single volume *The Apostolic Fathers* (Holmes 1999).

The citations of Justin Martyr come from the Eerdmans volume, edited by Alexander Roberts and James Donaldson, *The Ante-Nicene Fathers: Translations of the Writings of the Fathers Down to A.D. 325*, volume 1 (Coxe 1867). I have updated this translation by only changing pronouns like *thee* and *thou* to current modern pronouns. The translation of the Nag Hammadi texts and the ante-Nicene fathers is rough in some places so that the result is awkward in English. However, no changes have been made.

"Mirror" readings—reading the opponents' texts to dis-cover what the other side taught—are not used: New Testament material is not noted to discuss the views of move-ments that were opposed by the gospel writers. Neither are Gnostic texts used to show what traditionalists taught. There are three reasons for this limitation.

1. It is often said that when people discuss their opponents in contentious debate, the result is skewed. Polemic is engaging someone in an effort to refute the opponent's view. This is exactly why modern study has become more hesitant in using the fathers to discuss those movements for which we do not have corroborative evidence. We know of cases where distortion took place. Evidence found only in the fathers has to be treated

with care as well as where the alternative view treats the traditional approach.

2. Mirror readings are difficult to do. How much do the little pieces we possess tell us? Is there enough in these allusions from opponents to really know what was essential to what was being taught? In many cases, different scholars spin out multiple hypotheses from mirror readings of the same evidence since these readings often are ambiguous.

3. What we can gain from such reading often is a general sense of what was taught. For example, we know that John's opponents in 1 John held to some kind of Docetism, that is, a view that strongly distinguished between the physical world and the spiritual world, so that the idea that Jesus really came in the flesh is contested. Beyond this we can tell very little.

On every topic, we face a spectrum of belief, not two clear categories. We also have to remember that each work expresses its own view and does not necessarily agree exactly with another work. This allows us to see the variations within a topic under consideration and will keep us sensitive to nuances among the views.

Each topic is discussed spanning two chapters. The first chapter examines the more recent materials, which I call *new materials* or *alternative materials* because they stand in contrast to the older sources. The second chapter examines traditional materials, looking especially for doctrinal summaries used for teaching in the earliest periods. We refer to them as *traditional* or *old* because they are sources we have known about for centuries. Once we have the full spectrum in front of us, comparison appears in the second chapter.

This tour compares historical ideas that have entranced people for centuries. On the one side are texts associated with traditional Christianity (what some call *orthodox* or *proto-orthodox*), and on the other are various alternative expressions of the first two centuries. Most texts from the traditional side predate Irenaeus because the claim of the new school is that he and Tertullian, who followed him, are primarily responsible for orthodoxy's formation. In these texts, we consider a core element in roots of Western culture—an exercise that is a lot like looking at our corporate genealogy.

Let's begin with the understanding of God and creation. We start by surveying the newly discovered materials in each topic, so they can be heard first on their own. Since there is extensive debate about whether our textual pool is selective and distorted by the political process of suppression or by natural causes of textual deterioration, proceeding chrono-logically gives a bias to the discussion for the traditional side we wish to avoid.

The gospels that have received the most attention—*Thomas, Mary Magdalene, Philip,* and *Truth*—will be our focus, along with other related nongospel texts that present Jesus. Some may charge that only a small selection of extra-biblical texts out of many others is being used since we do not cover the many extrabiblical Acts texts that are available. However, the key texts covered are the ones highlighted by the new school as those that show the need for reassessment. In addition, most of the other texts are variations from a tradi-tional point of view, and their inclusion would not change the basic emphases of our key themes.

THE NEW MATERIALS ON GOD AND CREATION

In the *Gospel of Thomas*
The *Gospel of Thomas*, found at Nag Hammadi, contains 114 sayings attributed to Jesus. It is our most important alterna-tive text, being the closest to what we have in the synoptic

Gospels (i.e., a summary name for Matthew, Mark, and Luke), and so demands careful attention.

The *Gospel of Thomas* presents wisdom sayings like proverbs or contains parables about the kingdom of God (sayings 22, 27, 46, 50, 57, 96–99, 107, 109, 113). For example, saying 27 reads, "If you do not fast as regards the world, you will not find the kingdom. If you do not observe the Sabbath as a Sabbath, you will not see the Father." It also has sayings that are prophetic in tone (51, 111), beatitudes (18–19), cries of lament (103), words of law (53, 104), and community rules (12, 25). Unlike the gospels of Matthew, Mark, Luke, and John, there is neither narrative sequence nor a clear outline. The work is not clearly Gnostic as it lacks discussion about how the world was created. However, some concepts sound Gnostic (2–3, 37, 50–51, 60, 77, 84, 86–87, 90). For example, saying 2 reads, "Jesus said, 'Let him who seeks continue seeking until he finds. When he finds, he will become troubled, he will be astonished, and he will rule over all.'" Finding knowledge is the key to ruling here. The end of saying 50 reads, "If they ask you, 'What is the sign of your father in you?' say to them, 'It is movement and rest.'" Rest is a key concept of salvation in Gnosticism. Another key idea in Gnosticism is the bridal chamber, a largely unknown Gnostic community rite. Saying 75 alludes to this idea in a way that looks not at the rite, but at what it pictured, entry into full relationship with God. It reads, "Jesus said, 'Many are standing at the door, but it is the solitary who will enter the bridal chamber.'"

The key debate over Thomas's *date and new school claims of an early* Thomas. *Thomas's* dating is disputed and important to our discussion. Many regard the book as reflecting the views of the Encratites. This connection means it holds to a strict ascetic lifestyle that was frequent among some Jewish Christians, as well as possessing less than fully developed Gnostic ideas. Most date the gospel to the second century and place its origin in Syria (Lapham 2003, 120, argues for mid- to late second century from eastern Syria or the Mesopotamian region; Klauck 2003, 108, dates it to ca. 120–40; Nordsieck 2004, 20, suggests 100–110). Walter Rebell (1992, 41) is probably right when he sees a mix of old and young material in *Thomas*. Perhaps some of the gospel contains a few genuine sayings from the Jesus tradition that come from sources independent of the Gospels. However, the bulk of the gospel seems to reflect recastings of synoptic material, that is, a reworking of material from Matthew, Mark, and Luke. Most scholars regard the book as an early second-century work.

Others place the gospel earlier, around the mid- to late first century (Koester 1990, 75–128). Koester argues that the gospel reflects first-century views (p. 84) and that its sayings tradition "pre-dates the canonical gospels" (p. 85). Finally he compares Q and *Thomas*, noting that both "must belong to a very early stage of the transmission of Jesus' sayings" (p. 95). He similarly handles the many parables of *Thomas* (p. 99). Koester is more cautious in his introduction to the translation of *Thomas* in *The Coptic Gnostic Library* (Robinson 2000, 2:39). Here he simply compares *Thomas* to Q, advocates its independence from the canonical Gospels, and concludes that the date is "well before Justin, possibly even in the first century AD." Koester's views on the early origin of *Thomas* have been central to the new school. The argument is that *Thomas* gives first-century evidence of an alternative Christianity, one of Jesus as a teacher of wisdom only. This existed alongside other, more traditional expressions of Christianity. This claim for a very early, alternative view of Jesus makes the date of *Thomas* important.

Most historical Jesus scholars largely reject this new school dating. James Dunn, professor of New Testament in Durham,

England, argues that Koester's observation that *Thomas* presents a Jesus who does not teach an apocalyptic coming of the kingdom is understandable when considering *Thomas*'s theological perspective (Dunn 2003, 164–65). Gnostic-like thought emphasized the fact that the kingdom had come and that knowledge places one in the kingdom. Dunn argues any themes in the Jesus tradition highlighting a kingdom to come and God's future vindication would have been edited out by those holding such views. *Thomas* is a gospel with this Gnostic-like point of view. In contrast to *Thomas,* Dunn claims that Jesus taught in a manner similar to Jewish expectations about the end, looking for God's vindication expressed in a kingdom to come.

Jesus scholars debate whether Jesus was a teacher of wisdom or held to Jewish views of the end. The debate is whether Jesus reflected such Jewish hopes and taught about apocalyptic themes that looked for God to vindicate the righteous in a final judgment. A significant majority of Jesus scholars hold that He did teach such ideas, just as Dunn argues.

Evidence against Koester's claim is the depth of distribution of apocalyptic themes in the traditional materials that have Jesus teaching about the end. These apocalyptic themes appear in multiple strands of the Jesus tradition, a piece of evidence known as the *criterion of multiple attestation.* The idea is that the more widely distributed a particular theme is across the various sources in the tradition about Jesus, the stronger the evidence that this material is old and rooted in Jesus' teaching. It is like having multiple witnesses to an event. These sources are seen as (1) Mark, (2) the teaching that Matthew and Luke share (also known as Q), (3) what is unique to Matthew, and (4) what is unique to Luke. Jesus' teaching on this theme appears in all levels of this tradition. The wide distribution suggests that Jesus taught about God's vindication in the end. So it is likely Dunn has the better of this argument (Bock 2002, 199–203, discusses all these criteria that assess the strength of the evidence within the Jesus tradition).

Thomas may contain an authentic saying of Jesus here and there, making parts of it early. However, for most scholars, the bulk of it is later, reflecting a second-century work. Each saying of *Thomas* has to be assessed on its own terms, but as a whole, *Thomas* is later than Matthew, Mark, and Luke. Efforts to argue it is early as a whole distort the historical record for our first-century sources.

God and creation in the Gospel of Thomas. *Thomas* says very little about God or the creation. This lack of detail about God is not entirely surprising because in Gnostic or Gnostic-like movements, God was unknowable in any direct way.

The lack of detail about the creation, however, gives pause to saying this work is Gnostic. Saying 89 echoes a well-known traditional gospel text (Luke 11:40) and reads, "Jesus said, 'Why do you wash the outside of the cup? Do you not realize he who made the inside is the same one who made the outside?'" This saying sees God as Creator of human life.

In fact, the name God appears only twice, both in saying 100, which reads, "They showed Jesus a gold coin and said to him, 'Caesar's men demand taxes from us.' He said to them, 'Give Caesar what belongs to Caesar, give God what belongs to God, and give me what is mine.'" This is a longer variation of verses found in Matthew 22:21; Mark 12:17; and Luke 20:24–25. It includes a claim by Jesus of His own authority, an interesting heightening of Jesus' self-understanding in a gospel that is not supposed to have such themes! The saying tells us very little about how *Thomas* sees God, and it is questionable that this longer version really reflects what Jesus said because the saying is too personally focused on Jesus.

More common are references to the *father* or being *sons of the father.* The last part of saying 3 reads, "'Rather, the kingdom is inside of you, and it is outside of you. When you come to know yourselves, then you will become known, and you will realize that you are sons of the living father.' But if you do not know yourselves, you dwell in poverty and it is you who are that poverty." Such sayings point to Gnostic-like ideas, in which sonship with God is directly connected to self-understanding and knowledge. This emphasis on self-understanding and sonship with God through proper knowledge makes the teaching in *Thomas* reflective of an alternative way of thinking about Jesus.

Another text with this emphasis is saying 50, which reads, "Jesus said, 'If they say to you, 'Where did you come from?', say to them, 'We came from the light, the place where the light came into being on its own accord and established [itself] and became manifest through their image.' If they say to you, 'Is it you?' say, 'We are its children, and we are the elect of the living father.' If they ask you, 'What is the sign of your father in you?' say, 'It is movement and rest.'" The emphasis on light has parallels in the earlier writings. Ephesians 5:7–14 speaks of the children of God being light, as does the letter of 1 John. However, there is a difference. In those letters, the work of Jesus makes it possible for one to become a child of light. The closest *Thomas* comes to this is saying 61, where Jesus states that "I was given some of the things of my father." This limited delegation to Jesus is another point of difference between *Thomas* and the biblical Gospels. The lack of discussion about the work of Jesus in *Thomas* is yet another difference showing it has an alternative perspective.

The mystery that surrounds God in *Thomas*'s view is evident in saying 83: "Jesus said, 'The images are manifest to man, but the light in them remains concealed in the image of the light of the father. He will become manifest, but his image will remain concealed by his light.'" In other words, God and His power will become evident, but He will remain unseen.

Thus, *Thomas* says next to nothing about God as Creator other than that He creates. God is light. The goal of life is related to attaining knowledge of who we are, discovering that we are children of this God, and finding the presence of the kingdom that is in us.

In the *Gospel of Mary Magdalene*

The *Gospel of Mary Magdalene* exists only in partial form. We know this because of the nature of the breaks in the three manuscripts we have (King 2003b). The bulk of these manuscripts describes a discussion between the resurrected Jesus and Mary Magdalene about the afterlife. The new gospel finds often have a dialogue format between post-resurrection Jesus and a disciple. Using extended dialogues is unlike the biblical Gospels. The form suggests the special and secret nature of the revelation, something coming directly from the raised Jesus. This message Mary reports to the Twelve, some of whom are jealous that Jesus has given it to her while others come to her defense. Bock (2004, 25–26) presents the entire final exchange from *Mary* 17:10–18:21. Klauck (2003, 168) describes its contents as reflecting nothing of the real relationship between Mary and Jesus but presenting "cosmological and ethical speculations, and with a description in mythical language about the ascent of the soul" (p. 167). One theme of Gnostic eschatology is the return of the soul (but not the body) to God.

The issue of dating is complex, although there is consensus on its literary character. One manuscript in which the *Gospel of Mary Magdalene* appears (the Berlin Codex = BG 8502 = Akhmim Codex) has it alongside other well-known Gnostic works like the *Apocryphon of John* and *Sophia of Jesus Christ*

(Klauck 2003, 160). This codex has only chapter 7 of this gospel. That manuscript find dates to 1896 and comes from the fifth century, but the gospel was not published until Nag Hammadi showed where it fit. The find's small size makes dating difficult. King (2003b, 3) places it in the early second century, while Klauck (2003, 160) places it in the second half of the second century and calls earlier dates "not convincing." Lapham (2003, 167) speaks of it being relatively early and no later than the mid-second century and places its roots in Egypt. The introduction in *The Coptic Gnostic Library* (Robinson 2000, 3:454) simply says its date must come before the third century, the date for one of the manuscripts we have.

Thus, this gospel is not usually treated as a major source because of its fragmentary nature, which leads to uncertainty about its date. The fragmentary text means that translations often have brackets [ ] to indicate where the manuscript is blank with the likely idea filled in. Parentheses ( ) indicate that an incomplete idea has been filled in.

This gospel lacks a direct discussion of God. It does refer to "the Good" (7:17) as a way of presenting Him but vaguely presents the material creation. In 7:1–2, the question often treated in Gnostic teaching is whether matter will be destroyed or not. The answer appears in 7:2b–9. It reads, "The Savior said: 'All natures, all formations, all creatures exist in and with one another, and they will be resolved again into their own roots. For the nature of matter is resolved into the (roots) of its nature alone. He who has ears to hear, let him hear'" (Robinson 2000, 3:457; Robinson 1990, 524). Later in 8:2b–11 Jesus says, "[Matter gave birth to] a passion that has no equal, which proceeded from (something) contrary to nature. Then there arises a disturbance in the whole body, That is why I said to you, 'Be of good courage,' and if you are discouraged be encouraged in the presence of different forms of nature. He who has ears to hear, let him hear'" (Robinson 2000, 3:459; Robinson 1990, 525). Here, evil comes from matter because matter gave birth to what is contrary to nature. This deprecation of the physical world is common for Gnosticism. In 9:18–20, Mary notes that God's grace makes people into new creatures. It reads, "But rather let us praise his greatness, for he has prepared us and made us into men" (Robinson 2000, 3:461; Robinson 1990, 525). These three sayings on God and creation in the *Gospel of Mary Magdalene* tell us very little other than suggesting the evil nature of matter. As with *Thomas*, there is no division in God and His role in creation evident from these texts.

In the *Gospel of Philip*

This gospel also was found at Nag Hammadi. The fourth-century church father Epiphanius may have noted it in his work *Panarion*. It has conceptual overlaps with *Thomas*, but there are some differences between *Philip* and *Thomas* that make a connection between the two less than certain (Klauck 2003, 123). This gospel is not like *Thomas* in form. It has very few simple sayings that directly cite Jesus. It is a combination of small theological treatises and short, often puzzling sayings. The work feels like a collection of materials. Its name comes from the fact that Philip makes a cryptic remark in chapter 91. The work appears to have its roots in Syria, given that some wordplays work only in Syriac. *Philip* is seen as "broadly Gnostic" (Lapham 2003, 95). The mention of the "bridal chamber" (65:12; 67:16, 30; 69:1; 70:27–28) is a clue of its origin since this rite belongs to Gnosticism. Much of the material relates to sacraments: the Eucharist, baptism, anointing, and the bridal chamber. The list shows how some of these sacraments are familiar and others are new.

Rebell (1992, 61) dates it to the second half of the second century. Klauck (2003, 124) places its dating in the very late second or early third century. Lapham (2003, 99) dates the work to the early third century, if not in the later half of the second. Wesley Isenberg in *The Coptic Gnostic Library* (Robinson 2000, 2:134–35) dates it to the second half of the third century. So it is a late gospel.

This gospel begins by discussing the issue of names. Names reflect God's transcendence and mystery; 53:23–54:5 reads:

Names given to the worldly are very deceptive, for they divert our thoughts from what is correct and incorrect. Thus one who hears the word "God" does not perceive what is correct, but perceives what is incorrect. So also with "the father" and "the son" and "the holy spirit" and "life" and "light" and "resurrection" and "the church" and all the rest—people do not perceive what is correct but they perceive what is incorrect, [unless] they have come to know what is correct. The [names which are heard] are in the world [. . . deceive. If they] were in the eternal realm [aeon], they would at no time be used as names in the world. Nor were they set among worldly things. They have an end in the eternal realm. (Robinson 2000, 2:147; Robinson 1990, 142)

The text goes on to say how the name of the father, which is given to the son, is unutterable. Those who have this name, those who belong to the son, do not utter it. Here we see the elements of dualism noted as a key to Gnosticism. The world above is distinct from the world below, so much so that names used below do not belong to the world above. The world and the understanding of God are shaded in the mystery that exists between the two realms.

What about creation? Wisdom is called "the mother [of the] angels" (63:33) and is described as Mary's companion. In 73:19–27, we have dualism in the contrast between the created world and the truth as a place from which Jesus came: "This world is a corpse-eater. All things eaten in it themselves die also. Truth is a life-eater. Therefore no one nourished by [truth] will die. It was from that place Jesus came and brought food. To those who so desired he gave [life, that] they might not die" (Robinson 2000, 2:189; Robinson 1990, 153).

The clearest text on creation is 75:2b–14, which reads, "The world came about through a mistake. For he who created it wanted to create it imperishable and immortal. He fell short of attaining his desire. For the world was never imperishable, nor, for that matter, was he who made the world. For things are not imperishable, but sons are. Nothing will be able to receive imperishability if it does not first become a son. But he who has not the ability to receive, how much more will he be able to give?" Creation was always imperfect. It was not created "good," to use the language of Genesis 1. Not only that, the creator failed in his efforts and is not eternal. This hints at a distinction between the true God above, who is full spirit, and the creator of the world, who is something less. In this text and the ideas tied to it, we see a move away from the idea of one God who is Creator, which is basic to Judaism and to traditional Christianity.

In the *Gospel of Truth*

Besides *Thomas* and *Philip*, a third work called a gospel found at Nag Hammadi is the *Gospel of Truth*. Irenaeus noted this work or a version close to it in *Against Heretics* 3.11.9, so we knew of this gospel before it was discovered. Irenaeus attributes the work to the disciples of Valentinus, which would place it in the second half of the second century, a view some scholars accept. Others attach it to only one of his disciples or to Valentinus himself. These options place the work in the mid-second century. The introduction in *The Coptic Gnostic Library* by Attridge and MacRae vacillates between a connection to Valentinus or to a follower of his (Robinson 2000, 1:76–81). Klauck (2003, 135–36) discusses the options and rejects a connection to Valentinus. A second version of this gospel was found at Nag Hammadi, attesting to its importance, but this second version is less complete.

The work cycles through its topics without discernable structure, covering an array of themes from creation and the origin of error to the Redeemer's coming. It discusses a book of revelation, presents various parables, and mentions redemption, rest, the good shepherd, works of mercy, the anointing, and names. It moves from searching to finding. Such themes are certainly Gnostic.

It does not take long to get this work's complex flavor. The manuscript opens in 16:31–17:4: "The gospel of truth is joy for those who have received from the Father of truth the grace of knowing him, through the power of the Word that came forth from the pleroma, the one who is thought and the mind of the Father, that is, the one who is addressed as the Savior, (that) being the name of the work he is to perform for the redemption of those who were ignorant of the Father, while the name of the gospel is the proclamation of hope, being discovery for those who search for him" (Robinson 2000, 1:83; Robinson 1990, 40). *Pleroma* refers to the "fullness," which is a product of God. God is known through discovery that removes ignorance. This is defined later in 41:14–19, "Therefore all the emanations of the Father are pleromas, and the root of all his emanations is in the one who made them all grow up in himself."

The story of chapter 17 continues discussing the pleroma, seen as a plural, corporate totality. When the totality went searching for the one from whom they had come forth, missing that the answer was inside of them, the ignorance of the incomprehensible, inconceivable one led to anguish and terror. This pleroma performed the creation, "preparing with beauty and power a substitute for the truth" (17:19–20). The creation is the work of others and is error. Success came for the elect: "Through this, the gospel of the one who is searched for which [was] revealed to those who are perfect through the mercies of the Father, the hidden mystery, Jesus, the Christ, enlightened those who were in darkness through oblivion. He enlightened them; he showed (them) a way; and the way is the truth which he taught them" (18:11b–21; Robinson 2000, 1:85; Robinson 1990, 40–41).

Again the language of knowledge discovery dominates as we read in 35:8–14: "The deficiency of matter came to be not through the limitlessness of the Father, who is coming to give time for the deficiency, although no one above could say that the incorruptible one could come in this way." The failure in matter lies not at God's feet even though the way He will deal with it was not anticipated. These texts fit Gnostic emphases of knowledge and creation's deficiency.

In the *Apocryphon of John*
If any work embodies a fully developed Gnostic perspective, it is the *Apocryphon of John*. Found at Nag Hammadi, it is "a dialogue with the risen Jesus," presenting a full description of the creation with emanation after emanation (Klauck 2003, 169). Four copies of this work exist in two versions, one longer and another shorter. It is agreed that the longer version emerged from the shorter one (Waldstein and Wisse in Robinson 2000, 2:7). The four distinct copies are indicated by abbreviations that let us know which one is being cited (III and BG—earlier short versions; II and IV—later long versions). Versions II and IV match. The second half of *Apocryphon* treats the early chapters

of Genesis. Irenaeus's reference to "Barbelo Gnostics" is probably a version of this work (*Against Heresies* 1.29.1–4). This potential use dates the basic ideas to 150–60 at the latest (see Rebell 1992, 51–52, who calls it a key Gnostic text). Klauck (2003, 169–70) and Waldstein and Wisse (in Robinson 2000, 1:1) argue that the shorter version we have comes from about 200, and the longer version, which is later, comes from sometime in the third century.

A full citation indicates how *Apocryphon* views the creation. First, Jesus introduces himself in II 2:9–25:

> He said to me, "John, Jo[h]n, why do you doubt, and why are you afraid? You are not unfamiliar with this image, are you?— that is, do not [be] timid! I am the one who [is with all of you] always. I [am the Father]; I am the Mother; I am the Son. I am the undefiled and incorruptible one. Now [I have come to teach you] what is [and what was] and what will come to [pass], that [you may know the] things that are not revealed [and those which are revealed, and to teach you] concerning the [unwavering race of] perfect [Man]. Now, [therefore, lift up] your [face that] you may [receive] the things that I [shall teach you] today, [and] may [tell them to your] fellow spirits who [are from] the [unwavering] race of the perfect Man." (Robinson 2000, 1:17, 19; Robinson 1990, 105–6)

The mystery theme dominates these texts. God is a complex figure, consisting of Father, Mother, and Son. Many Gnostic texts portrayed God as a dyad, with the divine mother as part of the original couple. The recognition of the divine feminine distinguishes Gnosticism from the Jewish and Christian presentations of God. The Judeo-Christian tradition argued that God lacks gender. In fact, males *and* females were made in

God's image (Gen. 1:27). The closest that these other Jewish and Christian views of God came to such feminine understandings appears in the metaphorical portrayal of Wisdom as a female (Prov. 8; Bock 2004, 74–76).

The *Apocryphon of John* II 2:33–4:10 is a long description of God's uniqueness. He is "more than a god, nothing is above him" (2:35). He is illimitable, total perfection, immeasurable, invisible, eternal, unnameable, pure, holy, not corporeal, and superior from other beings among a variety of attributes. He is an "aeon giving aeon" (4:3). He is at rest (4:11). It was his thought that performed a deed and she came forth (4:27). She is the "forethought of the All" (4:31–32) and the glory of the Barbelo (4:36). The Barbelo is the invisible, virginal Spirit (5:13). Next is named a series of aeons that came from the Father (6.2–10). In 7:11, "Christ, the divine Autogenes created everything." A series of lights and aeons are the product (8:25–28).

The key event follows. Sophia, an aeon herself, conceives of a thought from herself (9:25–26). She sought to conceive without her consort's consent (9:34). What she produced was "imperfect and different from her appearance" (10:4), a lion-faced serpent called Yaltabaoth, the first archon to take power from his mother (10:9–19). He is also called the Great Ruler. Here is the start of evil, emerging from an act independent of the highest God. A woman, Sophia, acts on her own. She repents and asks for forgiveness (13:36–14:10). Yaltabaoth moves to create the first man, which chapters 15 and 16 detail part by part. Later, the command of "the Mother-Father of all" sends five lights to Yaltabaoth to tell him to breathe into the being a breath. Unknown to him, Yaltabaoth breathes into the body an element of power from his mother. The being moves, coming to life (19:15–33). The archons will have power over the "natural and perceptible body," but in him was an Epinoia (a Greek word meaning "thought"), hidden in Adam that was the correction of the mother's deficiency (20:9–29).

This complex creation story has God tied indirectly to creation, which involves the work of underlings and was created with flaws. Evil resulted from a female deity's failure to seek out God's will. Matter is evil with an evil impulse. But the potential for the right kind of life exists, hidden from within, so evil forces cannot get to it. Creation is the work of others with God the Facilitator working to recover what his divided Godhead lost. This portrait will be important when we compare accounts.

In the *Hypostasis of the Archons*

This work, also found at Nag Hammadi, is a defense of the "reality of the Archons (or rulers)," which is what the title means. It is not a gospel or even in the genre of a gospel. However, it is included because it appeals to Genesis 1–6 with clear Gnostic elements. It is believed to have originated in Egypt and dates most likely to the third century.

The key element of this narrative begins at 86:20. Here is a complex deity, existing in a series of worlds, revealing a conflict between multiple heavenly authorities. Once again, similar to *Apocryphon,* we have a female deity responsible for the creation of authorities. The name of the figure here has changed to Pistis Sophia, but her function is the same as in *Apocryphon.*

The story continues in 87:11–26:

> As Incorruptibility looked down into the region of the waters, her image [Pistis Sophia] appeared in the Waters; and the Authorities of the Darkness became enamored of her. But they could not lay hold of that Image, which had appeared to them in the waters, because of their weakness—since beings that merely possess a soul cannot lay hold of those that possess a

Spirit—; for they were from Below, while it was from Above. This is why "Incorruptibility looked down into the regions [of the waters]": so that by the Father's will, she might bring Entirety into union with the Light. The rulers (Archons) laid plans and said, "Come, let us create a man that will be soil from the earth." They modeled their creature as one wholly of the earth. (Robinson 2000, 2:237; Robinson 1990, 163)

After this, they form the soul-filled man who lies lifeless on the ground. The Pleroma (the Incorruptible) sends the Spirit to indwell the man and give Adam life (88:10–17). These verses then complete the creation of man: "Now all these events came to pass by the will of the father of the entirety. Afterwards, the spirit saw the soul-endowed man upon the ground. And the Spirit came forth from the Adamantine Land; it descended and came to dwell within him, and that man became a living soul. It called his name Adam since he was found moving on the ground" (Robinson 2000, 2:239; Robinson 1990, 163).

So the material world and humanity emerged as part of a fallen world from the beginning. The God of the highest realm provides the breath of spiritual life, but the creation primarily was the act of others. This creation theology is distinct from Genesis. The creation of humanity was a group project of heaven and lesser forces. God is a facilitator in creation, at the top of a corporate effort. However, a major role in the creation goes to beings jealous of God. This is why matter is evil. Such a view of an evil creation by many is common, as Segal (1977, 252, n. 20) shows. He cites an additional Nag Hammadi text that makes this point: the *Origin of the World* 103:6–20, where Yaldabaoth becomes insolent and declares himself the one true God (Robinson 2000, 2:41; Yaldabaoth functions like Yaltabaoth in *Apocryphon*). A similar view appears in the *Gospel of the Egyptians*, our next text.

In the *Gospel of the Egyptians*

This gospel is a "typical work of mythological Gnosticism," according to its translators Alexander Böhlig and Frederik Wisse (Robinson 2000, 2:24). An alternate title is the *Holy Book of the Great Invisible Spirit*. It presents a report from Seth, one of Adam's descendants, and comes across almost as a gospel from Seth (Robinson 2000, 2:21–22). *Egyptians* is a work unrelated to the apocryphal Christian gospel of the same name, which is a fragmentary text known to us through Clement of Alexandria. The work described by Clement contains a dialogue where Jesus instructs Salome about an ascetic life of sexual restraint. That is a work of the middle second century. *Gospel of the Egyptians/Invisible Spirit* exists in two versions found at Nag Hammadi, distinguished by abbreviations (III, IV). They are very similar. The work deals with the origin of the heavenly world (III 41:8–55:16), the path taken by Seth and his descendants (III 55:16–66:80), followed by hymnic and closing sections (Klauck 2003, 60). Klauck (2003, 59) and Robinson (2000, 2:38) note dates range between the second and early third centuries.

The view of creation in III 41:8–55:16 is so complex, here's a summary. Under the Father God stands a Trinity that contains another Father of a lower degree, Mother, and Son. Each part of the Trinity is an ogdoad, each having its own sphere. *Ogdoad* is a Greek word, meaning "group of eight," but it is used to refer to a complex, primeval force. The Father is mind, word, incorruptibility, and will. The Mother is simply called Barbelo. The Son has himself and seven voices. In addition an aeon, Domedon (also known as Doxomedon), comes into existence to be the aeon that envelops the world of light. Through a complex interaction of Spirit and Barbelo, the Christ comes into existence, along with the "thrice-male" child (III 53:23–24;

Robinson 2000, 2:26–28; Robinson 1990, 213). This treatment reflects a highly developed Gnostic cosmology. Monotheism has disappeared.

The second section on Seth (III 55:16–66:8) is equally complex. Seth's seed is created through the work of Plesithea, the virgin with four breasts, the mother of angels, and the mother of lights. A review of creation shows that Gamaliel, minister of the light Oroiael, and Sophia share in the creation. Plesithea proclaims himself to be a jealous Creator God. He is rebuked by a voice from heaven that then moves to create a man with the help of a figure called *metanoia*. This word means "repentance" in Greek. This act creates the line of Seth through the work of yet another figure, Hormos, and the Holy Spirit. Later, a third story of Seth's origin is put forward as Edokla, an otherwise unidentified figure, gives birth to truth and justice, the beginning seed of eternal life, as well as to Seth's children. These children face dangers in the world left by the devil. Seth prays for their protection, and angels rush in to protect them and to create truth.

In this book, there is a separation between the Highest God and the Creator(s). The multiplication of aeons is evident from the outline of the account as well, so there is dualism. The competition within the spiritual realm for honor is also evident, with creation the partial responsibility of an evil force, a defector from God.

This reflects a Gnostic view of creation, even though in each account the details vary. Various figures create, functioning as a *demiurge* or an assistant in the creation. Sometimes, that term as a summary description is misleading since in many of these accounts, creation is not an act of a figure assisting God but is the result of the figure acting on his or her own. As we have discovered, these ideas about creative assistants form the backdrop to several of the Nag Hammadi texts.

In the *Gospel of Peter*

The *Gospel of Peter* is one of the few texts that treats Jesus' death and resurrection exclusively. It is a passion narrative.

Eusebius, *Ecclesiastical History* 6.12.1–6, names the *Gospel of Peter* and notes that some churches of the area initially read this gospel. However, it came to be adopted by some docetic groups, which distinguished between Jesus in the flesh and the spiritual Christ that inhabited him. The association of this work with these groups led, in the latter part of the second century, to the end of its being read in church through the instruction of Serapion, bishop of Antioch. Two examples of potential docetic influence appear: 4:10, where Jesus hangs on the cross but feels no pain; and 5:19, where Jesus notes power is departing from him, rather than God is forsaking him. At the same point, it is said Jesus "was taken up," possibly indicating that his ascension took place at the cross although this meaning is debated (Lapham 2003, 91–92).

John Dominic Crossan proposed a date of AD 50–70, but that is an idiosyncratic view. Klauck (2003, 87) notes that many themes are a development of the gospel tradition, with material like that in Matthew, Mark, and Luke. Klauck lists these developed ideas: calling Jesus "Lord," the lack of knowledge about Jewish custom, the transfer of responsibility for Jesus' death away from Pilate to Herod and the Jews, the presence of direct eyewitnesses to the resurrection itself, a descent into hell, huge angelic figures, and a cross that talks. Elements that are parallel to other apocryphal gospels also indicate it is not as old as Crossan suggests, as Raymond Brown's critique shows (Brown 1994, 1317–49). Lapham (2003, 94) and Rebell (1992, 98) note the connection to Serapion means this is a second-century work, probably rooted in Syria and from the middle of that period. This work's history shows it operated on the edges of the church from the time of its composition until the judgment was made that it was docetic.

Because this is a passion account, there is little about the doctrine of God or creation in it. The one key text is in 10:38–11:49. Here God is directly mentioned in a scene where the centurions guarding Jesus' tomb saw three large men emerging from it with a cross following them. The men were apparently large since two had heads reaching to the heaven and one had a head that "overpassed the heaven." When asked if preaching had taken place to those who sleep, the cross, which could talk, replied yes. The centurions then ran to tell Pilate that, indeed, Jesus was the Son of God. They asked Pilate to let them face God's judgment for their sin, but not to hand them over to the Jews to be stoned. Pilate told them to tell no one what had taken place. All we learn from this text about God is that he had a son and that God will judge.

In the *Gospel(s) of Bartholomew*

This is another passion narrative. In fact, two traditions tied to Bartholomew exist in two distinct versions. Jerome (347–419) and the *Decretum Gelasianum* (a sixth-century church decree) also refer to a gospel tied to this figure, but we cannot be sure if this or another work is in view since they give no details. The *Decretum* is a list of material viewed as apocryphal by the sixth-century church (Klauck 2003, 3–5, cites the decree). The first Bartholomew tradition involves a Coptic work also known as "the book of the resurrection of Jesus Christ." It is late, dating from the fifth or sixth century (Klauck 2003, 99). The second tradition, *The Questions of Bartholomew*, is probably earlier. Dates for it run from the second to sixth centuries. The work reflects a heightening of Mary's role but to a lesser degree than later works that makes a third-century date possible (Klauck 2003, 99). M. R. James

(1924) notes and discusses this tradition and presents a translation of *Questions*. As cited below, *Questions* provides a glimpse into the abyss; a discussion of Mary and her conception; a treatment of the devil, also called Beliar, who gives testimony to his work; a discussion of the deadly sins; and a commissioning of the apostles. In addition, Bartholomew receives a glimpse of the seventh heaven. There also are scenes involving Thomas, who is not among the Twelve when Jesus appears because Thomas's son, named Siophanes, has died. Thomas raises his son from the dead, leading to thousands believing. Thomas returns, hears about the resurrection, and doubts. However, Jesus appears to Thomas, and having touched Jesus' wounds, Thomas believes.

In *Questions* 4:27–28, Satan, the first created angel, confesses that he cannot hide anything from God. In fact, the son existed before and created Satan. The Father will render judgment in the end (6:2).

One text discusses God and creation. In 4:52–61, Bartholomew has a vision of heaven and sees the creation of Adam repeated. Also Bartholomew sees Jesus. God tells Michael to bring him a clod of dirt out of which God forms Adam. Michael worships the creation of God's image and tells Satan to follow his example, but Satan refuses.

This idea also appears in first-century Jewish tradition in the *Life of Adam and Eve* 12–16. It describes a similar satanic refusal. In *Adam and Eve,* Satan's refusal causes him to be cast from the garden, just as he is in *Questions*.

When Bartholomew completes his vision involving Satan's testimony, he falls at Jesus' feet and prays (4:61–62). This prayer in Latin contains some forty lines. There is even a reference later in the prayer to the "consubstantial Trinity," a detail about the nature of the Trinity that shows the work to be slightly later than the second century (4:63). At the end, Bartholomew asks Jesus as "My God, and Father, the greatest, My King" to save the sinners (4:64).

This work's view of God perceives Jesus as Father and Son in a manner that shows it predates the detailed teaching of the Trinity. What we see also is that God is the Creator and a uniquely exalted figure. These views place this work on the spectrum somewhere between the developed hostile, divine dualism of the *Apocryphon of John* or *Hypostasis of the Archons* and the more familiar traditional texts.

SUMMARY

God appears in a variety of ways in this new material. Some speak only of God (*Thomas*) while others have several heavenly figures participating in creation (*Apocryphon of John; Hypostasis of the Archons*). In most cases, the resulting creation is seen as evil, inherently evil (*Philip*), imperfectly created, so it will perish. Other texts have similar ideas. Texts we have not examined, such as *2 Apocalypse of James* 58:2–6; 63:1–2, 10–11, note an imperfect creation. In other texts we have not treated, the creation is inhabited by evil forces (*1 Apocalypse of James* 25:18–19; *Dialogue of the Savior* 142:6–9). Majella Franzmann (1996, 57–60) summarizes and notes a few texts are more positive toward the Creation or, at least, are not as strongly dualistic (*Dialogue of the Savior* 129:20–21). So these later texts are not uniform. In other words, the alternative views have many subalternatives, even though in most cases they go in the same basic direction. These differences among the texts make visualizing a spectrum more helpful than considering merely two views. Nonetheless, as we shall see, a line of difference will exist for the most part between these texts and their traditional counterparts.

Now that we have surveyed the new works for their complex views of God, let's consider how the traditional texts view God and creation. Is there a difference between the new and the more traditional texts?

STUDY QUESTIONS

1) *Why is the* Gospel of Thomas *an important text, and what is at stake in determining its date for this discussion?*

2) *Who creates, and what is the fundamental character of the creation, according to these texts?*

3) *What role does Sophia play in some of these texts, and is it pro-female?*

SEVEN

THE NATURE OF GOD AND CREATION, PART 2

GOD AND CREATION IN THE TRADITIONAL MATERIALS

The works of the New Testament date from the first century even though they encompass a series of distinct writers of apostolic background like Paul, Peter, and John as well as other figures who likely had contact with the apostles and their circles, such as Mark and Luke. Thus, the age of these texts as our earliest sources gives them historical importance.

Some complain about an approach that gives these texts precedence. They claim that this reflects a theological bias for the Canon, inappropriate for historical study. Other critics say this is the inappropriate use of a rule rather than historical analysis (Franzmann 1996, 8–14). Such claims about a "subtle tyranny" of the Canon or the biblical Gospels are misguided. These texts have value *because of when they were written, and because of the persons who did the writing and their relationships to Jesus or those around Him.* In historical work, sources rule. The best sources are the most important. Thus, it is not a rule or a theological bias that elevates these sources. Solid historical ground undergirds the material. To say otherwise is to ignore basic historical method.

The term *New Testament* is a theological term that postdates the period we are considering. The traditional church recognized this collection of works in its Pauline-gospel core by the end of the second century and as a total collection by the early to mid-fourth century. In the earliest centuries, the church's teaching was passed on orally through circulating *traditions* about Jesus and the church's theology. That is why we call the teaching *traditional*. These were summaries of the church's theology learned through short theological statements or hymns as well as by appeal to individual books of what became the New Testament.

These important books were read during Christian services as a means of instruction and encouragement to those present. However, communities in this early period did not have, or even think in terms of, a functioning New Testament. No one carried a Bible to church. Thus, to speak of the New Testament in this historical context is to use a grouping of convenience.

Rather than having one witness to the theology of this period (that of the New Testament), we have several witnesses. Each of the writers whose work ended up in that collection is an independent witness to what was believed; therefore, each will be treated individually, so the scope of the witness is clear.

•

In the New Testament

One compelling element of evidence from this material includes extracts of church confessions or short theological statements. These short pieces of theological summary or praise taught people the theological core of the church's teaching. When it comes to the Creation, two ideas are consistently set forth: (1) God is the Creator, not some substitute figure, and (2) Jesus participated in that Creation and is not a creature.

Such a piece of material that discusses God and Creation comes from Paul in the fifties of the first century. The text is 1 Corinthians 8:5–6, which reads, "If after all there are so-called gods, whether in heaven or on earth (as there are many gods and many lords), yet for us there is one God, the Father, from whom are all things and for whom we live, and one Lord, Jesus Christ, through whom are all things and through whom we live." Paul contrasts Greco-Roman belief and its polytheism with Christian teaching. He presents a basic confession of the role of the one God in terms of two *cooperating* figures in the Creation. Each one of them bears a title of sovereignty and performs an act of sovereignty, but they are confessed together as God. There are the Father, who is the source of all creation, and the Lord, Jesus Christ, who mediated that one and same Creation. The text's conciseness and balance reveal a theological summary confession. It is easy to contrast this simple confession with the involved discussions of the Creation from the *Apocryphon of John* or *Hypostasis of the Archons* or *Gospel of the Egyptians*. For the Jewish-Christian Paul to associate Jesus with the Creation, as an act of one God, was to point to Jesus' divinity because only the one God is the Creator. Paul says similar things again in Romans 1:25 and 1 Corinthians 10:26, where he affirms God as the Creator, Maker of all. This difference with many alternative texts is significant.

Another key text from the Pauline tradition is hymnic, sung as a word of praise to God. As such, it expressed the theology of the singers. Referring to Jesus, Colossians 1:15–17 states, "He is the image of the invisible God, the firstborn over all creation, for all things in heaven and on earth were created by him—all things, whether visible or invisible, whether thrones or dominions, whether principalities or powers—all things were created through him and for him. He himself is before all things and all things are held together in him." Here we see 1 Corinthians 8 set out in more detail. Jesus is a reflection of God and shared in the act of Creation that reveals God. His position reflects sovereignty over that creation.

The author of the book of Hebrews shares this view of Jesus and creation. Hebrews 1:10–12 asserts the Son's role in creation with the one God by citing Psalm 102:25–27 and applying its language about God to the Son, while arguing that Jesus is superior to any angel.

A simpler confession from the Pauline tradition appears in Ephesians 3:9, which discusses the riches found in Christ. Paul preached this message "to enlighten everyone about God's secret plan—a secret that has been hidden for ages in God who has created all things." What Paul taught and preached was not a secret to be kept or special knowledge only for a select few. It was to be preached to all in the world.

Other texts make passing remarks about Creation but have a similar thrust. In Matthew 19:4 Jesus discusses marriage: "Have you not read that from the beginning the Creator made them male and female?" Here Adam's and Eve's creation is tied to God alone. Jesus says about the future events that harbor the end, "In those days there will be suffering unlike anything that has happened from the beginning of the creation that God created until now, or ever will happen" (Mark 13:19). These remarks come as asides while another topic is in view, functioning as virtually assumed ideas from the first century for their authors.

Peter shares this view: "Let those who suffer according to the will of God entrust their souls to a faithful Creator as they do good" (1 Peter 4:19). These several citations show that the church accepted the idea of one Creator God through Judaism. Hebrews even rooted it in Jewish praise psalms to God. Creation, then, did not involve a series of subdeities as set forth in several alternative texts.

The Pauline tradition makes practical points from the world's creation by God. First Corinthians 10:25–26 reads, "Eat anything that is sold in the marketplace without questions of conscience, for 'the earth and its abundance are the Lord's'" (citing Ps. 24:1 or 50:12). Here Paul asserts the essential goodness of the creation and the food God provides. First Timothy 4:3–5 speaks of people in the last days who have a seared conscience: "They will prohibit marriage and require abstinence from foods that God created to be received with thanksgiving by those who believe and know the truth. For every creation of God is good, and no food is to be rejected if it is received with thanksgiving. For it is sanctified by God's word and by prayer." The perspective parallels 1 Corinthians 10 and stands in contrast to an evil, material creation of many alternative texts.

This teaching does not mean that God lacks transcendence. First Timothy 6:15–16 refers to God as "the blessed and only Sovereign, the King of kings and Lord of lords . . . He alone possesses immortality and lives in unapproachable light, whom no human has ever seen or is able to see." For this writer, God must reveal what is known about Him (2 Tim. 3:16).

More witnesses exist. Acts includes a series of such references in 4:24; 14:15; and 17:26. Acts 4:24 addresses the "Master of all . . . who made the heaven, the earth, the sea, and everything that is in them." Here is the basic confession of God as the one Creator. Acts 14:15 speaks of a living God, "who made the heaven, the earth, the sea, and everything that is in them." Acts 17:26 notes, "from one man he [God] made every nation of the human race to inhabit the entire earth." God is directly responsible for humanity's existence.

John 1:1–3 declares, "In the beginning was the Word, and the Word was with God, and the Word was fully God. The Word was with God in the beginning. All things were created by him, and apart from him not one thing was created that has been created." Later, John 1:14 states, "the Word became flesh." This connection shows that for this author the Word and Jesus were the same figure. It also shows that Jesus as God participated in the Creation. John 1 parallels Paul's statement in 1 Corinthians. The role of Jesus in the Creation is the fresh Christian element in what had been the Jewish view of the Creation through one God. The Creator God mediated the Creation *through Jesus.*

The writer of Revelation also uses hymnic language about the Creator. He writes in Revelation 4:11: "You are worthy, our Lord and God, to receive glory and honor and power, since you created all things, and because of your will they existed and were created." Revelation 10:6 speaks of God as the Creator of the heaven and everything in it, the earth and everything in it, and the sea and everything in it. The match of this conception with the heaven, earth, and sea language of Acts suggests a kind of confession about God as Creator. In 14:7 there is a call to worship "the one who made heaven and earth, the sea and the springs of water."

James says it this way in 1:17–18: "All generous giving and every perfect gift is from above, coming down from the Father of lights, with whom there is no variation or the slightest hint of change. By his sovereign plan he gave us birth through the message of truth, that we would be a kind of firstfruits of all he created." James compares the new birth of faith to all the good things that God provides as Creator.

Every major writer of the New Testament makes a statement about the work of the one God in creation. Most note that good intent grounded the creation. Matter is not inherently evil. This conception of God and creation differs from what we saw in many of the alternative works.

Jaroslav Pelikan, dean of contemporary historical theologians and former professor at Yale University, discusses systems of cosmic redemption and says that this confession of "one God and one Lord" stands "against all Gnostic mythology and polytheism." Most important here are the oneness of God and the unique role of God as the one Creator (Pelikan 1971,

95–96). Here is a core element of Christian orthodoxy. This core teaching surfaced in confession and worship as well as in asides. There was one God who was the Creator, and the Son participated in that Creation.

In the Apostolic Fathers

This teaching appears in the fathers. Our treatment here is selective, but a full list of texts appears in Appendix 2 on the apostolic fathers. Many of the remarks about God from these fathers come in the context of worship, praise, prayer, or exhortation.

Writing from Rome to Corinth, Clement composed *1 Clement* in AD 95. In 19:2–3, he gives an exhortation: "Seeing, then, that we have a share in many great and glorious deeds, let us hasten on to the goal of peace, which has been handed down to us from the beginning; let us fix our eyes upon the Father and Maker of the whole world, and hold fast to his magnificent and excellent gifts and benefits of peace. Let us see him in our mind, let us look with the eyes of the soul on his patient will. Let us note how free from anger he is toward all his creation." Reviewing God's gifts, he says, "All these things the great Creator and Master of the Universe ordered to exist in peace and harmony, thus doing good to all things, but especially abundantly to us who have taken refuge in his compassionate mercies through our Lord Jesus Christ. To whom be the glory and the majesty for ever and ever. Amen" (20:11–12). Later on he adds, "By his majestic word he established the universe, and by a word he can destroy it" (27:4).

On his view of creation, Clement affirms:

> For the Creator and Master of the universe himself rejoices in His works. For by his infinitely great might he established the heavens, and in his incomparable wisdom he set them in order.

Likewise he separated the earth from the water surrounding it, and set it firmly on the sure foundation of his own will; and the living creatures which walk upon it he called into existence by his decree. Having already created the sea and living creatures in it, he fixed boundaries by his own power. Above all, as the most excellent and by far the greatest work of his intelligence, with his holy and faultless hands he formed man as a representation of his own image. (33:2–4)

Clement sees the creation as the good work of the one God. Man also results from His direct creative action.

Ignatius wrote a series of letters in the middle of the second century. His remarks are less direct about creation, but confess a Jesus from the beginning closely associated with the God who willed all. In writing to the Magnesians, he notes that "bishops and presbyters . . . having been entrusted with the service of Jesus Christ, who before the ages was with the Father and appeared at the end of time" (6:1). Jesus shared divine glory before there was time. Ignatius affirms the unity of God: "Let all of you run together as to one temple of God, as to one altar, to one Jesus Christ, who came forth from One Father and remained with the One and returned to the One" (7:2).

In greeting the Romans, Ignatius confesses his faith in the God who willed all: "Ignatius, who is also called Theophorus, to the church that has found mercy in the majesty of the Father Most High and Jesus Christ his only son, beloved and enlightened through the will of him who willed all things that exist, in accordance with faith in and love for Jesus Christ our God" (1:1). Ignatius confesses the unity of God and the work of God's will in creation.

The *Didache* puts things simply: "There are two ways, one of life and one of death, and there is a great difference between these two ways. Now this is the way of life: first, 'you shall love the Lord your God who made you'; second, 'your neighbor as yourself'; and 'whatever you do not wish to happen to you do not do to another'" (1:1–2). One of the basic elements of faith is that God is the Creator, whom we love (see also 10:3).

In the *Shepherd of Hermas,* we get another early second-century summary confession like those we saw in the New Testament. We read, "First of all, believe that God is one, who created all things and set them in order, and made out of what did not exist everything that is, and who contains all things but is himself alone uncontained" (26:1). Here is the first doctrine to believe—the unity of God who is the Creator. In 47:2*b,* *Shepherd* speaks of God creating humanity: "Don't you understand how great and mighty and marvelous God's glory is, because he created the world for the sake of man, and gave him all authority to rule over everything under heaven?" In 59:5, 7 there is elaboration on the Creation and the role of the Holy Spirit who occupied human flesh and was involved in the Creation. The Holy Spirit as flesh is another way to discuss Jesus as well since He is the "flesh" being discussed. The text reads, "The preexistent Holy Spirit, which created the whole creation, God caused to live in the flesh that he wished. This flesh, therefore, in which the Holy Spirit lived, served the Spirit well, living in holiness and purity, without defiling the Spirit in any way . . . For all flesh in which the Holy Spirit has lived will, if it proves to be undefiled and spotless, receive a reward."

The letter of *Diognetus* dates from the mid- to late second century. It speaks of God's patience with his creation: "God, the Master and Creator of the universe, who made all things and arranged them in order, was not only tender-hearted but also very patient" (8:7). The idea of the maker and arranger of all things recalls the language of *Shepherd.*

The apostolic fathers hold a traditional view of the Creator God. There is one God behind a good creation. He has created while being patient with humanity.

In Justin Martyr

Justin, the first apologist, wrote in the middle of the second century. Citing tradition, he discusses the creation and writes:

> We have been taught that he in the beginning did of his good-
> ness, for man's sake, create all things out of unformed matter;
> and if men by their works show themselves worthy of this his
> design, they are deemed worthy, and so we have received—of
> reigning in company with him, being delivered from corrup-
> tion and suffering. For as in the beginning he created us when
> we were not, so do we consider that, in like manner, those who
> choose what is pleasing to him are, on account of their choice,
> deemed worthy of incorruption and of fellowship with him. (1
> Apology, chap. 10)

Here, God is the Creator of all and of humanity.

In his *2 Apology*, chapter 6, Justin elaborates on God's and Jesus' relationship, explaining their names as well:

> To the Father of all, who is unbegotten there is no name given.
> For by whatever name He be called, He has as His elder the per-
> son who gives Him the name. But these words Father, and God,
> and Creator, and Lord, and Master, are not names, but appella-
> tions derived from His good deeds and functions. And His Son,
> who alone is properly called Son, the Word who also was with
> Him and was begotten before the works when at first He created
> and arranged all things by Him, is called Christ, in reference to
> His being anointed and God's ordering all things through Him;
> this name itself also containing an unknown significance; as

also the appellation "God" is not a name, but an opinion implanted in the nature of men of a thing that can hardly be explained. But "Jesus," His name as man and Savior, has also significance. For He was made man also, as we before said, having been conceived according to the will of God the Father, for the sake of believing men, and for the destruction of the demons.

Creation is the work of the one God, who created through Jesus, who is begotten, not created. Jesus being begotten refers to the unique connection of Jesus to God within the Godhead. He was not made. This fits the relationship we saw in the works of the New Testament where Jesus shares in the Creation. Justin also refers to God creating and giving an order to creation, matching earlier traditional language about creation.

In the *Dialogue with Trypho*, chapter 61, the term *begetting* is explained as wisdom born of God. It is not the same as something created. Justin argues that he has the support of Scripture; he is making claims from the Jewish Scripture, what we call the Old Testament. Later in this same discussion he cites Proverbs 8:

> I shall give you another testimony, my friends, said I, from the Scriptures, that God begat before all creatures a Beginning, [who was] a certain rational power [proceeding] from himself, who is called by the Holy Spirit, now the Glory of the Lord, now the Son, again Wisdom, again an Angel, then God, and then Lord and Logos; and on another occasion he calls himself Captain, when he appeared in human form to Joshua the son of Nave (Nun). For he can be called by all those names, since he ministers to the Father's will, and since he was begotten of the Father by an act of will; just as we see happening among ourselves.

In chapter 128, Justin returns to this idea, making it clear that there is no division in the Godhead between Father and

Son. He states, "I have discussed briefly in what has gone before; when I asserted that this power was begotten from the Father, by his power and will, but not by abscission, as if the essence of the Father were divided; as all other things partitioned and divided are not the same after as before they were divided: and, for the sake of example, I took the case of fires kindled from a fire, which we see to be distinct from it, and yet that from which many can be kindled is by no means made less, but remains the same."

Justin sees a tight unity between Father and Son, as well as a single creation by God.

SUMMARY

Our instructive survey of God and Creation is finished.

In the new materials, there is a range of discussion about God, aeons, emanations, and creation. Some works, like *Thomas*, do not seem to divide the Godhead, but do suggest the creation's evil nature. Other new works operate on the other end of the spectrum with an elaborate series of creative acts, so that God is not the single Creator, but a permissive Facilitator. In some of these works, the female principle in God, Sophia, is responsible for an evil creation. Often she is not alone in that work, which she regrets, seeking restitution. The Gnostic story of redemption will seek to restore the creation. This will be a topic of discussion in Chapters 10 and 12.

In the traditional materials, there is far less variety of belief and much more simplicity. When it comes to God and creation, the traditional materials are united. God is one and is the Creator. This idea of one God and one Creator was inherited from Judaism. The only additional factor in this essentially Jewish picture is Jesus' mediatory role in Creation. Jesus participates in Creation, but not in a way that challenges God's oneness or that prevents Jesus from being worshipped. The earliest, confessional text we have from Paul indicates this when he says that the one God who is worshipped is Father and Lord Jesus Christ.

This view of God was fundamental to this early Christian period. *Shepherd* calls it the first teaching. The earliest church creeds of the third and fourth centuries lead off with the statement, "I believe in God the Father, maker of heaven and earth." That point of faith is rooted in the very earliest texts, reflecting the earliest beliefs. Whatever orthodoxy became and whatever detail it added, that God was a good Creator was the initial core element.

This major point explains why some traditional believers reacted negatively when alternative movements began to multiply agents involved in the Creation and began to assert that the creation or matter was inherently evil. It was seen as turning one's back to basic teaching about God as Father and Creator of a good creation. This departure in belief was regarded as a fundamental challenge to one of the most basic ideas of the faith about the Creator, the Creation, and His creatures.

Alternatives to traditional faith did exist from early days, pointing to a variety of views making claims about being Christian. However, many of those alternative views were not seen as holding to the traditional view of God, a view rooted in the Jewish belief of one God, Maker of heaven and earth. Such alternative views immediately raised doubt about the faithfulness of their teaching to that of Jesus and the apostolic roots of the faith.

One important difference between traditional Christianity and the alternatives is a fundamental disagreement about the person and work of God as the faith's core figure.

Our tour's first stop has been quite fruitful. We have seen how one of the issues that could separate traditional faith from alternative faith is the differing view of God and Creation (see Irenaeus, *Against Heresies* 2.1–2a; 9.1–2; 11.1–2.28.1). As J. N. D. Kelly of Oxford puts it, "The Doctrine of one God, the Father and Creator, formed the background and indisputable premise of the Church's faith. Inherited from Judaism, it was her bulwark against pagan polytheism, Gnostic emanationism and Marcionite dualism" (Kelly 1978, 87). These two chapters on God and Creation have shown why and that Kelly is correct.

STUDY QUESTIONS

1) *As a matter of historical record, why are these texts so important?*

2) *What are the key affirmations of these texts about God and Creation?*

3) *What key differences exist between alternative and traditional texts, and why is that important?*

· EIGHT ·

JESUS: DIVINE AND/OR HUMAN? PART 1

How is Jesus, Christianity's central figure, portrayed in both the new and also the more traditional texts? A spectrum of views exists. Nonetheless, is there a dividing line along this spectrum? In Chapters 12 and 13 we shall consider in detail Jesus' work. Some mention of that theme surfaces here because in the sources, Jesus' person and work often are treated together.

When it comes to Jesus' person, there are basically four options: (1) He is a heavenly being but in a form that permits human contact. The question this category often raises is whether there is a dualist Jesus, where a distinction is made between the human Jesus and the divine Christ. Or is there a docetic Jesus, where Jesus only seems to have one nature versus another? (2) Jesus takes on a human form that complements his heavenly existence. This is often known as the two-natures view. (3) Does Jesus take on a form that requires he abandon some (but not all) of his heavenly characteristics? Is his divinity stated expressly as limited? [Franzmann (1996, 25–55, 71–111, esp. 71) notes these first three options. We add one more view because of the way that people today often perceive Jesus. (4) Jesus is a mere human figure, a great teacher or prophet.

The first three options share the basic idea that the Christ is primarily a figure sent from beyond, who is more than human. The actual options within the texts narrow the theoretical spectrum some, but the variation is still there, running from humanity added to purely heavenly.

JESUS IN THE NEW MATERIALS

In the Gospel of Thomas
Thomas has very few developed statements about who Jesus is. Those we have indicate a "high" Christology, a unique Jesus sent by the Father who is light. Christology is teaching about who the Messiah is and what He does. In the church this meant teaching about Jesus. "Low" Christology points to a human Jesus. "High" Christology sets forth Jesus as a divine figure, or at least a figure uniquely related to God. *Thomas* has a "high" Christology, but the work does not specify its exact nature.

The most important sayings about Jesus in *Thomas* are 77, 13, and 61. Saying 77 reads, "Jesus said, 'It is I who am the light which is above them all. It is I who am the all. From me did the all come forth, and unto me did the all extend. Split a piece of wood, and I am there. Lift up the stone, and you will find me there'" (Robinson 2000, 2:83; Robinson 1990, 135). Here Jesus affirms he is light. The text also affirms Jesus' unique position as above all, as the all, as the one to whom the all extends, and as source of the all. He is present everywhere as the saying about the wood and stone indicates. Jesus' role in the creation also reflects a high Christology. Those who imply that *Thomas* lacks a high Christology ignore this text to make that claim (e.g., Pagels 2003, 68). This passage suggests that Jesus bears unique, creative authority, but *Thomas* never spells out this authority. For *Thomas,* Jesus is more than a teacher of wisdom or a great philosopher who merely points the way to light.

Saying 13 also affirms this unique role. It reads, "Jesus said to his disciples, 'Compare me to someone and tell me whom I am like.' Simon Peter said to him, 'You are like a righteous angel.' Matthew said to him, 'You are like a wise philosopher.' Thomas said to him, 'Master, my mouth is wholly incapable of saying who you are like.' Jesus replied, 'I am not your (2nd person singular) master. Because you (singular) have drunk, you (singular) have become intoxicated from the bubbling spring which I have measured out'" (Robinson 2000, 2:59; Robinson 1990, 127–28). Jesus then takes Thomas aside for a private discussion. When the disciples ask Thomas about the conversation, he replies that if he mentioned any of the things, they would pick up stones, and fire would come out of the stones and burn them. Several things stand out here. First, there is high Christology because Jesus' role is inexpressible. Second, there is emphasis on a held secret, not to be revealed to everyone, reflecting the elite and secret side of this movement. Third, Jesus' response has Thomas's reply about being incomparable especially in mind and affirms the inexpressible Jesus over the other options. Those who embrace Thomas's reply know something that others do not. Should such things be broadcast to those who do not embrace them, they will be burned by their reaction.

In saying 61 Jesus states, "I am he who exists from the undivided. I was given some of the things of my father" (Robinson 2000, 2:75; Robinson 1990, 133). Here Jesus has a close link to God, but less than a complete sharing of authority. The identification of Jesus and God involves a less than equal status, even though Jesus is a unique, heavenly figure.

Saying 15 also may be important. There Jesus teaches, "When you see one who was not born of woman, prostrate yourselves on your faces and worship him. That one is your father" (Robinson 2000, 2:61; Robinson 1990, 128). Scholars debate whether this text describes worship only of God the Father (Nordsieck 2004,

80–81) or teaches that Jesus should be worshipped as the one who represents the Father (Franzmann 1996, 80). Many take the second sense. If so, this text also reflects a high Christology with Jesus having a position worthy of worship.

A few texts in *Thomas* are descriptive of Jesus, referring to him as "living" (Prologue, 52). Another passage describes the blessing of one who "came into being before he came into being" (saying 19). So Jesus existed before he came to Earth as a human being. This double form of existence becomes a model for blessing for anyone who is born twice (first physically, then spiritually).

In *Thomas*, Jesus has a unique relationship with God. He is a heavenly figure with a position that only the elite with inside knowledge understand. Such understanding will "burn" outsiders. Jesus' authority is not absolute as the Father has given him only some things, but Jesus is more than a philosopher or an angel. This position for Jesus will place *Thomas* somewhere in the middle of our spectrum. There does not seem to be a dualism in Jesus as in more typically Gnostic texts, a fact suggesting that *Thomas* is not a pure Gnostic text. However, there also is enough distinction between Father and Son that the Son has a limit in his authority. Nonetheless, Jesus' role is greater than that of the angels and the greatest thinkers among humanity. As such, *Thomas* teaches a high Christology since Jesus is a major heavenly figure, uniquely tied to the Father. This does not, however, reflect the highest conceptual Christology possible as other works show.

In the Gospel of Philip

This gospel has a complicated and less-than-clear presentation of Jesus (Franzmann 1996, 49–50, 72–73). The text denies the virgin birth and argues that Mary did not conceive by the Holy Spirit because a woman does not conceive by another woman. In other words, *Philip* sees the Holy Spirit (= Sophia Achamôth) as feminine (55:23–27), so this rules out a creation by the Spirit through Mary. Jesus is of the seed of Joseph (73:9–15), but he also is the product of a union of the "Father of all" and the "virgin who came down," Sophia Achamôth, in the great bridal chamber (71:4–13). He exists at two levels. Jesus is also the first begotten in rebirth at his baptism at the Jordan where he is anointed and redeemed (70:34–71:2). This rectifies Adam's fall (71:18–21).

It also looks as if Jesus' status as a human, at least after his baptism, is uncertain; his flesh is called Logos, and his blood is called the Holy Spirit. The argument is by analogy. *Philip* 56:32–34 denies that the flesh will inherit God's kingdom on the basis of 1 Corinthians 15:50 ("Flesh and blood cannot inherit the kingdom of God"). Instead of a physical redemption or attributing any value to physical existence, *Philip* 57:3–8 quotes John 6:53 and states, "Because of this he said, 'He who shall not eat my flesh and drink my blood has not life in him.' What is it? His flesh is the word, and his blood is the Holy Spirit. He who has received these has food and he has drink and clothing" (Robinson 2000, 2:155; Robinson 1990, 144). The argument is that if flesh and blood do not partake of God's kingdom, then by analogy Jesus as a human being is not important. This saying affirms that the primary way to relate to Jesus is as a spiritual being, not as a human (more on 1 Corinthians 15:50 in Chapter 11).

Another key text is 57:28–58:10:

> Jesus took them all by stealth, for he did not appear as he was, but in the manner in which [they would] be able to see him. He appeared to [them all. He appeared] to the great as great. He [appeared] to the small as small. He [appeared to the] angels as an angel, and to men as a man. Because of this his word hid

itself from everyone. Some indeed saw him, thinking they were seeing themselves, but when he appeared to his disciples in glory, on the mount he was not small. He became great, but he made his disciples great, that they might be able to see him in greatness. (Robinson 2000, 2:155, 157; Robinson 1990, 144–45)

Jesus operates in a mystery, not appearing as he really was. He is not human, but much more. Here the heavenly and spiritual takes precedence over the human. The human is an accommodation to humanity.

So in *Philip*, Jesus recedes as an earthly being in importance; he is seen primarily as a spiritual, heavenly being.

In the Gospel of Truth

Here Jesus is a part of a Trinity that belongs to a formula, "into the Father, into the Mother, Jesus of the infinite sweetness" (24:6–7). The Mother here may function in the role of the Holy Spirit (Franzmann 1996, 30). According to 31:5–12, Jesus comes "by means of fleshly form, while nothing blocked his course because incorruptibility is irresistible, since he, again, spoke new things, still speaking about what is in the heart of the Father, having brought forth the flawless word" (Robinson 2000, 1:101; Robinson 1990, 46). Jesus is the Christ and the way, showing the way out of oblivion (18:15–21). He is the name of the Father (38:7–40:23). Jesus is tied to a series of names and heavenly figures. Jesus is a guide, restful and leisurely (19:17–18), patient in suffering (20:11), as well as being knowledge and perfection, and proclaiming the things that are in the heart (20:38–39).

In this gospel, there is little speculation about Jesus. He is a heavenly figure who is related to Father and Mother, but otherwise possesses a connection to knowledge, an interior knowledge he reveals.

In the *Letter to Rheginos* (= Treatise on the Resurrection)
This Nag Hammadi work bears two titles and discusses the resurrection, which has already taken place for all. Rebell (1992, 48) notes that 2 Timothy 2:18 and 1 Corinthians 15:12 challenge such a view. *Rheginos* 49:9–16 tells Rheginos that he already has the resurrection, described as the imperishable swallowing up the perishable, so that the flesh is not a part of resurrection (47:30–49:9). This reflects Gnostic views.

This work is a teaching letter with Rheginos as the recipient, which explains one of the titles for the work. Although the work claims Valentinus as author, most see it as a product of the Valentinian school, not the founder. Thus, it is a late second-century work (Robinson 2000, 1:131–33, 146). Beyond this connection to Valentinian Gnosticism, its origin is unknown.

Rheginos teaches that the visible world is an illusion (48:13–15). Jesus is "the Seed of Truth" (44:35). He existed in the flesh (44:14–15) and lived on Earth where believers are (44:17–19). Flesh is a temporary form of existence (47:4–16). Jesus is Son of Man, who will restore the Pleroma (44:33–38). The key summary text is 44:13–37:

> How did the Lord proclaim things while he existed in Flesh and after he revealed himself as Son of God? He lived in this place [Earth] where you remain, speaking about the Law of Nature—but I call it "Death!" Now the Son of God, Rheginos, was Son of Man. He embraced them both, possessing the humanity and divinity, so that on the one hand he might vanquish death through his being Son of God, and that on the other through the Son of Man the restoration to the Pleroma might occur; because he was originally from above, a seed of Truth, before the structure (of the cosmos) had come into

being. In this (structure) many dominions and divinities came into existence. (Robinson 2000, 1:149; Robinson 1990, 54)

Jesus has two natures. He vanquished death and restores the Pleroma, an act that causes the unity of spiritual beings. And the resurrection involves only a spiritual component. This is a high Christology with Jesus possessing two natures.

In the *Teachings of Silvanus*

This Nag Hammadi work is exceptional because it is regarded as one of its few non-Gnostic texts. It is a wisdom text, more like Proverbs in style and reflecting several texts found also in Jewish Wisdom literature. Christ comes to give the gift of light (88:25–89:1). The ignorant person follows passion (89:34–90:4). Such texts combine warnings and teaching. Creation is portrayed as good in the work (116:5–9). *Silvanus* dates from the mid-third to early fourth century (Robinson 2000, 4:272–74). The work probably comes from Egypt because it reflects the views of Alexandrian Christianity.

In this work, the Christ is a teacher of understanding and wisdom: "Accept Christ, [this true friend,] as a good teacher" (90:33–91:1; Robinson 2000, 4:297). *Silvanus* 91:14–20 exhorts, "But return, my son, to your first Father, God, and wisdom your mother, from whom you came into being in order that you might fight against all your enemies, the powers of the Adversary" (Robinson 2000, 4:297; Robinson 1990, 384).

Christ also appears as a divine figure. *Silvanus* 96:19–97:3 declares: "Accept Christ who is able to set you free, and who has taken on the devices of that one [the Adversary] so that through these he might destroy him by deceit. For this is the king whom you have who is forever invincible, against whom no one will be able to fight or say a word. This is your king and your father, for there is no one like him. The divine teacher is with you always. He is a helper and meets you because of the good which is in you" (Robinson 2000, 4:309, 311; Robinson 1990, 368). Here is high Christology. Jesus is the divine teacher and helper, who also is king and cannot be defeated. He also is Father.

Silvanus 98:18–28 is about Jesus' authority. It reads, "Be pleasing to God, and you will not need anyone. Live with Christ, and he will save you. For he is the true light and sun of life. For just as the sun which is visible makes light for the eyes of the flesh, so Christ illuminates every mind and the heart" (Robinson 2000, 4:315, 317; Robinson 1990, 387). Jesus functions as light, available for all, appealing for understanding.

We read about Jesus' nature: "Similarly, Christ has a single being, and he gives light to every place" (99:12–15). This is a clear statement that Christ is a unity in his person. His light extends to every locale. Both ideas are unlike full Gnostic texts, which split Jesus' person and where light exists only for the few. Similar is *Silvanus* 100:13–29, which declares that God is difficult to know, but is knowable. In verses 23–29, the writer teaches, "You cannot know God through anyone except Christ who has the image of the Father, for this image reveals the true likeness in correspondence to that which is revealed" (Robinson 2000, 4:321). *Silvanus* 101:22–24 continues, "Christ is All, he who has inherited all from the Existent One" (Robinson 2000, 4:323; Robinson 1990, 388). Here Jesus' authority is comprehensive. Christ is also light shining undefiled (101:30). In 106:21–28, Christ bears a series of titles: Tree of Life, Wisdom, Word, Life, Power, Door, Light, the Angel, and the Good Shepherd. In 108:30–32, the exhortation is to make oneself like God, just as Paul made himself like Christ. *Silvanus* 109:10–11 states where Christ is, sin is idle while 110:17–19 calls Christ "God and teacher." The verse continues on Jesus' nature, "This one, being God, became man for your sake."

Silvanus 111:13–20 offers a cry to the King to hear the writer's words and give forgiveness. Later the text states that this one had a hand in the Creation and is the Father's hand (115:3–6). The work closes in praise to "Jesus Christ, Son of God, Savior, Wonder Extraordinary" (118:8; Robinson 2000, 4:369; Robinson 1990, 395).

This work has the marks of a traditional text. Jesus has two natures, human and divine. He has a very clear, unique relationship to God, and He is Creator with full authority.

In the *Apocalypse of Peter*

This Nag Hammadi work is not the same as another work known to the church fathers that exists today in Ethiopic. The *Apocalypse* consists of visions of Peter with interpretations from the Savior. There is debate whether two or three visions exist because the second vision, a long discourse, is sometimes viewed as an explanation of the first. The topics are Jesus' death and a debate about what his death involved. This work defends a docetic view of Christ's death and is dualistic (Desjardins's introduction in Robinson 2000, 4:201–14). Desjardins dates it anywhere between AD 150 and 250, although most place it in the third century.

In contrast to the portrait of Jesus in *Silvanus*, the presentation here is very complex. This work presents a Petrine vision of the passion. Jesus has a variety of forms. First, Jesus is the intellectual Spirit filled with radiant light (83:8–10). Second, he is servant, the living Jesus, the incorporeal body of the Savior (81:15–18). Jesus' flesh is a third form (81:18–24). He also is the intellectual Pleroma of the Savior, who resembles the living Jesus and is filled with the Spirit (82:4–9).

This portrait's complexity is evident in the Crucifixion's description. When the figure to be crucified goes to the cross, a laughing Jesus appears above the cross. Those on Earth think they are crucifying Jesus, but they are not (81:7–23). That text reads:

> I [Peter] said, "What am I seeing, O Lord? Is it you yourself whom they take? And are you holding on to me? Who is this one above the cross, who is glad and laughing? And is it another person whose feet and hands they are hammering?" The Savior said to me, "He whom you see above the cross, glad and laughing, is the living Jesus. But he into whose hands and feet they are driving the nails is his physical part, which is the substitute. They are putting to shame that which is his likeness." (Robinson 2000, 4:241, 243; Robinson 1990, 377)

This division of Jesus' person, so that the living Jesus does not suffer, is called *Docetism* because Jesus *appears* to be present but is not. The Greek word for seeming or appearing to be something (*dokeo-*) supplies the derivation for the term *Docetism*. *Apocalypse* 83:1–3 explains that the figure laughs because of the false perception of those who think they crucify Jesus. Jesus knows they have been born blind.

Jesus' body is like a container, not a real part of him. The human Jesus and the heavenly Jesus are divisible. This is the other end of our spectrum. This is a very high Christology. Jesus is so heavenly, he cannot be human.

In a *Valentinian Exposition*

This Nag Hammadi work reflects a Valentinian Gnostic exposition from the late second century. It treats creation, the nature of humanity, salvation, and the final redemption. It parallels ideas that Irenaeus describes for some opponents in *Against Heresies*. In that work, Irenaeus treats Ptolemaeus in I.1.1–8.5.1. In I.11.1–5, Irenaeus covers Valentinus, and

I.13.1–21.5 examines Marcus (Pagels's introduction in Robinson 2000, 5:89). Ptolemaeus and Marcus were Valentinian Gnostics of the second half of the second century.

Valentinians had split into two camps by then. Ptolemaeus represented the "Italian" group, holding that Jesus had a psychic body in which the Spirit (= the Logos of Sophia) entered at his baptism. Marcus represented the "Anatolian" or "oriental" school, holding that Jesus already had a pneumatic (or spiritually indwelt) body at birth (Rudolph 1983, 323). *Exposition* shows how Gnostics did not agree with each other, as Tertullian, *Prescriptions* 42, also noted. Pagels suggests that the views here are like those of the Gnostic Heracleon, a representative of Italian Valentinianism. The work focuses on the secret doctrine of Sophia and her role in a less than perfect creation. Jesus joins with Sophia to restore the creation that the Demiurge currently controls (36:10–16). In 37:12–15, the world's creation is a domain of this Demiurge.

Our treatment is brief because creation is the main topic. The Son of God is a reflection of God, a hypostasis, who is his revelation. Specifically the Son is goodness, the one who descends, and the All (22:31–36). He is paired with truth (39:20–24). Jesus is merely his image (39:15–24). The heavenly Christ is the portrait's dominating figure. This Christ is the one sent to restore the disgraced Sophia, who acted in creation without her pair (33:28–32). These are themes covered in Chapter 6.

The key text, 39:28–35, describes the reconciliation: "Moreover whenever Sophia [receives] her consort and Jesus receives the Christ and the seeds and the angels, then Pleroma will receive Sophia joyfully, and All will come to be unity and reconciliation" (Robinson 2000, 5:141; Robinson 1990, 487). The book reflects a Gnostic view where Jesus and the Christ are distinguished, united only at the end.

In the *Second Treatise of the Great Seth*

This Nag Hammadi work is a Gnostic sermon, presented by the ascended Christ to his followers. It calls for disciples to rest in their redemption and to maintain unity with each other. They are to stand strong in the face of opposition from those in ignorance, an allusion to the traditional church (68:25–69:19). It is that great church that teaches Jesus' actual suffering and death, "the doctrine of a dead man" (60:22). Real knowledge knows this is not so because the heavenly and divine son descends into the creation of Yaldabaoth and takes over the body of an earthly man. The Christ is not associated with "worldly matter" (52:2–6; 61:7; 68:28–69:10). In fact, Christ cast out the one who was in the body he visited when he came to Earth. This act disturbed the archons of Earth (51:20–26). Christ did not resemble the one who was in that body previously (51:31–34). In this way he becomes the Christ on Earth. Jesus only appears to suffer at the passion, so the suffering does not really involve the Christ. This work's perspective on Jesus and the Christ is docetic—Jesus only appears to be human. Epiphanius, the fourth-century church father, discusses the Gnostic works tied to Seth in his *Panarion* 40.7.4, calling their works forgeries in the name of Seth. The work is tied to Seth because for Sethian Gnostics, Jesus is a later incarnation of Seth (Riley's introduction in Robinson 2000, 4:129–33). *Treatise* is a late second-century work.

One text suffices, 55:9–56:19. It describes who the Christ is, while discussing his suffering:

I was in the mouth of lions. And (as for) the counsel which they had planned about me against destruction of their deception and their foolishness, I did not give into them as they had devised. And I was not afflicted at all. Those there punished me, yet I did not die in solid reality but in what appears, in order that I not be put to shame by them, because these are part of me. I cut off the shame from me and I did not become fainthearted at what happened to me at their hands. I was about to become a slave to fear, but I was struck (merely) according to their sight and thought, in order that no word might ever be found to speak about them. For my death, which they think happened, (happened) to them in their error and blindness. They nailed their man up to their death. For their minds did not see me, for they were deaf and blind. But in doing these things, they render judgment against themselves. As for me, on the one hand, they saw me; they punished me. Another, their father, was the one who drank the gall and vinegar; it was not I. They were hitting me with the reed; another was the one who lifted the cross on his shoulder, who was Simon. Another was the one on whom they put the crown of thorns. But I was rejoicing in the height over all the riches of the archons and the offspring of their error and their conceit, and I was laughing at their ignorance. (Robinson 2000, 4:163, 165, 167; Robinson 1990, 365)

This text is clear. It was not the heavenly Christ who suffered but one who appeared to be him, a classic Gnostic view at the end of the spectrum.

In the Gospel of the Egyptians

This gospel is another Sethian work. Jesus is the one "whom the great Seth has put on" (III 64:2–3 = IV 75:16–17; Robinson 2000, 2:146–47). Jesus is "Logos-begotten" (III 64:1 = IV 75: 15–16). Nothing is said of his human existence. So for this work, "although Jesus is the means by which Seth moves from the heavenly to earthly region, he cannot be considered to have a true human existence" (Franzmann 1996, 73).

Here is another Gnostic work, presenting only a heavenly figure of Jesus. Such texts consistently teach an elevated Christology where the human Jesus is swallowed up in his heavenly dimension or he disappears through an illusionary appearance of humanness.

In *Sophia of Jesus Christ*

This work we possess in two manuscripts, one of which appeared at Nag Hammadi, while the other manuscript is called the *Berolinensis Gnosticus* or BG 8502.3. They are distinguished by abbreviations (III is the Nag Hammadi text; BG points to the other version). The work overlaps significantly with another work known as *Eugnostos the Blessed*, also found at Nag Hammadi in two manuscripts (identified as III and V). In fact, *Eugnostos* and *Sophia* are so close, parallel columns can show their relationship.

The question of which came first is debated. Most regard *Eugnostos* as the earlier version, seeing it as a philosophical treatise reflecting middle Platonism (Klauck 2003, 147). Others argue that the use of Son of Man in *Eugnostos* represents a title that is not free of Christian influence, showing it may well be later than *Sophia*. Others argue that to move from a clear system (*Eugnostos*) to a less structured, dialogue form (*Sophia*) is an unnatural direction for development (Yamauchi 1983, 104–7). Those who contend for the priority of *Sophia* make these last two arguments. So the issue of order has not produced a clear consensus. This debate creates a variation in the suggested dating of these works.

Sophia discusses the relationship between Wisdom-Sophia and Jesus. She is his spiritual consort, and together they form a pair. It is a dialogue gospel, with disciples, including Mary Magdalene, asking questions. However, its contents are difficult to understand because of its complex treatment of origins.

Sophia likely dates from the second century (Klauck 2003, 147). Parrott's introduction (Robinson 2000, 3:6) places *Sophia* in the late first or early second century and its earlier relative, which he sees as *Eugnostos,* in the first century BC. The likelihood of these early dates depends on when one places the rise of a developed Gnosticism, how developed middle Platonism is in these works, and whether *Eugnostos* has traces of Christian expression in it. R. McL. Wilson (1968, 116), an expert in Gnostic materials, warns that the resemblances in these works "demand a due measure of caution against assertions that *Eugnostos* is entirely non-Christian or shows no signs of Christian influence." Pearson (2004, 70, 75–77) places *Eugnostos* in the late first century AD at the earliest and *Sophia* in the second century, with the works coming from Egypt. Regardless of the dispute over dating and sequence, this important work is likely the oldest dialogue gospel we possess, which is why our tour of new texts on this theme ends here.

This work makes a distinction between Jesus in his ascended form and his flesh. His ascended form is like "a great angel of light" (III 91:12–14; 93:10–11). No mortal flesh can bear to see the pure and perfect flesh (91:15–17). Jesus exists in the form of the invisible Spirit, not in the previous form (91:10–12). This teaching suggests that "perhaps his earthly form was not in the Spirit" (Franzmann 1996, 84).

In III 91:10–20 (= BG 78:11–79:9), the text reads, "The savior appeared not in his previous form, but in the invisible spirit. And his likeness resembles a great angel of light, but his resemblance I must not describe. No mortal flesh could endure it, but only pure (and) perfect flesh like that which he taught us about on the mountain called 'Of Olives' in Galilee" (Robinson 2000, 3:39; Robinson 1990, 222). Jesus is from the Light and reveals truth (III 93:8–12).

In III 100:1–3 (= BG 92:12–15), the ascended figure speaks of "Sons of the Unbegotten Father, God, Savior, Son of God, whose likeness is in you" (Robinson 2000, 3:77; Robinson 1990, 227). This reference is to a divine element within the elect revealed to them. In III 101:7–8 (= BG 94:5–10) there is a reference to the androgynous Man who was in the creation, while Wisdom, the consort, appears in III 101:15–19 (= BG 94:19–95:4). The Holy One, that is, First Man, and Sophia together reveal "First Begetter Son of God" (III 104: 15–16 = BG 99:7–8), who is called "'Christ.' Since he has authority from his father, he created a multitude of angels" (III 104: 22–24 = BG 99: 16–19). The account then runs through a series of creations. Salvation involves being redeemed from a defective creation by the work of the "great Savior," who brings light and removes forgetfulness (III 107:22–108:14 = BG 105:1–106:8).

This text, even though possibly early, reveals a very developed story of origins. The heavenly Christ is part of a series of creative acts.

SUMMARY

None of these ancient texts presents a strictly human Christ. That option is popular in many modern-day appeals to this material as *The Da Vinci Code* exemplifies and some theologians teach. A strictly human Jesus, however, simply does not exist in any of these sources.

1. *Silvanus* has a portrait of Jesus as human and heavenly. Both are to be held together in a way that is left unspecified. This text is exceptional and represents one end of our spectrum.

2. Other texts are vague about how Jesus is viewed, other than he is alive and has great power. *Thomas* belongs in this category. However, unlike the claims of many who present this gospel to the public, *Thomas* does not lack a high Christology.

Jesus is above all, is responsible for the creation, and is every-where. Jesus is *not* a mere teacher of wisdom in *Thomas*.

3. As we move further across the spectrum, we meet in most texts a heavenly Jesus who dominates the picture. This Christ is such a heavenly person that His humanity is mentioned in passing. This is a dualistic Jesus; the earthly Jesus and the heavenly Christ can be distinguished or are brought together only on occasion.

4. In other works, Christ's heavenly portrait so dominates that His earthly existence is seen as one of appearance only. Sometimes His suffering is portrayed as not really His. This final type of text is called docetic, most exemplified in the *Apocalypse of Peter* and the *Second Treatise of the Great Seth*.

We have considered a large number of texts from the new materials. Although these works contain some variation, they also possess certain basic themes. Foremost is Christ's heavenly nature. This portrait frequently surfaces in the description of His involvement in the creation. Some texts also speak of a defect in the original creation, so that the material world is unredeemable. Christ is the Savior, only because He reveals creation's corruptness, as well as the liberating knowledge of light and truth. Jesus reveals the divine inner spark of spiritual presence to those who understand Him.

STUDY QUESTIONS

1) *What four options exist for how Jesus' person is seen, and to which period (ancient or modern) does each view belong?*

2) *Do these texts as a group affirm a human Jesus? Why or why not?*

3) *What range of views about the person of Jesus do these texts show? Name one example for each view (Note: some may not have an example).*

· NINE ·

JESUS: DIVINE AND/OR HUMAN? PART 2

JESUS IN THE TRADITIONAL MATERIALS

The key issue here revolves around the unity of Jesus as human and divine. Of special importance will be how Jesus' humanity is presented and the relationship of the Savior or the Christ to Jesus.

In the New Testament

First, the four Gospels take seriously Jesus' humanity. The bulk of these Gospels presents the story of His work and teaching on Earth. With the new materials from Nag Hammadi and other such texts, often the settings involve the ascended Christ. His teachings in these alternative texts are words from above after His death. In contrast, virtually none of the teaching material from the four Gospels is given this post-Cross setting (Bock 2002b for details). In fact, the pre-Cross nature of this teaching is clearly marked as a literary feature. Even the exalted opening of John 1:1–18 is an introduction by John and not Jesus' direct teaching, standing in contrast to the earthly setting of virtually everything else Jesus teaches in John's gospel. This point is a significant difference between the new materials and their older counterparts.

Parallel to this difference of setting is the reappearance in the traditional materials of the short doctrinal, confessional teaching.

Paul, writing in the fifties, presents one such teaching in Romans 1:1–4: "From Paul, a slave of Christ Jesus, called to be an apostle, set apart for the gospel of God. This gospel he promised beforehand through his prophets in the holy scriptures, concerning his Son who was a descendant of David with reference to the flesh, who was appointed the Son-of-God-in-power according to the Holy Spirit by the resurrection from the dead, Jesus Christ our Lord."

In Paul's famous summary, we have Jesus Christ in one package. The Son is both "descendant of David with reference to the flesh" (a human) and "Son-of-God-in-power" by resurrection, reflecting His divine role as Son. The Greek term here often translated "appointed" more precisely means "marked out." It has the idea of showing a horizon or giving someone a frame of reference. The combined name of Jesus Christ also presents the unity of His person. His name, Jesus, and His office as anointed (what Christ means) often appear together to express this unity of function within His person.

This context involves the gospel being summarized. The gospel is connected to Scripture's promise from what Christians call the Old Testament. This opening association claims that the gospel's roots are tied to the long revealed promise of God. Thus, works that reject the God of Genesis and of Israel stand in opposition to this message. In tying the God of promise and the gospel together with Jesus Christ, this summary pulls together the themes of the first two topics of our tour. In 1 Corinthians 8:4–6, the role of Jesus Christ as Creator is affirmed to the Corinthians. There is no splitting of the person in these summaries.

Another summary from the Pauline tradition makes this point. Titus 2:11–14 discusses God's grace in the gospel, and at the core is Jesus Christ. It reads:

> For the grace of God has appeared, bringing salvation to all people. It trains us to reject godless ways and worldly desires and to live self-controlled, upright, and godly lives in the present age, as we wait for the happy fulfillment of our hope in the glorious appearing of our great God and Savior, Jesus Christ. He gave himself for us to set us free from every kind of lawlessness and to purify for himself a people who are truly his, who are eager to do good.

Here we have deity as well as sacrifice and suffering side by side. Jesus is God and a Savior who truly suffered on behalf of His people.

John 1:1–18, although it starts back before the Creation, lacks any of the kind of cosmic detail that we see in many new works. We have the Word with God, the Word as divine, and the Word sharing in Creation. In Him are life and light, themes also struck by the new materials. This Word became flesh and tabernacled (or dwelled) among us. There is no sense of any deceptiveness or the presence of seeming appearance here. In fact, the related letter of 1 John 1:1–4 says it clearly as a teaching summary:

> This is what we proclaim to you: what was from the beginning, what we have heard, what we have seen with our eyes, what we have looked at and our hands have touched (concerning the word of life—and the life was revealed, and we have seen and testify and announce to you the eternal life that was with the Father and was revealed to us). What we have seen and heard we announce to you too, so that you may have fellowship with

us (and indeed our fellowship is with the Father and with his Son Jesus Christ). Thus we are writing these things so that our joy may be complete.

Jesus Christ had a real physical, material presence. Such teaching is key to fellowship among believers.

Even more clear is the test in 1 John 4:2–3: "By this you know the Spirit of God: Every spirit that confesses Jesus as the Christ who has come in the flesh is from God, but every spirit that does not confess Jesus is not from God." What is important here is the use of the name Jesus Christ in the positive affirmation and the use of the name Jesus on the negative side. The confession of the heavenly Christ was common in all kinds of Christian materials; the debated issue was whether Jesus and the divinely sent Christ were the same figure. Second John 7 says it even more compactly: "Many deceivers have gone out into the world, people who do not confess Jesus as Christ coming in the flesh. This person is the deceiver and the antichrist!" These texts were written not in the second, third, or fourth century, but from the end of the first century. They do not use the word *heresy*, but the teaching that Jesus did not come in the flesh is branded as false teaching.

In the Johannine tradition, we find in Revelation 1:17–18 this declaration: "Do not be afraid! I am the first and the last, and the one who lives! I was dead, but look, now I am alive—forever and ever—and I hold the keys of death and of Hades!" Earlier in Revelation 1:8, Jesus spoke of Himself as the Alpha and the Omega, another way to say the first and the last. These are the words of "the Lord God—the one who is, and who was, and who is still to come—the All-Powerful!" In 1:5, Jesus Christ is called the firstborn from the dead and ruler of the kings on earth. Unity of person is affirmed again.

These texts are as direct as possible and represent a historical record that those who were associated with teaching rooted in Paul and John saw these issues as reflective of a core faith, not an alternative option.

Hebrews also presents Jesus as Son, who reflects God and humanity. The author says that the Son is "the representation of his [God's] essence" (1:3). The author also affirms Jesus' full humanity as a true human sympathetic High Priest, an embrace of Jewish imagery lacking in most of the new materials (2:14–18; 4:14–16). Hebrews 2:14–18 states:

> Since the children share in flesh and blood, he likewise shared in their humanity, so that through death he could destroy the one who holds the power of death (that is, the devil), and set free those who were held in slavery all their lives by their fear of death. For surely his concern is not for angels, but he is concerned for Abraham's descendants. Therefore *he had to be made* like his brothers and sisters *in every respect,* so that he could become a merciful and faithful high priest in things relating to God, to make atonement for the sins of the people. For since he himself suffered when he was tempted, he is able to help those who are tempted. (emphasis added)

To the author of Hebrews, a full connection to humanity was necessary. This view is in contrast to that of many alternative texts where it was impossible for Jesus to be human because His humanity would compromise His heavenly incorruptibility. The author is aware of this issue as well, as he says in 4:15, "We do not have a high priest incapable of sympathizing with our weaknesses, but one who has been tempted in every way just as we are, yet without sin." He calls this portrait of Jesus, the Son of God, "our confession" (4:14).

First Peter is no different. This epistle highlights the example of Jesus' actual suffering as the model for the believer's own life. The parallel structure in 1 Peter 2:21–25 has a hymnic or confessional feel. The first two verses of this unit read, "To this you were called, since Christ also suffered for you, leaving an example for you to follow in his steps. He committed no sin nor was deceit found in his mouth." The example is Christ's real suffering. In 1:2, the chosen are destined "according to the foreknowledge of God the Father by being set apart by the Spirit for obedience" to Jesus Christ, a formula that points to devotion to Jesus. In 3:21–22, Jesus Christ has ascended into heaven where He is "at the right hand of God with angels and authorities and powers subject to him." The Jesus Christ who suffered is the Jesus Christ of heavenly authority.

Once again a survey of New Testament writers shows that the unity of the person of Jesus Christ was a core element of belief.

Acts 2:16–36 makes the same point. On the one hand, we have "Jesus the Nazarene, a man clearly attested to you by God" (2:22). This is the One who was crucified and raised according to God's plan and promise (2:24–31). On the other hand, we have in this same person, the One who now is raised to God's right hand. Acts 2:32–36 reads:

This Jesus God raised up, and we are all witnesses of it. So then, exalted to the right hand of God, and having received the promise of the Holy Spirit from the Father, he has poured out what you both see and hear. For David did not ascend into heaven, but he himself says,

"The Lord said to my lord,
'Sit at my right hand
until I make your enemies a footstool for your feet.'"

> Therefore let all the house of Israel know beyond a doubt that
> God has made this Jesus whom you crucified both Lord and
> Christ.

This text speaks of what God did with Jesus of Nazareth
(2:32). It also cites part of Israel's Scripture, Psalm 110:1, to support the claim. The result is that the One who was known as Jesus
of Nazareth is revealed to be Lord and Christ, the very Lord we
call upon to be saved. Acts 2:21 reads, "Everyone who calls on the
name of the Lord will be saved." Acts 2:21 is actually a citation of
Joel 2:32 from the Old Testament. Whom Joel referred to as the
God of Israel (2:27), Peter says also includes the lordship of Jesus
(Acts 2:21 with 2:36, with Jesus the Lord who is being called
upon). Here we have an appeal to the Scripture of the God of
Israel and to events of real suffering, death, and resurrection that
show Jesus is confessed as the Christ, the Lord. The affirmation is
that God has shown through events the unity of Jesus' person. He
is Jesus, Christ, and even the Lord on whom we call for salvation.

These witnesses share a core belief that Jesus Christ was one
and the same figure, uniquely connected to divinity and fully
human. There was no "appearance" to His humanity. And no
matter how great Jesus was seen to be, His entire person—as
both a human and a being uniquely related to God—performed the work God called Him to carry out. This is the core
high Christology of the early faith, with all witnesses dating
back to the first century.

In the Apostolic Fathers

As we move toward the second century, *1 Clement* makes the
same point. In 36:1–2, Clement writes to Corinth:

> This is the way, dear friends, in which we found our salvation,
> namely, Jesus Christ, the high priest of our offerings, the

Guardian and Helper of our weakness. Through him let us look steadily into the heights of heaven; through him we see as in a mirror his faultless and transcendent face; through him the eyes of our hearts have been opened; through him our foolish and darkened mind springs up into the light; through him the Master has willed that we should taste immortal knowledge, for "he, being the radiance of his majesty, is as much superior to the angels as the name he has inherited is more excellent."

Clement cites Hebrews 1:4 and notes that Jesus is a human high priest of offerings. He is light and the way to knowledge, being also the radiance of divine majesty.

The work known as *2 Clement* comes from an unknown author. In 1:1–2 he tells his readers how to think about Jesus:

Brothers, we ought to think of Jesus Christ, as we do of God, as 'Judge of the living and the dead.' And we ought not to belittle our salvation, for when we belittle him, we also hope to receive but little. And those who listen as though these are small matters do wrong, and we also do wrong, when we fail to acknowledge from where and by whom and to what place we were called, and how much suffering Jesus Christ endured for our sake.

Jesus Christ suffered and yet should be thought of in a manner similar to God, as Judge of the living and the dead. There also is a text that echoes newer materials with its theme of the transitory nature of our earthly existence and the need for rest: "You know, brothers, that our stay in this world of the flesh is insignificant and transitory, but the promise of Christ is great and marvelous: rest in the coming kingdom and eternal life!" (*2 Clement* 5:5).

Lest we think this is parallel to an evil creation that excludes the flesh and the material world from salvation, we read in *2 Clement* 9:1–5:

> Let none of us say that this flesh is not judged and does not rise again. Understand this: In what state were you saved? In what state did you recover your sight, if it was not while you were in this flesh? We must, therefore, guard the flesh as a temple of God. For just as you were called in the flesh, so you will come in the flesh. If Christ, the Lord who saved us, became flesh (even though he was originally spirit) and in that state called us, so also we shall receive our reward in this flesh.

In *2 Clement*, Jesus really suffered and is the Christ who redeems His children, including their flesh.

Ignatius is similar. In *Ephesians*, he compares false teachers to wild beasts. In 7:2, Ignatius says, "There is only one Physician who is both flesh and spirit, born and unborn, God in man, true life in death, both from Mary and from God, first subject to suffering and then beyond it, Jesus Christ our Lord." Reinforcing this, Ignatius teaches, "Our God Jesus the Christ was conceived by Mary according to God's plan, both from the seed of David and of the Holy Spirit. He was born and was baptized in order that by his suffering he might cleanse the water" (18:2). In 19:3*b*, he declares, "The ancient kingdom was abolished, when God appeared in human form to bring newness of eternal life; and what God had been prepared by God began to take effect." And he sums up in 20:2, "Continue to gather together, each and every one of you, collectively and individually by name, in grace, in one faith and one Jesus Christ, who physically was a descendant of David, who is Son of man and Son of God." Ignatius sees one person, reflecting both God and man. He also appeals to a new idea that he in particular emphasized. It involves being responsible to the bishop and the presbytery, an appeal to be faithful to the one church that Jesus founded.

Ignatius has many such texts (Appendix 2 has a partial listing). One more text shows what he might be opposing. He writes in *Magnesians* 11:1, "I want to forewarn you not to get snagged on the hooks of worthless opinions but instead to be fully convinced about the birth and the suffering and the resurrection, which took place during the governorship of Pontius Pilate. These things were truly and most assuredly done by Jesus Christ, our hope, from which may none of you be turned aside" (see also *Philadelphians* 9:2).

Ignatius teaches the unity of Jesus' person and the reality of His suffering. Its historical place rings like a chorus through his letters, echoing the refrain from other traditional texts.

In *Philippians* 7:1, Polycarp cites his teacher John, "Everyone 'who does not confess that Jesus Christ has come in the flesh is the antichrist'; and whoever does not acknowledge the testimony of the cross 'is of the devil'; and whoever twists the sayings of the Lord to suit his own sinful desires and claims that there is neither resurrection nor judgment—well, that person is the first-born of Satan." The term *heresy* may not appear here, but for Polycarp, there is little doubt about how he regards such views. Polycarp holds to such a thing as orthodoxy. It is found in the core themes we are considering.

The epistle known by the name *Barnabas,* but not tied to the Barnabas of the New Testament, also discusses this theme. In the midst of a long discussion in 5:1–14, he says about Jesus' suffering:

> If he had not come in the flesh, men could in no way have been saved by looking at him. For when they look at merely the sun they are not able to gaze at its rays, even though it is the work of

his hands and will eventually cease to exist. Therefore the Son of God came in the flesh for the reason, that he might complete the full measure of the sins who persecuted his prophets to death. It was for this reason, therefore, that he submitted. For God says that the wounds of his flesh came from them: "When they strike down their own Shepherd, then the sheep of the flock will perish." But he himself desired to suffer in this manner, for it was necessary for him to suffer on a tree. For the one who prophesies says concerning him, "Spare my soul from the sword" and "Pierce my flesh with nails, for bands of evil men have risen up against me." And again he says, "Behold, I have given my back to scourges, and my cheeks to blows, and I have set my face like a solid rock."

Again it is the Son of God in the flesh who truly suffers. The appeal is to Scripture's language and promise, Jewish texts that revealed the Creator God of Israel, even as he challenges the Jewish leadership's rejection of Jesus.

Shepherd of Hermas reveals a parallel theme in one of its citations of the Lord. It comes in a vision that has a similar feel to the dialogue gospels of the new materials. "Because," he said, "God planted the vineyard, that is, he created the people, and turned them over to his Son. And the Son placed angels over them to protect them, and the Son himself cleansed their sins with great labor and enduring much toil, for no one can cultivate a vineyard without toil or labor. So, when he himself had cleansed the sins of the people, he showed them the paths of life, giving them the law which he received from his Father" (59:2–3). The people's cleansing takes place by His enduring much toil and labor, an allusion to His suffering as Son.

So the apostolic fathers have a core belief about the unity of Jesus and His real suffering as a human and a divine figure. They do not work out the specific details of this relationship between Jesus and God or between Jesus' two natures. That task is something the church does later in the third century and beyond, but a core belief was being echoed repeatedly in these earliest writers. That core belief focused upon Jesus of Nazareth, both human and divine, whose suffering was real. For these early church leaders, to divide Jesus' person, to say He did not come in the flesh, or to teach His suffering was not real was false teaching. It might not have been named heresy, but that is how it was seen (Davids 1973).

In Justin Martyr

Justin Martyr has the same core idea. He says of Jesus:

> Our teacher of these things is Jesus Christ, who also was born for this purpose, and was crucified under Pontius Pilate, procurator of Judaea, in the times of Tiberius Caesar; and that we reasonably worship him, having learned that he is the Son of the true God himself, and holding him in the second place, and the prophetic Spirit in the third, we will prove. For they proclaim our madness to consist in this, that we give to a crucified man a place second to the unchangeable and eternal God, the Creator of all; for they do not discern the mystery that is herein, to which, as we make it plain to you, we pray you to give heed. (*1 Apology* 12–13)

Justin gives a ranking in the Godhead but also claims that the man who taught these things is the Son, Jesus Christ. This Jesus is also to be worshipped, an important point for a movement that claims to venerate one true God.

In Chapter 7, we noted Justin's *2 Apology,* elaborating on God's and Jesus' relationship and explaining their names, but this text also points out the unity of Jesus' person:

> His Son, who alone is properly called Son, the Word who also was with Him and was begotten before the works when at first He

created and arranged all things by Him, is called Christ, in reference to His being anointed and God's ordering all things through Him . . . For He was made man also, as we before said, having been conceived according to the will of God the Father, for the sake of believing men, and for the destruction of the demons.

In his *Dialogue with Trypho*, chapter 128, Justin engages his Jewish protagonist with a remark about how the Father and Son are related. He declares that the essence of the Father cannot be divided while discussing the Father and His begotten Son. For Justin there is no division in the person of God. Jesus is as much deity as God is, just as fire is fire, no matter in how many different, distinct spots it appears.

In Melito of Sardis

Our final citation is from the bishop of Sardis, who wrote circa 160. His preserved work is a collection of fragments from various works that do not have verse numbers, so his work is referred to by the title of the fragment topic. Melito's *Discourse on the Cross* virtually summarizes the traditional view. Melito affirms the humanity and the divinity of Jesus side by side:

On these accounts He came to us; on these accounts, though He was incorporeal, He formed for Himself a body after our fashion—appearing as a sheep, yet still remaining the Shepherd; being esteemed a servant, yet not renouncing the Sonship; being carried *in the womb* of Mary, yet arrayed in *the nature of* His Father; treading upon the earth, yet filling heaven; appearing as an infant, yet not discarding the eternity of His nature; being invested with a body, yet not circumscribing the unmixed simplicity of His Godhead; being esteemed poor, yet not divested of His riches; needing sustenance inasmuch as He was man, yet not ceasing to feed the entire world inasmuch as He is God; putting on the likeness of a servant, yet not impairing the likeness of His Father. He sustained every character *belonging to Him* in an immutable nature: He was standing before Pilate, and *at the same time* was sitting with His Father; He was nailed upon the tree, and *yet* was the Lord of all things.

Melito does not discuss how this works philosophically, but he affirms in eloquently balanced statements a human and a divine Jesus. Jesus is incorporeal and has a body. He is sheep and Shepherd. He is servant, yet Son. He is infant and yet eternal in nature. He is man and God. He stood before Pilate and was seated with the Father. Nailed to the tree, He was still Lord. At the beginning of the *Discourse on Body and Soul*, Melito summarizes this way: "For this reason did the Father send His Son from heaven without a bodily form, that, when He should put on a body by means of the Virgin's womb, and be born man, He might save man, and gather together those members of His which death had scattered when he divided man." Such views reacted instinctively against the dualism found in most alternative Gnostic works.

SUMMARY

Jesus' role and His relationship to God are among the most crucial topics being discussed. Our broad sample of new materials made clear the full scope of what was discussed in the early centuries among those who claimed Jesus' name. Again, there is no doubt that a spectrum of views existed. There were three or four diverse conceptions of Jesus. For some, Jesus was human and divine; His role in the Creation was significant. Could Jesus be fully human? Was what Jesus redeemed a good creation worth saving? Most of the new materials hesitated either about Jesus as an earthly figure or the reality of His suffering or about a redemption that included the physical world in a creation that was seen as flawed from the start. This was done in one of two ways: by highlighting Jesus' heavenly character so that the discussion of any humanity was muted or by arguing Jesus only appeared to be human.

Exceptions to this in the new materials were *Silvanus*, which most have never grouped with an alternative view, and *Thomas*, which is most vague about how the relationship within Jesus works. What the new materials do share is an extremely high view of Jesus. Even *Thomas*, which is often held up as a source that presents Jesus merely as a teacher, has an exalted Jesus. In fact, many new materials show a Jesus who is so exalted that His humanity is lost or almost hidden, the exact reverse of what many popular treatments of such works claim today.

The more traditional materials go in a completely different direction. They contain a consistent refrain, affirming the humanity *and* the divinity of Jesus Christ as Lord and Son of God. Having come in real flesh, Jesus' suffering is real. This is a core belief. This is not to say that the traditional materials have sorted out in detail how this works. That would be a task of later forms of the traditional faith as they sought to define philosophically and theologically their understanding of a human and divine Jesus. However, what we do see in the first two centuries is a clear, confessed declaration of faith. The community affirmed such a figure because they believed that was what Jesus taught. That faith also affirmed that Jesus did this in fulfillment of God's promise. Jesus came as Son of David *and* Son of God, the chosen Christ who truly suffered.

Like the belief in God as Maker of heaven and earth, so there was a belief in Jesus Christ, truly God and truly man. When the later creeds affirmed this statement, they did not create the view in the third century or fourth century as many popular writers today imply. This teaching was a core belief of those closest to Jesus in the earliest period as virtually every work they produced in the first two centuries shows.

When Robert Wilken (1981, 106) introduced a new journal on the study of the second century, he made this observation about the Bauer thesis and the second century: "We have overlooked the ineluctable fact that the Christian tradition did solidify around certain practices and beliefs and that catholic Christianity not only seized the center but was able effectively to shape and form the main trunk of Christian tradition." Our tour shows he is right. (For clarification, when Wilken refers to catholic Christianity, he is thinking not of what we mean by Roman Catholicism, but of the early church's work in this early period before the "catholic" church became so Roman in its hierarchical structure. *Catholic* simply means "universal," and this is how Wilken uses the term.)

Our tour is not yet complete, but the first two stops suggest that the early church possessed core beliefs reflected in its tradition. Such ideas were affirmed in the church's collection of sacred texts that also provided a basis for the church's identity. There is far more evidence for this core of faith being solidly in place by the second century than there is evidence for the mere existence of competing alternatives.

STUDY QUESTIONS

1) *How do traditional texts see Jesus in terms of divinity and humanity?*

2) *How consistent is this view in this material?*

3) *What differences exist between alternative and traditional materials when it comes to Jesus' person?*

4) *Are these significant differences?*

· TEN ·

THE NATURE OF HUMANITY'S REDEMPTION: SPIRITUAL OR ALSO PHYSICAL? PART 1

Our tour turns to the nature of humanity. Several questions are in view. What is said of man's creation as a being with the potential to have spiritual knowledge? Is the human made up of body and soul or body, soul, and spirit? What is redeemable in humanity: only the spiritual element? Does redemption include the soul or the body? Is there a physical dimension to salvation? The new materials open our tour with traditional ones following. The scope of the questions and the number of sources surveyed require more summarizing than citation. We shall see a spectrum of views and sense more overlap among all the materials on this topic. Yet key differences will surface. The primary question here is whether an individual is redeemed as a unit or divided up. In other words, is it only the person's soul that is saved? Or does salvation include a transformed body as part of the deliverance of the material part of creation?

It is difficult to distinguish soul from spirit in Greek thought. Both refer to the nonmaterial part of a person that animates life and also describes the part of a person that is sensitive to religious expression. They can function as synonyms. When a person is divided into simply body and soul, then the soul covers the spiritual part of a person. When there is seen body, soul, and spirit, then it is normally the spirit that is said to be the part of a person that relates to God or the gods.

MAN IN THE NEW MATERIALS

In the Gospel of Thomas

Thomas has a few relevant texts. In saying 28, Jesus declares that he took his place in the midst of the world and appeared in the flesh. He then reports on what he found: "I found all of them intoxicated; I found none of them thirsty. And my soul became afflicted for the sons of men, because they are blind in their hearts and do not have sight; for empty they came into the world, and empty too they seek to leave the world. But for the moment they are intoxicated. When they shake off their wine, they will repent." This passage points to people in need, and it uses the metaphors *blindness* and *drunkenness*, humanity's condition upon entering the world. Usually metaphorical blindness and drunkenness speak of a lack of understanding.

In another saying, Jesus comments on the wonder of a person's creation: "If the flesh came into being because of the spirit, it is a wonder. But if the spirit came into being because of the body, it is a wonder of wonders. Indeed, I am amazed at how this great wealth has made its home in this poverty" (saying 29; Robinson 2000, 2:67; Robinson 1990, 130). Metaphor again appears and makes the point. We have two elements that make up life: spirit and body. What is amazing is that the spirit is able to live in the "poverty" of the body. That is why body giving a place of life to spirit is a "wonder of wonders."

Saying 22 treats the question about who will enter the kingdom. Here Jesus replies that one can enter the kingdom when two are made one, the inside is made like the outside, the above is made like the below, when the male and female become one, when eyes are fashioned in the place of the eye, when a hand is made in the place of the hand, a foot is made in the place of the foot, and likeness is made in place of likeness. The reply is an extended metaphor about oneness and a new creation. Beyond that one point it tells us little. Saying 37 is similar but pictures disrobing and putting on "new life" garments. Salvation means a new existence.

Saying 53 asks whether circumcision is beneficial. The reply is that if it were, then children would have been born circumcised. What is profitable is "true circumcision in the spirit." The spirit is superior to the flesh.

Saying 87 states this body-soul contrast more starkly: "Wretched is the body that is dependent upon a body, and wretched is the soul that is dependent on these two." This saying also devalues the body. Similar is saying 112: "Woe to the flesh that depends on the soul; woe to the soul that depends on the flesh." The one additional feature here is that this passage sees neither soul nor body as positive. Such sayings suggest why an activated or discovered spirit is needed to participate in the kingdom.

This point about the living spirit is made by the last saying in the gospel, saying 114. In it, Peter seeks to send Mary away because she is not worthy of kingdom life as a woman. Jesus replies, "I myself shall lead her in order to make her male, so that she may become a living spirit resembling you males. For every woman who will make herself male will enter the kingdom." This saying is hardly politically correct. It shows that women were not elevated in these texts as some claim. For our current topic, the "living spirit" makes one able to share in the kingdom. In other texts, we shall see that maleness is associated with the mind that knows. This is another metaphor and helps us understand saying 114 and its strange, "no salvation for women" imagery, for to be saved is to have a mind that knows.

Saying 85 suggests that Adam's creation comes up short. He was created by great power and wealth, and yet he was not worthy of those Jesus enlightens. For "had he been worthy [he would] not [have experienced] death."

In discussing death in saying 11, Jesus notes that the dead are not alive, nor will the living die. In fact, there will be a day of light when two are made one. So in the end, salvation involves reconciliation within creation, but some things that die stay dead. In this reconciliation, great things will be done. According to saying 106, when the two are made one, "you will become sons of man, and when you say, 'Mountain, move away,' it will move away."

Thomas says a variety of things about humanity. Soul and body make up life with potential access to the living spirit. Body and soul are something less as substances, but *Thomas* does not spell out how this works. There also is a sense that creation, which Adam represents, is a place of death and lacks something, but no details appear about this view. Spirit and the knowledge are needed for reconciliation in the end when all things are made one. As saying 111 notes, when the heavens are rolled up, "the one who lives from the living one will not see death."

In *Pistis Sophia*

Pistis Sophia: The Books of the Savior was one of the few Gnostic works we had before Nag Hammadi. The Askew Codex contains this work. As early as 1778 C. G. Woide discussed it (Logan 1996, xiii; Rudolph 1983, 27). Jesus answers questions from his disciples, so it is a dialogue gospel, parallel to the *Apocryphon of John* (Logan 1996, 260). In *Pistis*, Jesus as Savior is related to an entity called the First Mystery, but nowhere is he called the Christ. The work reveals the labor of this Jesus as a preexistent, cosmic being. Thus, it parallels many new works that treat cosmology and creation. However, its primary topic is the afterlife and who is saved, presenting eleven years of secret teaching and true knowledge that Jesus gave to his followers after his resurrection. The teaching leads to ethical exhortation and includes appeals to magic and the invocation of special names. This work includes five hymns from the *Odes of Solomon,* an early second-century Jewish or Gnostic work. Yamauchi (1983, 91, 94) questions whether the *Odes* are Gnostic, while Rudolph (1983, 29) holds they are. Either way, this usage places *Pistis* in the second century at the earliest. Most see it using the *Apocryphon of John* (Logan 1996, 260; Rudolph 1983, 27). Such usage places *Pistis* in the later second century if not into the third.

This book divides into chapters. *Pistis* sees the existence of souls tied to Jesus' work to call others to himself. He cast twelve powers into the wombs of their mothers when he came to earth. These twelve powers, members of the Treasury of Light, produce power that now resides in believers (chap. 7). So Jesus tells his followers they are not from the world, just as he is not. The souls in the world who lack the light come from the power of the archons of the aeons, namely, rulers from the spiritual world. But the souls of believers come from Jesus and belong "to the height" (chaps. 7–8).

Jesus also transformed John the Baptist's soul and, in the form of "Gabriel," addressed Mary. He cast into her the power of Barbelo, which was his body from above. This power replaced the soul in her. Thus, believers are born without souls from the archons while Jesus' work in Mary sets the stage for his coming (chap. 7).

In chapter 23, Jesus turns a multitude of souls onto the right path by saving them so they can ascend. In chapter 25, Jesus describes how the archons created matter and the souls of the imperfect. In chapter 27, the souls of the saved receive the mysteries. The disciples worship Jesus in response to this news. A hymn appears in chapter 32, and verses 35–36 sum things up: "God will save their souls out of all matter, and a city will be prepared in the light; and all souls which will be saved will dwell in that city, and they will inherit it. And the soul of those who will receive mysteries will be in that place, and they who have received mysteries in his name will be within it." Chapter 37 calls these special people the "pneumatics," or spiritual ones. This book describes a special people different from the start than others in creation.

Chapter 39 presents Sophia's battle with the evil archons. During it she says that she had her light taken from her so that her power dried up. She was like "a peculiar demon which dwells in matter, in whom is no light." She was like "a spirit counterpart, which is in a material body in which there is no light-power" (vv. 4–6). Here is dualism between the material world and the spiritual world, between darkness and light. In 41:3, her dilemma is summarized: "I have become like a material body, which has no one in the height who will save it." Her hymns are called hymns of repentance, seeking forgiveness for her transgression, an allusion to the flawed creation she generated (46:7–8). Eventually in answer to her pleas, the First Mystery sends Jesus to bring her back to the Light from the Chaos of creation (chaps. 58–59). In chapter 71, she praises her deliverance, noting that creation will be dissolved.

Pistis is a developed Gnostic work. There are two types of humanity, those indwelt by the power of light and those made without it. Those of the light reflect spiritual awareness and have a spirit. Those who are not of the light lack a spirit and have only an evil soul. *Pistis* has a different emphasis from *Thomas*. It represents one end of our spectrum, where those headed for redemption are completely distinguished from everyone else.

In the Letter to Rheginos (= Treatise on the Resurrection)
Resurrection and humanity are the topics in chapters 47–49
and explain this book's alternate title, the *Treatise on the
Resurrection*. It challenges the resurrection of the flesh. The
body is not saved. What comes from the All is much better.
The deliverance of what is inside us gives life, an allusion to
the spirit.

> Nothing, then, redeems us from this world. But the All which
> we are, we are saved. We have received salvation from end to
> end. Let us think this way! Let us comprehend this way!
>
> But there are some (who) wish to understand, in the
> enquiry about those things they are looking into, whether he
> who is saved, if he leaves his body behind, will be saved imme-
> diately. Let no one doubt concerning this, . . . indeed, the visible
> members which are dead shall not be saved, for (only) the liv
> ing [members] which exist within them would arise.
>
> What, then, is the resurrection? It is always the disclosure of
> those who have risen. (47:24–48:6; Robinson 2000, 1:153–55;
> Robinson 1990, 55–56)

The resurrection is "the revelation of what is, the transformation of things, and a transition into newness" (48:34–38).
The imperishable and light swallow up the perishable, and the
Pleroma fills up the deficiency (48:38–49:5). Rheginos should
consider himself as already risen, sharing in this deliverance as
he flees the things associated with the flesh (49:9–25).

So the resurrection is one of spirit, not body. The nature of
resurrection forms an ethical base for behavior now and a
separation from the things tied to this world. This account of
resurrection is less radical than that in *Pistis,* but the essence
of resurrection is similar. The body will not be raised. As
45:39–46:2 summarizes, "This is the spiritual resurrection which

swallows up the psychic in the same way as the fleshly." In resurrection, the body passes away, but the spirit abides forever.

In the Teachings of Silvanus

In *Silvanus* the person is a combination of body, soul, and mind. It teaches, "Understand that you have come into being from three races: from the earth, from the formed, and from the created. The body has come into being from the earth with an earthly substance, but the formed, for the sake of the soul, has come into being from the thought of the Divine. The created, however, is the mind, which has come into being in conformity with the image of God" (92:15–24; Robinson 2000, 4:301; Robinson 1990, 384). So live in accord with the mind and do not think about the things of the flesh (93:3–5). The soul is the wife to the image of God (92:29–31), but to cast out the mind is to cast out "the male part," leaving the female part to itself (93:9–13). This suggests that one needs mind and soul to really be complete, to be able to defeat the passions as well as ignorance (Franzmann 1996, 61).

Summarily, a person consists of three parts, but the spirit is the reflection of God's image.

In the Apocryphon of John

Apocryphon II 25–27 treats the afterlife as things understood only by those who belong to the immovable race. The saved and the perfect are those on whom the Spirit of life will descend, those with whom he will be in power. They are purified from all wickedness and involvement with evil, caring only about incorruption. They "are not affected by anything except the state of being in the flesh alone, which they bear while looking expectantly for the time when they will be met by the receivers (of the body). Such then are worthy of the imperishable, eternal life and the calling" (II 25:33–26:3). Anyone who has the Spirit will be saved (II 26:7–19). Those on whom a counterfeit spirit falls will also be saved, for the power will eventually overcome the despicable spirit (II 26:20–32). What of the ignorant, those who had no interest in the spirit? These souls are purged over a period of time until the soul "awakens from forgetfulness and acquires knowledge" (II 26:32–27:8). The advantage of real life is knowing early on who you are.

Apocryphon teaches not only that the body is left behind but also that eventually all come to such knowledge. So all are saved.

In the *Apocryphon of James*
This Nag Hammadi work claims to be a letter from James to an unknown recipient and gives James a lead role over Peter. The letter, written 550 days after resurrection, has a report about a "secret writing" from the Savior to James and Peter (2:19–20). The work encourages and threatens, ending with a description of Jesus' ascension. It may not be Gnostic although most scholars regard it that way. It is unlike traditional materials because it condemns the flesh, emphasizes the soul's ascent, and lacks a bodily resurrection and a return by Jesus. It denies remission of sin of one for another (Williams's introduction in Robinson 2000, 1:21). It dates from the late second or early third century.

This work contrasts Spirit and reason as revealed in chapter 4: "Hence become full of the Spirit, but be in want of reason, for reason [belongs to] the soul; in turn it is (of the nature of) the soul" (vv. 18–22; Robinson 2000, 1:35; Robinson 1990, 31). The work explains that the Father knows what the flesh needs, and the flesh desires the soul. Chapters 11:38*b*–12:16 discuss the relationship of body, soul, and sin:

For without the soul, the body does not sin, just as the soul is not saved without [the] spirit. But if the soul is saved (when it is) without evil, and the spirit is also saved, then the body becomes free from sin. For it is the spirit that raises the soul, but the body that kills it; that is, it is it (the soul) which kills itself. Verily I say unto you, He will not forgive the soul the sin by any means, nor the flesh the guilt; for none who have worn the flesh will be saved. For do you think that many have found the kingdom? Blessed is he who has seen himself as a fourth one in heaven!

In *Apocryphon*, the soul is like a force choosing between following the spirit or the flesh. It has responsibility for the person's spiritual welfare. According to 14:8–14, faith and knowledge give life.

Loving the flesh involves self-protection from suffering. In 5:6–9, the author asks, "So will you not cease loving the flesh and being afraid of sufferings?" In 6:15–18, Jesus teaches that those who fear death will not be saved.

The new materials conceive of the spirit, soul, and flesh in various ways. The body is usually seen negatively. The variation is how one speaks of a soul and/or spirit. Usually the soul is negative and needs the spirit. But in the case of the *Apocryphon of James*, the soul is like a judge, capable of going either way in choosing between good and evil. Unique to this book is a call to be ready for martyrdom.

In the Apocalypse of Peter

This *Apocalypse* argued that some teach falsely when they seek to respond to a dead man, an allusion to Jesus' death and resurrection. Such belief is called blaspheming (74:24–25). The error is that "they will hold fast to the name of a dead man, while thinking that they will become pure" (74:13–15). In 75:12–76:2, the author elaborates:

Not every soul comes from the truth, nor from immortality. For every soul of these ages has death assigned to it, in our view. Consequently, it is always a slave. It is created for desires and their eternal destruction, for which they exist and in which they exist. They (the souls) love the material creatures which came forth with them. But immortal souls are not like these, O Peter. But, indeed, as long as the hour has not yet come, she (the immortal soul) will indeed resemble a mortal one. But she will not reveal her nature, although she alone is the immortal one and thinks about immortality. (Robinson 2000, 4:231, 233; Robinson 1990, 375)

The *Apocalypse of Peter* has mortal and immortal elements in the soul. Less clear is whether the distinction is between two classes of people as other works hold. In that case, the immortal soul belongs to those with knowledge and the mortal soul to those who lack it. Another possibility is that this refers to the inner individual, which does not gain an immortal soul until there is a response. This apocalypse is probably like other Gnostic works. We have two classes of people, the slave to the material world with his mortal soul and the liberated person of spiritual knowledge with his immortal soul touched by divine knowledge. The text makes it clear that whoever does not abide with the immortal soul "will dissolve into that which does not exist" (76:18–20). Either way the soul is viewed, *Apocalypse* rejects the material world.

In the Gospel of Philip

Philip possesses a clear view of the soul and the spirit. The work teaches, "No one will hide a large valuable object in something large, but many a time one has tossed countless thousands into a thing worth a penny. Compare the soul. It is a precious thing and it came to be in a contemptible body"

141

(56:20–26). The distinction between the soul's value and the worthless body is powerfully stated.

A similar contrast appears with the sons of Adam and of the perfect man: "If the sons of Adam are many, although they die, how much more are the sons of the perfect man, they do not die but are always begotten" (58:17–22).

Salvation involves reconciliation, a return to the original creative condition, and 68:22–26 points to Adam and Eve's example: "When Eve was still in Adam death did not exist. When she was separated from him death came into being. If he enters again and attains his former self, death will be no more." This theme of two becoming one or woman coming back into man has appeared in several texts. It is about the creation's reunification, but almost looks as if it treats women as a "tack on" to creation. Interestingly 70:9–11 returns to this idea and speaks about Adam's separation as death's beginning. Christ comes to repair this separation and unite them again (70:11–22).

The text notes that Adam came into being by a breath (70:22–29). The partner of his soul is the spirit, which represents the giving to him of a mother, something the powers envied. The archons' jealousy for humanity's position was noted earlier in the *Gospel(s) of Bartholomew*.

Philip reflects Gnostic texts. It is the spirit that gives life to the soul. The flesh reflects a flawed creation. Creation has two types of people: sons of Adam and sons of the perfect man.

In the Gospel of Truth

This work also highlights two types of people but devotes more time to discussing those from above (42:11–43:2):

> This is the manner of those who possess (something) from above of the immeasurable greatness, as they wait for the one alone and the perfect one, the one who is there for them. And

they do not go down to Hades nor have they envy nor groaning nor death within them, but they rest in him who is at rest, not striving nor being twisted around the truth. But they themselves are the truth; and the Father is within them and they are in the Father, being perfect, being undivided in the truly good one, being in no way deficient in anything, but they are set at rest, refreshed in the Spirit. And they will heed their root. They will be concerned with those (things) in which he will find his root and not suffer loss to his soul. This is the place of the [blessed; this is their place.]

For the rest, then, may they know, in their places, that it is not fitting for me having come to be in the resting-place, to speak of anything else. (Robinson 2000, 1:117; Robinson 1990, 51)

The gift from the Father is the Spirit that refreshes the soul and prevents it from suffering loss. About those who lack blessing, it is not fitting to say anything.

In the Second Treatise on the Great Seth

Our final two works possess the most developed pictures of creation. What does this developed portrait mean for humanity and redemption? The deliverer came "to reveal the glory of my kindred friends and the brethren of my spirit" (50:23–24). He goes on to explain that he visited a bodily dwelling and cast out the one first in it and went in, causing a tumult among the archons (51:20–32). Only what is from above is worth delivering. What was originally created in the person must go. The work closes in 69:20–70:1 in praise:

But these things I have given to you—I am Jesus the Christ, the Son of Man, exalted above the heavens—, O perfect and undefiled ones, on account of the mystery, undefiled and perfect and unutterable. But they think that (. . .) we decreed them before the foundation of the world in order that, when we emerge from the places of the world we may present there symbols of incorruption from the spiritual union with knowledge. You do not know this because the fleshly cloud overshadows you. But I alone am friend of Sophia. I have been in the bosom of the Father from the beginning, in the place of the sons of Truth, and the Greatness. Rest with me, my fellow spirits and my brethren, for ever. (Robinson 2000, 4:199)

In this obscure text, the fog of the flesh is treated as a cloud needing union of the spirit with knowledge. This idea parallels other Gnostic texts. The ultimate fellowship in *Second Treatise* involves kindred spirits.

In the Hypostasis of the Archons

Chapter 89 opens with Eve's creation. Here she is not the introduction of separation and death, as in the *Gospel of Philip,* but causes desire in the archons, who seek to have a child through her. However, when they attempt to seize her, she escapes by becoming a tree (89:3–26). This incident had precedent earlier in the book. At creation, when a female form appeared in the waters, the authorities of darkness also wanted to seize her (87:11–14) but could not because "beings that merely possess a soul cannot lay hold of those that possess a spirit, for they were from below, while it was from above" (87:17–19).

Adam is created by the forces below (87:33–88:5). They breathe into him so that he possesses a soul, but he does not move for days. The will of the father of the entirety allows all these events to take place. In a comic and pathetic scene, the forces continually try to breathe life into the man but fail. Finally, the spirit saw the soul-endowed man. He came and descended into the man to dwell within him and make him a living soul. So Adam is a figure with a soul made alive by the spirit that gave him life.

Hypostasis 90:13–19 describes the Fall. The carnal woman, Eve, eats of the tree and gives her husband the fruit. The Fall exposes that these beings were directed only by a soul because when they ate, "their imperfection became apparent in their lack of acquaintance; and they recognized that they were naked of the spiritual element, and took fig leaves and bound them upon their loins" (Robinson 2000, 2:243; Robinson 1990, 165). This final text shows that the soul was defective from the start. They needed to follow the most important element, the living spirit. Even though a spirit had come into them and gave them life, something was not right.

At the end of the work, the vision's recipient asks if he shares the matter of the archons (96:17–19). The reply is revealing: "You, together with your offspring, are from the primeval father, from above, out of the imperishable light, their souls are come. Thus the authorities cannot approach them because of the spirit of truth present within them; and all who become acquainted with this way exist deathless in the midst of dying mankind. Still that sown element will not become known now" (96:19–28; Robinson 2000, 2:257; Robinson 1990, 169). Two kinds of humanity exist, but the seed of new life that shows birth from above is not yet evident. Nonetheless, the presence of this spirit in them protects them from the authorities.

SUMMARY

These accounts on creation and humanity's makeup come in various packages while sharing certain features. The creation is defective. The material world is fallen. Mankind is divided into two classes. Redemption is about understanding one's real origin and seeking to embrace the spiritual dimension of existence.

One day all will be made clear, when those who are spiritual are united with the world above and the light. Redemption only will involve the ascent of spiritual ones back into the perfect, nonmaterial world. Humanity may be composed of flesh, but redemption involves only the enduring, spiritual person. Almost all the texts from Nag Hammadi reflect these ideas. How does this portrait compare with traditional materials?

STUDY QUESTIONS

1) *What is the central feature of salvation in these texts?*

2) *Is there a range of views about salvation in these texts?*

3) *According to many of these texts, what happens to the material creation (that is, physical matter)?*

• ELEVEN •

THE NATURE OF HUMANITY'S REDEMPTION: SPIRITUAL OR ALSO PHYSICAL? PART 2

MAN IN THE TRADITIONAL MATERIALS

What parts of the person get redeemed? Does salvation include the physical body or the soul? How does the rest of creation relate to this reconciliation? These questions are central to this topic.

In the New Testament

In 1 Corinthians, Paul has a long chapter on resurrection, arguing that Jesus was physically raised from the dead. Two portions of this passage affect our discussion, 15:1–19 and 15:35–58.

In 15:1–19, Paul stresses that what he teaches is something he received as tradition. He has not made up this doctrine. In addition, the resurrection hope reflects the experience of several people, placing this teaching well before the mid- to late fifties when Paul writes. The passage in part reads:

> Now I want to make clear for you, brothers and sisters, the gospel that I preached to you, that you received and on which you stand, and by which you are being saved, if you hold firmly to the message I preached to you—unless you believed in vain.

For I passed on to you as of first importance what I also received—that Christ died for our sins according to the scriptures, and that he was buried, and that he was raised on the third day according to the scriptures, and that he appeared to Cephas, then to the twelve. Then he appeared to more than five hundred of the brothers and sisters at one time, most of whom are still alive, though some have fallen asleep . . .

Now if Christ is being preached as raised from the dead, how can some of you say there is no resurrection of the dead? But if there is no resurrection of the dead, then not even Christ has been raised. And if Christ has not been raised, then our preaching is futile and your faith is empty. Also, we are found to be false witnesses about God, because we have testified against God that he raised Christ from the dead, when in reality he did not raise him, if indeed the dead are not raised. For if the dead are not raised, then not even Christ has been raised. And if Christ has not been raised, your faith is useless; you are still in your sins. Furthermore, those who have fallen asleep in Christ have also perished. For if only in this life we have hope in Christ, we should be pitied more than anyone.

Six points emerge from this text:

1. This teaching was "passed on" to Paul. So it is tradition circulating through the church with roots going back to the apostolic circle. Martin Hengel (2001, 119–83) has made a detailed study of resurrection teaching and its background in Judaism. He also works through 15:3–5 in some detail (pp. 119–38). This teaching belongs to those key doctrinal summaries. Resurrection sits at the top of this teaching list. It is of first importance, a core element of the faith.

2. Some were clearly denying this teaching. This is not entirely surprising because there was no idea of physical resurrection in Greco-Roman culture. Most heirs of the Greek culture believed

in the immortality of the soul or in some form of soul ascent they held to an afterlife.

3. The idea of physical resurrection is Jewish (Dan. 12:1–2). It is a hope that came from the God of Israel, who is Creator and thus can re-create life. In fact, Jews stressed physical resurrection in texts on martyrdom. Physical death was not significant, given that the body will be raised and restored. Second Maccabees 7, written in the first century BC, illustrates this view. Here seven sons faced execution for their faith as their mother exhorted them to be strong. In verses 10–11, the third son's turn to die comes. The text states, "After him, the third was the victim of their sport. When it [his death] was demanded, he quickly put out his tongue and courageously stretched forth his hands and said nobly, 'I got these from Heaven, and because of his laws I disdain them, and from him I hope to get them back again'"(RSV). Hope of a new life includes physical restoration. The belief was that this restoration occurs at one time during God's final deliverance for all people.

4. The last idea—a resurrection for all at the end—means that the idea of an individual being resurrected in the midst of history, before the resurrection of all at the end, was a Christian innovation. It is often claimed that the apostles or other disappointed followers of Jesus made up the New Testament resurrection accounts.

Yet this claim of a made-up resurrection for Jesus has two historical problems. The first is that had such a story been concocted on the basis of past Jewish or Greco-Roman precedent, there would have been no category of resurrection of a single person to turn to for the story. In other words, the story we have does not match the ideas of what such a story would have looked like (Wright 2003). There was no category of individual resurrection as a belief widespread enough to generate the new story. Something has to explain why the story was not that

Jesus' soul alone ascended or that Jesus will judge when He and everyone else are raised at the end. Those were the two key contemporary categories. Something generated this new doctrine of an individual rising from the dead. Paul's claim according to this older tradition was that the event of resurrection itself generated this new belief.

A second problem for a made-up resurrection account is that the allegedly made-up story relies on the presence of women witnesses at its start. In this culture females could not be witnesses. If one were making up this story, why would one create it with women as witnesses? The key role of women in the account suggests the women are there because the women were there at the start, not that this resurrection was made up.

5. The later remark about Jesus' resurrection as a "firstfruits" indicates what happens to us (1 Cor. 15:20). There also will be a physical resurrection for people. Paul ultimately is defending this real physical resurrection.

6. Paul's argument for resurrection is so central in his view that if he were wrong, Christians would be the most pitied of people. If he and those who hold to this tradition are wrong, they have hoped in an illusionary lie. Knowing what is at stake, Paul is quite honest here about his options. He does not believe that there is a chance the other option is true, as his many witnesses to a raised Jesus stand against it, but he knows that the alternative exists. Paul presents resurrection as fundamental to the faith.

How does physical resurrection work? First Corinthians 15:35–57 treats this idea:

> Someone will say, "How are the dead raised? With what kind of body will they come?" Fool! What you sow will not come to life unless it dies. And what you sow is not the body that is to be, but a bare seed—perhaps of wheat or something else. But God gives it a body just as he planned, and to each of the seeds a

body of its own. All flesh is not the same: People have one flesh, animals have another, birds and fish another. And there are heavenly bodies and earthly bodies. The glory of the heavenly body is one sort and the earthly another. There is one glory of the sun, and another glory of the moon and another glory of the stars, for star differs from star in glory.

It is the same with the resurrection of the dead. What is sown is perishable, what is raised is imperishable. It is sown in dishonor, it is raised in glory; it is sown in weakness, it is raised in power; it is sown a natural body, it is raised a spiritual body. If there is a natural body, there is also a spiritual body. So also it is written, "The first man, Adam, became a living person"; the last Adam became a life-giving spirit. However, the spiritual did not come first, but the natural, and then the spiritual. The first man is from the earth, made of dust; the second man is from heaven. Like the one made of dust, so too are those made of dust, and like the one from heaven, so too those who are heavenly. And just as we have borne the image of the man of dust, let us also bear the image of the man of heaven.

Now this is what I am saying, brothers and sisters: Flesh and blood cannot inherit the kingdom of God, nor does the perishable inherit the imperishable. Listen, I will tell you a mystery: We will not all sleep, but we will all be changed—in a moment, in the blinking of an eye, at the last trumpet. For the trumpet will sound, and the dead will be raised imperishable, and we will be changed. For this perishable body must put on the imperishable, and this mortal body must put on immortality. Now when this perishable puts on the imperishable, and this mortal puts on immortality, then the saying that is written will happen,

"Death has been swallowed up in victory."
"Where, O death, is your victory?
Where, O death, is your sting?"

> The sting of death is sin, and the power of sin is the law. But thanks be to God, who gives us the victory through our Lord Jesus Christ!

Paul argues that there are kinds of flesh in the world. The analogy is bodies of the heavens, earth, animals, birds, and fish. The physical body we have is like a seed that will be transformed and will emerge different and more glorious. However, it is of the same substance as it started. So Paul can say that flesh and blood will not inherit the kingdom (15:50), and yet there is a physical, material element to the redemption. The redeemed body is both like and unlike the physical body we now have. It is more than flesh and blood, but it is also material. When Paul makes his concluding point, he affirms it is the *mortal body* that is clothed with immortality (15:53). Redemption delivers an immortal body. For Paul and those of this early tradition, redemption covers the entire creation.

Other Pauline texts nuance this teaching. For example, in the midst of teaching about a redeemed body, Paul affirms the perishable and temporary nature of elements of the original body. Second Corinthians 5:1–3 speaks of the earthly tent we live in being destroyed. We groan for a heavenly dwelling with the Spirit being the key new ingredient. Earlier in 2 Corinthians 4, he notes the treasure of our person being encased in earthen vessels, another image of contrast between being made in God's image and having a fragile body. Another difference emerging from Paul's teaching is that not only people groan for redemption, but so does the entire creation (Rom. 8:18–24). When restoration comes, it will be for all of what God made as good, body included.

Nothing shows the difference between Paul and the new materials on the flesh as clearly as 1 Corinthians 6:12–20. Paul argues that it matters what one does with the body in this life, especially when it comes to sexual activity, because the body, contrary to what others teach, will be redeemed. When it comes to the body, Paul has a type of dualism but with crucial differences. The body is weak, fragile, even flawed, but it is part of the originally good creation that will be redeemed.

Another key difference about the original body's perishable nature exists in the midst of all the materials. For many of the new materials, the body is the product of an originally defective creation; for Paul, death emerges from humanity's failure to respond to God (Rom. 5:12–21). What is defective in creation is not the Creator's work, but the result of human failure and responsibility.

First Corinthians 15 and its companions are the texts for this discussion. Such teaching on God's creative work, Jesus, and hope of the resurrection encapsulates traditional thinking. A good creation includes redemption of its physical element.

This example is significant because it shows that although similar things may have been believed in the affirmations of the new and the traditional materials, they were not believed for the same reasons or ends. Sometimes the difference between similar ideas and their contexts are more important than surface similarities. All these texts regard current creation as corrupt, but the alternative texts mostly do away with the material world while the traditional texts argue for its redemption.

Such teaching also appears in Romans 7:13–25. The background for its argument exists in the already noted Romans 5:12, which says, "So then, just as sin entered the world through one man and death through sin, and so death spread to all people because all sinned." In Romans 7, Paul picks up the argument and condemns the evil that is in the flesh. The text presents an intense back-and-forth argument between what Paul wishes to do and what the flesh causes him to do. Paul presents humanity's struggle between what it would like to do and what it does. As he puts it in 7:14: "I am unspiritual, sold into slavery to sin." What is interesting about the way Paul says this is his sense of personal responsibility for this failure. Neither a defective creation nor outside spiritual forces are to blame. Paul looks in the mirror and sees the enemy as himself. Sin is at work in and through him. He says, "But now it is no longer me doing it, but sin that lives in me. For I know that nothing good lives in me, that is, in my flesh. For I want to do the good, but I cannot do it" (7:17–18). He concludes in verse 24, "Wretched man that I am!"

This self-analysis sounds pretty grim, but it also is quite different from the new materials. There the issue was finding goodness in us. Spiritual problems lay outside of us, either the fault of a defective creation or the terrorization of hostile beings. The closest we come to being responsible is for our ignorance and blindness. We are responsible to fix the problem, but what got us into this mess was not primarily our fault. To see the divine spark is to light up our lives. Paul's view differed. To light up our lives, we also must see our own flaws, not merely those of the creation, of others, or of our environment. Sin and responsibility have fallen on hard times in our day. Such ideas can teach us something about accepting responsibility for sin, being accountable before God.

Of course, Paul's story does not end in Romans 7:24. He goes on to say, "Thanks be to God through Jesus Christ our Lord! So then, I myself serve the law of God with my mind, but with my flesh I serve the law of sin." Romans 8 explains this praise. The path of spiritual awakening and enablement comes through Jesus, who gives the life-awaking spirit of adoption that makes us God's children.

Matthew 22: 23–33 = Mark 12: 18–27 = Luke 20: 27–39 are other works that teach a physical resurrection. In these texts, Jesus defends the teaching about resurrection to the Sadducees, who did not accept the doctrine. In comparing the heavenly body to angels, Jesus makes the point that the resurrection body means not only life after death but also that it is both spiritual *and* physical. Someone might ask is Jesus defending only the resurrection's reality and not its physical nature since He says the resurrection body is like an angel. Jesus is reacting to the presentation of the Sadducean denial of resurrection. His reply is met with acceptance by the Pharisees, whose view of resurrection was traditionally Jewish and so was also physical. The point of resurrection for a Jew is that the suffering one endures will be paid back in the end, as 2 Maccabees 7 showed.

John refers to the resurrection of the living and dead in John 5:26–29. If this is an analogy with Jesus' appearances in John, then this gospel also fits into this emphasis. While John tends to treat the idea of the world negatively, he speaks of God so loving the world that He sent His Son to save it (3:16–19). This brings us into the theme of redemption along with John's epistles reinforcing this view. First John 3:2 states that when Jesus appears "we will be like him," an allusion to Jesus' own resurrection body, an idea John calls a purifying hope. Various resurrection appearance texts in the Gospels also support this view of physical resurrection. Jesus' physical characteristics include His eating, the nail marks in His raised body, and features pointing to a new body that are indicated by the way He suddenly appears in a closed room (Luke 24:29–31, 41–43; John 20:19–29).

Like some new materials, there are images of rest in traditional material. Hebrews 3:1–4:16 speaks of entering God's rest, a rest made possible by Jesus' high priestly, sacrificial work. Hebrews 11:16 discusses a better country, a heavenly one, that will come. In 12:22–24 the author of Hebrews calls the new home the heavenly Jerusalem made possible by Jesus' shed blood that brings a new covenant with God.

Peter also expresses this hope: "By his great mercy he gave us new birth into a living hope through the resurrection of Jesus Christ from the dead, that is, into an inheritance imperishable, undefiled, and unfading. It is reserved in heaven for you" (1 Peter 1:3–4). Peter calls this obtaining of redemption the "salvation of your souls" (1:9). In 1 Peter 5:10, the hope involves enduring suffering for a little while with the promise that "the God of all grace who called you to his eternal glory in Christ will himself restore, confirm, strengthen, and establish you." Restoration, for Peter, looks to the entire person. The Petrine tradition expresses this hope as well in a dualistic contrast of the burning up of the heavens and earth and a replacement by a new heavens and a new earth where righteousness dwells (2 Peter 3:11–13). What is significant here is the picture of a new earth. Redemption is not just an ascent into the above.

Acts shares this expectation. Acts 3:19–21 says it this way: "Repent and turn back so that your sins may be wiped out, so that times of refreshing may come from the presence of the Lord, and so that he may send the Messiah appointed for you—that is, Jesus. This one heaven must receive until the time all things are restored, which God declared from times long ago through his holy prophets." The picture is of creation's restoration to its original design and goodness, something Revelation 21–22 also portrays in imagery. The detail, according to Acts, can be found in the teaching of the prophets of old, yet another affirmation that the God of Israel is the God of Christians.

All the early traditional materials, for all their variety of imagery and even their recognition of a kind of dualism in the creation, go a different way than most of the new materials. Here, fallenness and defect in creation are tied to human responsibility. Redemption extends to the entire person, including the body. In fact, restoration extends to the entire creation, heavens and earth. It is into this scenario that sin is mentioned, with sin involving more than primarily ignorance or blindness; it is a willful reaction against God.

In some things, all our texts, old and new, agree. The flesh is seen as corrupt, and judgment will dissolve evil. However, in traditional texts, judgment will not mean the end of matter nor does it mean that salvation is merely about ascent into an otherwise, undefined place of light. Rather, it will be a restoration of what humanity lost when man rebelled and brought death because of sin. What man foolishly brought together—namely, death, sin, and creation—God through Jesus Christ puts asunder, from head to toe and from heaven to earth.

Does the second century say the same?

In the Apostolic Fathers
In writing to Corinth, Clement focuses in *1 Clement* 25–26 on resurrection in treating redemption. In 26:3, he cites a version of Job 19:26 approvingly. That text affirms, "You will raise up this flesh of mine, which has endured all of these things." This citation comes after chapter 25 where Clement has used the ancient story of the famous phoenix, a bird that dies and rises again, as an example of resurrection. In 49:6, he develops the image: "In love the Master received us. Because of the love he had for us, Jesus Christ our Lord, in accordance with God's will, gave his blood for us, and his flesh for our flesh, and his life for our lives." Jesus' work covers the entire person. Clement goes on to note that God's kingdom is coming to earth (50:3), saying, "All the generations from Adam to this day have passed away, but those who by God's grace were perfected in love have a place among the gospel, who will be revealed when the kingdom of Christ visits us."

At the end of his letter in 59:3, this hope causes Clement to pray:

Grant us, Lord, to hope on your name, which is the primal source of all creation, and open the eyes of our hearts, that we might know you, who alone is "Highest among the high, and remains Holy among the holy." . . . You alone are the Benefactor of spirits and the God of all flesh, who "looks into the depths," who scans the works of man; the Helper of those who are in peril, the "Savior of those in despair"; the Creator and Guardian of every spirit, who multiplies the nations upon the earth, from among all of them have been chosen those who love you through Jesus Christ, your beloved Servant, through whom you instructed us, sanctified us, honored us.

Clement prays to the God of all flesh; it is a way of speaking of God as Creator of all people. All His creatures should hope in His name and the work of this Creator God through Jesus Christ, for only God can bring what is needed to make people sanctified, that is, make them holy.

The work of *2 Clement* sounds like the dualism of the new materials when he contrasts our transitory stay in this world of the flesh to the promise of Christ, namely, rest in the coming kingdom and eternal life (5:5). Yet this same writer declares in 9:1–4, "Let none of us say that this flesh is not judged and does not rise again . . . If Christ, the Lord who saved us, became flesh (even though he was originally spirit) and in that state called us, so also we shall receive our reward in this flesh." Redemption extends to the body.

When we come to Ignatius, one of his letters addresses the resurrection in detail. His *Letter to the Smyrneans* 1:1–2:1 introduces the topic:

I glorify Jesus Christ, the God who has made you so wise. For I have observed that you are established in an unshakable faith, having been nailed, as it were, to the cross of the Lord Jesus Christ, in both body and spirit, and firmly established in love by the blood of Christ, totally convinced with regard to our Lord, that he is truly of the seed of David with respect to human descent, Son of God with respect to divine will and power, truly born of a virgin, baptized by John, in order that all righteousness might be fulfilled by him, truly nailed in the flesh for us under Pontius Pilate and Herod the tetrarch (from this [the cross's] fruit we derive our existence, that is from his blessed suffering), in order that he might raise a banner for the ages through his resurrection for his saints and faithful people, whether among Jews or among Gentiles, in the one body of his Church. For he suffered all these things for our sakes, in order that we might be saved; and he truly suffered, just as he truly raised himself—not, as certain unbelievers say, that he suffered in appearance only (it is they who exist in appearance only!). Indeed, their fate will be determined by what they think: they will become disembodied and demonic.

Ignatius says that his opponents who deny a real, physical Jesus will suffer a judgment where they will be disembodied. The implication is that those who share in Christ's resurrection will have bodies, since disembodiment is a penalty for the crime of wrong belief. Ignatius continues to explain, "I know and believe that he was in the flesh even after the resurrection" (3:1). In 3:3, he says, "And after his resurrection, he ate and drank with them like one who is composed of flesh, although spiritually he was united with the Father." And in 5:2, he speaks of the implications for Jesus' being imprisoned for his faith: "If these things were done by our Lord in appearance only [the things Ignatius noted in chapter 3], then I am in chains in appearance only." Ignatius argues that he will be raised bodily, just as the Lord was. In another letter to Polycarp, he speaks appreciatively to him, "because your firmly rooted faith, renowned from the earliest times, still perseveres and bears fruit to our Lord Jesus Christ, who endured for our sins, facing even death, 'whom God raised up, having loosed the pangs of death'" (1:2). Ignatius alludes to the Psalms (18:6; 116:3) and a citation in Acts 2:24, where Peter defended Jesus' immediate, bodily resurrection.

In the epistle attributed to Barnabas, the author writes in 5:5*b*–7, "Learn! The prophets, receiving grace from him, prophesied about him. But he himself submitted, in order that he might destroy death and demonstrate the reality of the resurrection of the dead, because it was necessary that he be manifested in the flesh. Also, he submitted in order that he might redeem the promise to the fathers and—while preparing the new people for himself—prove, while he was still on earth, that after he has brought about the resurrection he will execute judgment." In *Barnabas* resurrection's reality points to the body's raising. What about the soul? Jesus has come to give new life to the soul, as 6:10–11 declares, "So, since he renewed us by the forgiveness of sins, he has made us men of another pattern, so that we should have the soul of children, as if he were creating us all over again." Redemption, then, means a new soul.

What about the spirit? In a detailed treatment, the author in 16:8–10 describes the new spiritual temple the Lord forms:

"It will be built in the name of the Lord." So pay attention, in order that the Lord's temple may be built gloriously. How? Learn! By receiving the forgiveness of sins and setting our hope on the name, we became new, created again from the beginning. Consequently God truly dwells in our dwelling place—that is, in us. How? The word of his faith, the calling of his promise, the wisdom of his righteous decrees, the commandments of his teaching; he himself prophesying in us; he himself dwelling in us; opening to us what had been in bondage to death the door of the temple, which is the mouth, and granting to us repentance, he leads us into the incorruptible temple. For the one who longs to be saved, looks not to the man, but to the One who dwells and speaks in him, and is amazed by the fact that he had never before heard such words from the mouth of the speaker nor for his part ever desired to hear them. This is the spiritual temple that is being built for the Lord.

The temple is called a spiritual temple because at its core is a newly formed being, one reborn by the One now indwelling the person. Redemption is a fresh creation, a completely new start—body, soul, and spirit.

The *Shepherd* speaks of the flesh being redeemed by the Spirit's work on the model Jesus provides. It teaches, "The preexistent Holy Spirit, which created the whole creation, God caused to live in the flesh that he wished. This flesh, therefore, in which the Holy Spirit lived, served the Spirit well, living in holiness and purity, without defiling the Spirit in any way . . . For all flesh in which the Holy Spirit has lived will, if it proves to be undefiled and spotless, receive a reward" (59:5, 7). Even more emphatically 60:2 affirms, "See to it that the idea never enters your heart that this flesh of yours is mortal, lest you abuse it in some defiling way. For if you defile your flesh, you also defile the Holy Spirit; and if you defile the flesh, you will not live."

Almost all the apostolic fathers speak of a complete redemption. The body is saved, and/or the kingdom comes to earth. Redemption deals with the entire person and all of creation.

In Justin Martyr

In *1 Apology*, Justin goes to great lengths to defend an idea that is not popular among Greek thinkers, namely, the physical resurrection. In chapter 19, he gives this long defense:

> To any thoughtful person would anything appear more incredible, than, if we were not in the body, and some one were to say that it was possible that from a small drop of human seed bones and sinews and flesh be formed into a shape such as we see? For let this now be said hypothetically: if you yourselves were not such as you now are, and born of such parents [and causes], and one were to show you human seed and a picture of a man, and were to say with confidence that from such a substance such a being could be produced, would you believe before you saw the actual production? No one will dare to deny [that such a statement would surpass belief]. In the same way, then, you are now incredulous because you have never seen a dead man rise again. But as at first you would not have believed it possible that such persons could be produced from the small drop, and yet now you see them thus produced, so also judge for yourselves that it is not impossible that the bodies of men, after they have been dissolved, and like seeds resolved into earth, should in God's appointed time rise again and put on incorruption . . . for we know that our Master Jesus Christ said, that "what is impossible with men is possible with God," and, "Fear not them that kill you, and after that can do no more; but fear Him who after death is able to cast both soul and body into hell." And hell is a place where those are to be punished who have lived wickedly, and who do not believe that those things which God has taught us by Christ will come to pass.

For Justin, resurrection is ultimately about the Creator God's power. If there can be a creation, there can be a resurrection.

With other traditional works, Justin's hope includes a physical resurrection that saves the entire person.

SUMMARY

Our tour has taken us through a host of texts where a spectrum of views exists. Hopes and dreams are summarized in thoughts about deliverance. Many ideas are parallel. Jesus brings knowledge of salvation. The Spirit is the key to that salvation. The flesh we now have is full of corruption. There is a need for God as well as for the knowledge that Jesus brings to take us to the light and give us a seat in heaven. He will make us new and deliver us.

But there also have been crucial distinctions. Most of the new materials see the flesh as being destroyed. Redemption applies either to both a soul and a spirit or to a spirit alone. The key image is of an ascent of the soul, that is, reconciliation into the spiritual world that comes from the true God above. The material world is left behind or will dissolve in judgment.

This is not the message of the older, traditional materials. There is renewed and reformed flesh as part of a physical resurrection. All the creation, including heaven and earth, shares in the redemption. Jesus' physical resurrection is the precursor to our own resurrection. Like a seed that sprouts, a phoenix that is reborn, or a human seed that produces a human being, so great is God's creative power that makes resurrection a real hope. The body to come with salvation is something new and yet like what it had been. This redemption will bring new heavens with a new earth or will take place when the Lord returns and establishes His kingdom. Some texts note that this promise takes place just as the old prophets of Israel said.

Later creeds speak of an actual resurrection of the dead and life in the age to come. That hope is most clearly expressed in the traditional materials, not in the alternative ones. Traditional teaching leads to the later creeds on this point. Abundant evidence exists of a core faith among key works of the first and second centuries. These beliefs excluded options that rejected a physical resurrection or that looked only to a spiritual redemption of humanity.

Much of this chapter applies to the next. The discussion of Jesus' work in salvation shows where the views of God as Creator, the person of Jesus, and the nature of redemption lead. What is Jesus' role in salvation? Why did He come?

STUDY QUESTIONS

1) *In the traditional texts, what does salvation cover, and how extensive is it (i.e., does it cover the physical world)?*

2) *How commonly is this idea expressed across these traditional texts?*

3) *Why is the resurrection an important part of the discussion in traditional texts?*

4) *What differences exist between many of the alternative texts and traditional texts, and are the differences significant?*

· TWELVE ·

JESUS' DEATH:
KNOWLEDGE, SIN, AND
SALVATION, PART 1

JESUS' WORK IN THE NEW MATERIALS

The traditional and the new works agree on a few things. Jesus' work has provided a way to salvation. He defeats powers hostile to God and humanity. A spectrum of views exists concerning Jesus' work: on one end, it is the knowledge that Jesus provides that brings salvation, and on the other, it is His activity that deals with sin. This sinfulness involves more than blindness or lack of knowledge about humanity's spiritual roots.

In the Gospel of Thomas
Jesus' work in *Thomas* involves revealing knowledge. The prologue reads, "These are the secret sayings which the living Jesus spoke and which Didymus Judas Thomas wrote down." Saying 13 reinforces this idea of secrecy. There Jesus took Thomas aside and revealed things to him that he did not repeat to the other disciples. In saying 62, Jesus explains, "It is to those worthy of my mysteries that I tell my mysteries."

Jesus also gives rest. Saying 90 reads, "Come unto me, for my yoke is easy and my lordship is mild, and you will find repose for yourselves." This saying is very similar to Matthew 11:28–29. Jesus announces the kingdom, but it is not found by waiting for it, because "it is spread out upon the earth, and men do not see it" (saying 113). Saying 111 summarizes what is found: "Jesus said, 'The heavens and earth will be rolled up in your presence. And the one who lives from the living one will not see death.' Does not Jesus say, 'Whoever finds himself is superior to the world'?" In *Thomas*, the key to God's kingdom is self-knowledge and self-understanding. Spiritual awakening produces life.

In the Apocryphon of James

This work is a "secret book" (1:10). It is not even the first secret book the author claims he sent (1:30). Entry into the kingdom does not take place at Jesus' bidding. His bidding them to come after him is not the answer to finding life. Rather, kingdom entry occurs because "only you yourselves are full" (2:30–33). The need of man is called an illness that Jesus heals (3:25–34). The healing in 4:19 involves becoming full of the Spirit and not reason. This teaching has an ethical thrust in calling for faith, love, and works (8:11–15). Jesus compares this word to a seed that produces food and more seed. Chapter 8 notes how the kingdom is received: "So also you yourselves can receive the kingdom of heaven; unless you receive this through knowledge, you will not be able to find it" (vv. 23–27). In 8:37–9:1, Jesus descends and suffers by dwelling on the earth in order to reveal this truth. The exhortation of 9:18–23 is, "Hearken to the word; understand knowledge; love life, and no one will persecute you, nor will anyone oppress you, other than you yourselves." A later passage, 14:8–10, reinforces the point: "You through faith [and] knowledge, have received life." In the *Apocryphon of James*, salvation means knowledge of the kingdom that Jesus reveals and the believer accepts.

In the Apocryphon of John

In this work, salvation takes a different direction. In II 30:3, *Apocryphon* discusses how death emerges from not knowing God's truth. The explanation continues about how Providence came into the world by entering the "middle of the prison" (II 30:11–18). He came yet a second time into the middle of the prison and to Hades to accomplish his task (II 30:25–26). Entering a third time, he summarizes the mission:

> I am the light which exists in the light, I am the remembrance of Providence—that I might enter into the midst of the darkness and the inside of Hades. And I filled my face with the light of the completion of their aeon. And I entered into the midst of their prison which is the prison <of> the body. And I said, "He who hears, let him get up from the deep sleep." And he wept and shed tears. Bitter tears he wiped from himself and he said, "Who is it that calls my name and from where has this hope come to me, while I am in the chains of the prison?" And I said, "I am the Providence of the pure light; I am the thinking of the virginal Spirit, who raises you up to an honored place. Arise and remember that it is you who hearkened, and follow your root, which is I, the merciful One, and guard yourself against the angels of poverty and the demons of chaos and all those who ensnare you, and beware of the deep sleep and the enclosure of the inside of Hades." (II 30:33–31:22; Robinson 2000, 2:171, 173; Robinson 1990, 122)

Deliverance involves knowledge and recognition of one's true roots, a move away from the forces of darkness. Jesus reveals the way out from the clutches of hostile forces. This belief falls into a new location on our spectrum, by highlighting the danger outside spiritual forces are for humanity.

In Letter to Rheginos (= Treatise on the Resurrection)
Rheginos, similar to *Apocryphon of John,* gives us another extended passage on the Lord's revelation. The context discusses those who seek rest but do not stand inside the Word of Truth (43:25–36). In 44:1–45:22, Rheginos is told of the way of rest, resurrection, and the restoration of the Pleroma in the cosmos. A later portion of Rheginos was considered when we looked at Jesus' person, but here we see how such understanding fits into the picture of Jesus' work:

> I know that I am presenting the solution in difficult terms, but there is nothing difficult in the Word of Truth. But since the Solution appears so as not to leave anything hidden, but to reveal all things concerning existence—the destruction of evil on the one hand, the revelation of the elect on the other. This (Solution) is the emanation of Truth and Spirit, Grace is of the Truth. (44:38–45:13; Robinson 2000, 1:149, 151; Robinson 1990, 54)

Reconciliation and knowledge come together as the Son of Man–Son of God defeats death and the forces hostile to humanity and God. The "solution" leads the elect, who are few, into truth, the Spirit, and grace. This has taken place courtesy of God and his work through the deliverer. So *Rheginos* adds detail to what we saw in *Apocryphon of John.* Salvation is about knowledge and victory over the hostile forces, as one appreciates the truth that evil is overcome and the Spirit is available.

In Sophia of Jesus Christ
In *Sophia,* a raised Jesus explains his work. In III 91:2–11 (= BG 77:16–78:15), twelve disciples and seven women gather to hear the Savior teach. The text explains, "When they gathered together and were perplexed about the underlying reality

of the universe and the plan and the holy Providence and the power of the authorities and about everything the Savior is doing with them in the secret of the holy plan, the Savior appeared, not in his previous form, but in the invisible spirit." Jesus in his resurrected state is pure Spirit. His discourse treats the secret plan. Much of *Sophia of Jesus Christ* is about the underlying world of aeons and forces. The Savior explains his coming in III 107:11–108:4:

> I came from the places above by the will of the great Light, (I) who escaped from that bond; I have cut off the work of the robbers; I have weakened that drop that was sent from Sophia, that it might bear much fruit through me and be perfected and not again be defective, but be <joined> through me—I am the Great Savior—that his glory might be revealed, so that Sophia might also be justified in regard to that defect, that her sons might not again become defective but might obtain honor and glory and go up to their Father and know the words of the masculine Light. (Robinson 2000, 3:131, 133, 135; Robinson 1990, 234–35)

Jesus presents knowledge of reconciliation, fixing the defect of Wisdom Sophia. In doing so, he brings all back to the masculine Light and defeats the forces of evil.

In the *Gospel of Thomas the Contender*
This Nag Hammadi work is a dialogue account distinct from the *Gospel of Thomas*. Jesus speaks to his brother Judas Thomas (138:1–4) just before Jesus' ascension. It dates to the first half of the third century and probably comes from Edessa of ancient Syria (now modern Turkey; Turner's introduction in Robinson 2000, 2:173, 177). It is Gnostic and calls for an ascetic life. The savior makes this possible.

The savior speaks to his "twin," that is, his true companion, and calls him to understanding "because it is not fitting that you be ignorant of yourself" (138:11–12). Thomas can do this because "you had already understood that I am the knowledge of the truth" (138:12–13).

This knowledge concerns "the depth of all" (138:18). In 139:4–8, Jesus notes the "bestial" body will perish. A metaphor explains the savior's work. Those who speak of things invisible and difficult before the revelation of the light are like those who shoot arrows at a target at night (139:13–16): "Yet when the light comes forth and hides the darkness, then the work of each will appear. And you, our light, enlighten, o lord" (139:18–20). The savior explains that the light's goal is not to have one remain where he was, but to be taken up to the essence (139:25–31). Thus, true wisdom gives one the ability "to make himself wings so as to fly, fleeing the lust that scorches the spirits of men. And he will make himself wings to flee every visible spirit" (140:1–5). This is doctrine for the perfect, who are not the ignorant (140:8–14). Truth is something in which one rests (140:42–141:1).

The savior goes on to urge that those who do not know the truth should be regarded "as beasts" (141:25–26). The question is then asked how this can be preached when those who share such a message are not esteemed. Jesus answers that the call is to discuss these things with people. If they sneer or smirk at them, then they are cast into the dark depths of Hades and Tartaros. There is no hope for them (142:26–143:7). Those who reject the message hope on the flesh. Most of the rest of chapters 143 and 144 are a series of woes against those who have wrong knowledge while chapter 145 presents beatitudes to those who respond with exhortations not to be in the flesh (145:1–16). The work closes noting that this is "The Book of Thomas The Contender Writing To the Perfect" (145:17–19).

Thomas the Contender argues that the savior brings the saving, proper knowledge of the spiritual. *Thomas* contends against those who hope in the flesh. Humanity has two types. The nature and judged fate of the opposition is clear. Secret knowledge is light that illumines only the elect.

In the Gospel of Truth

The emphasis on knowledge also fits this work. It begins in 16:31–35, noting that the "gospel of truth is joy for those who have received from the Father of truth the grace of knowing him, through the power of the Word that came forth from the pleroma." This pleroma performs redemption for those "who were ignorant of the Father" (16:39–17:1). Chapter 18 reads, "Oblivion did not come into existence from the Father, although it did indeed come into existence because of him. But what comes into existence in him is knowledge, which appeared in order that oblivion might vanish and the Father be known" (vv. 1–7). What is Jesus' role? It is showing the way to truth through revelation of knowledge. That is why the *Gospel of Truth* speaks of the gospel and ties it to Jesus' work of illumination: "Through this, the gospel of the one who is searched for, which <was> revealed to those who are perfect through the mercies of the Father, the hidden mystery, Jesus, the Christ, enlightened those who were in darkness through oblivion. He enlightened them; he showed (them) a way; the way is the truth which he taught them" (18:12–21).

After being nailed to a tree, Jesus, in the aftermath of his death, became "a fruit of knowledge of the Father" (18:24–26). In addition, "he discovered them in himself, and they discovered him in themselves" (18:30–31). This knowledge is now in a book "manifested in their heart the living book of the living—the one written in the thought and the mind" (19:35–36). This is a book about which "no one could have become manifest from among those who believed in salvation unless the book appeared" (20:6–9). Jesus took the book, the living book of the living, since "he knows his death is life for many" (20:13–14). Jesus "put on that book" (20:24); "he was nailed to a tree; he published the edict of the Father on the cross" (20:25–27). His death and new life reveal the new way. As 31:13–20 states, "When light had spoken through his mouth, as well as his voice which gave birth to life, he gave them thought and understanding and mercy and salvation and the powerful spirit from the infiniteness and the sweetness of the Father." Bonds and error "were destroyed with power and confounded with knowledge" (31:25–27).

The new materials about Jesus' work are consistent. Jesus' work is about knowledge, knowledge of the roots and origins of creation and man, as well as the spiritual need that Jesus reveals and supplies. It is easy to see why the view was labeled Gnosticism, or a belief about knowledge. *Gospel of Truth* is one of the few new texts to discuss the Cross. Jesus uses the Cross to show the real nature of existence and knowledge.

In the *Dialogue of the Savior*

This work is mostly a complex dialogue between Jesus and three disciples (Judas, Matthew, and Mary Magdalene) with Jesus answering their questions. Creation, wisdom, and apocalyptic themes are the key topics. This is a mid-second century text with Gnostic elements (Lapham 2003, 175–176; Klauck 2003, 185, against Koester's (1990, 173–187) dating in the early second century). Mary Magdalene is highly praised in this text for her understanding. As such, it is the most pro-female of these texts (Robinson 2000: 1–4). The work is not mentioned anywhere else in extant sources.

Beginning with a call to rest (120:3–5), the Savior explains why he has come: "When I came, I opened the path and I taught them about the passage they will traverse, the elect and the solitary, [who have known the Father having believed] the truth and [all] the praises while you offered praise" (120:23–121:3). *Dialogue* then describes the journey, the ascent to the above, as well as the nature of creation. The text of this second-century work is extremely broken up and fragmentary with many gaps, but we do know that this journey and its roots are its basic theme. In 139:55, we get this summary: "You are from the fullness and you dwell in the place where the deficiency is. And lo! His light has poured [down] upon me!" In 142:11–14, the Lord urges them to accept the things they understand by faith.

Jesus' work gives saving knowledge of the spiritual world.

In the Gospel of Philip

Philip has the most comprehensive discussion of this theme in the Nag Hammadi materials. It uses the formula "Christ came" to highlight the deliverer's activity (52:19, 35; 55:6; 68:17, 20; 70:12–13; 80:1). Alongside these formulae texts, other key passages appear. This activity combines all the themes we have seen: reconciliation, nourishing life, and punishment of the world.

Philip 52:19–24 starts with Christ coming and creation. Since Christ came, the world has been created, the cities adorned, and the dead are carried out. There was only a mother for God's children during the time of the Hebrews, a reference to the Jews. Now there are father and mother. This raises the themes of reconciliation with one's roots and full care of God's children. The imagery is important in declaring that the time of Jesus represents an advance in God's plan.

Christ came "to ransom some, to save others, to redeem others" (52:35–53:3). The *ransomed* were strangers whom he made his own children. He took his own by laying down his life from the time of the creation. This act was a pledge to accomplish this reconciliation and rescue the creation from

173

the hand of robbers. He redeemed the good people as well as the evil (53:4–14). On the one hand, that redemption means some will be dissolved. On the other hand, "those who are exalted above the world are dissoluble, eternal" (53:20–23).

Before "Christ came there was no bread in the world, just as Paradise, the place where Adam was, had many trees to nourish the animals, but no wheat to sustain man" (55:6–10). Jesus brought the food that sustains. This idea is like John 6. It refers to the spiritual sustenance Jesus provides.

Another enigmatic text is 68:18–22. Here, before Christ, some came from a place they were no longer able to enter. This is probably a reference to Adam and Eve in Paradise. After sin, they went where they were no longer able to come out, a reference to being stuck in a fallen world. "Then Christ came. Those who went in, he brought out, and those who went out, he brought in." Though the details are vague, the point is a work of reconciliation that reverses what Adam and Eve experienced.

The separation of man and woman sets the context of 70:12–13. Christ came "to repair the separation which was from the beginning and again unite the two, and to give life to those who died as a result of the separation and unite them" (70:12–17). Again reconciliation reverses something that came with the creation. It is important to note here that there is no explicit mention of sin. Separation is a basic defect in the creation, not in humanity, that Christ repairs. In 72:23, the children of the bridal chamber, where reconciliation is achieved, enter into rest. Forgiveness of sins is not discussed. *Philip* 75:14–21 gives the significance of the Supper, where the cup represents the Holy Spirit and the bread pictures the body of living, perfect man. *Philip* 77:14–15 puts it this way: "When the holy spirit breathes, the summer comes." This spiritual breath results from participating in baptism.

Jesus Christ came "to the whole place and did not burden any-one" (80:1–2). He is blessed as the perfect man. One is redeemed to a pure state where one does not rely on the flesh (82:5–6). *Philip* teaches, "Ignorance is a slave. Knowledge is freedom. If we know the truth, we shall find the fruits of the truth within us. If we are joined to it, it will bring fulfillment" (84:10–13). The work closes: "This is the way it is; it is revealed to him alone, not hidden in the darkness and the night, but hidden in a perfect day and a holy light." This teaching remains a mystery because it is still hidden. Only those of the day and light understand.

Jesus brings reconciliation and correct knowledge, allowing people to find their real roots in the spiritual self.

In the Apocalypse of Peter

This work begins explaining the Savior's role through an appearance to Peter. The opening uses the imagery of a built temple. In 70:14–71:5, the Savior is seated in the heavenly temple "at rest above the congregation of the living incorruptible Majesty." He says, starting in 70:21,

> Peter, blessed are those belonging to the Father, for they are heavenly. It is he (i.e., the Father) who revealed life, to those who are from life, through me. I reminded those who are built on what is strong, that they should heed my instruction and distinguish between words of unrighteousness and transgression of law (on the one hand), and righteousness (on the other), since they are from the height of every word of this fullness of truth. Graciously they have been enlightened by him whom the principalities sought (Robinson 2000, 4:219; Robinson 1990, 373).

The Savior's work is to inform and instruct about the difference between the spiritual, which lasts, and the physical, which perishes. For example, in this apocalypse, the Savior laughs at the crucifixion because those engaged in it think they are crucifying him (81:8–21; Robinson 2000, 4:241; Robinson 1990, 377). The real Christ cannot have a physical existence. Teaching about the Savior's glory and work of revelation and his distinctness from the physical world points the way to true knowledge.

In the *Gospel of the Savior*

This work is not from Nag Hammadi. At the Berlin Egyptian Museum, parchment fragments were pieced together in a manuscript called *Papyrus Berolinensis 22220*. The fragments came from a 300 deutsche mark purchase made in 1967. In 1991, Paul Mirecki pieced together 148 pieces. Work continued from 1991–1997 until publication in 1999 (Hedrick and Mirecki 1999, 1–4).

The manuscript of this dialogue gospel is incomplete with gaps and an unclear sequence. The savior's prominence explains the title (Hedrick and Mirecki 1999, 16). It alludes to both Matthew and John in eight places total, making this a work likely from the second half of the second century (Hedrick and Mirecki 1999, 21). *Gospel of the Savior* reflects Gnostic ideas and portrays heavenly journeys.

In 98:42–46, the savior gives the exhortation not to let matter rule them. The remark appears to take place just before the savior is betrayed. In 99:3–11, the savior notes that the sheep are about to be scattered. As he announces that they will flee at his arrest, he says, "Yet I am the good shepherd. I will lay down my life for you (plural). You (plural) yourselves also lay down your (plural) lives for your (plural) friends in order that you (plural) might be pleasing to my Father" (Hedrick and Mirecki 1999, 33). In 100:33–51, the followers appear to see the savior as he is pierced on the cross and converse with him. In 105:11–14, he says, "The one who does not receive my body [and] my blood, [this one] is a stranger to me." So the work perceives that followers share in the imagery associated with the Lord's Table.

In 106:44–47, the savior speaks to the cross, speaking of how the cross was eager for him, and he will be eager for it. In 107:12–20, those conversing with the savior ask him to come back with glory they can bear, not in his true glory. They are also told not to touch him before he goes to the Father (107:31–38). In 108:6–8, he declares, "I suffer because of the sins of the world." In 108:45–46, he announces that he "has overcome the world" as he exhorts them to be free of the world.

In the next unit, numbered 113, the apostles note that the world became darkness, and they became as those "among the Aeons" (113:6–7). The apostles experience a heavenly vision and see heaven worship the Father. There follows a discussion like Jesus' prayer in Gethsemane about letting the cup pass. So this heavenly scene looks to be a flashback to heavenly dialogue about the divine plan to have the savior die. Jesus accepts his call: "[I am ready] to die with joy and pour out my blood upon the human race" (114:32–36).

The text is quite broken until unit 122. Here the savior speaks to the cross and says the cross will be taken with him to heaven (122:35, 60–63).

At this point, the textual order is less than clear. In another unit, called 5F, the savior tells the cross that "that which is lacking will be perfected, and that which is diminished is full" (5F:23–26). This is followed by a declaration that in a little while "all the pleroma is perfected" (5F:30–32). The savior says this as he prepares to experience death on the cross. This is the last substantial portion from the manuscript.

This new gospel contains a conglomeration of themes. They reflect ideas we see in the new materials with its dialogue form;

its flashback, reflective character on events tied to the savior; and its direct address of the cross like the *Gospel of Peter*. The work also reflects traditional ideas: a call to share in the Lord's Table and the clear mention of Jesus' suffering for sin. Thus, this work falls in the middle of the spectrum, taking in almost every teaching available. In tone, it is like the *Interpretation of Knowledge*, reviewed later in this chapter.

In the *Tripartite Tractate*

Among the longest of the Nag Hammadi texts, this three-part work treats God's nature, the devolution from him, and the return to the Godhead. It also discusses what emanated from the Godhead, Adam's creation and fall, and the Savior's incarnation. It contains Western Valentinian Gnostic teaching with Christ redeeming psychic and spiritual Christians. Psychic Christians have an awakened soul but not an awakened spirit. Spiritual Christians have an alive spirit and greater knowledge. This third or fourth century text evidences a major break among Christians at this time (Attridge and Pagels's introduction in Robinson 2000, 1:176–78).

The third section covers the Savior's work. The Savior "became manifest in an involuntary suffering" (114:31–35). In 115:1–2, "the invisible one taught them invisibly about himself." He took up "the death of those whom he thought to save, but also accepted their smallness to which they had descended when they were <born> in body and soul" (115:4–11). He came exalted, conceived "without sin, stain and defilement" (115:14–16). Redemption, as defined in 117:23–24, is "the release from the captivity and the acceptance of freedom." The captivity involves "slaves of ignorance," while freedom is "the knowledge of the truth which existed before" (117:26–29).

The text treats the threefold division of humanity into spiritual, psychic, and material (118:14–21). These groups are known by their fruit (118:21–23). The spiritual receive "complete salvation in every way" (119:16–18). The material will receive "destruction in every way" (119:18–19). There remains the psychic: "The psychic race, since it is in the middle when it is brought forth and also when it is created, is double according to its determination for both good and evil" (119:20–24). This may refer to the double-minded and divided loyalty of psychic persons. Some of them will be delivered, eventually, when they embrace humility (121:29–38). Chapter 124 extends salvation into the larger creation by noting the salvation of angels (vv. 25–31).

This work has a fully developed concept of redemption, extending to both humanity and angels. Jesus engages in cosmic reconciliation. The Savior makes clear to humanity who they are and the reason for their creation. This fits the pattern of many new texts we have seen. It also leaves a future place of redemption for some who have not come as far in knowledge as those who have a full understanding. This seemingly new development about the scope of redemption in this late work has a degree of precedent as shown in the final new work from our tour.

In the *Interpretation of Knowledge*

This Nag Hammadi work parallels the *Gospel of Truth* and *Excerpta ex Theodoto*. Clement of Alexandria cites *Excerpta*, which is otherwise unknown. The manuscript is full of gaps, making the text unclear. The savior is "Teacher" (9:22). With many allusions to Matthew, it covers the savior's teaching and the Passion. It also exhorts believers to repair division between two sets of teachers: one, a school with writings, and another with a savior giving superior teaching (9:20–27). The work reflects a mix of New Testament and Gnostic ideas probably from the Valentinian school (Pagels's introduction in Robinson 2000, 5:24–30). Pagels argues for a second-century work, but it belongs to the latter part of that century because of its Gnostic ideas.

This work's importance comes from its evidence of some Gnostics who tried to mediate between the divisive factions who were claiming Christ's name. This attempt to hold things together eventually failed. This characteristic is why I have treated this work last.

The key texts for our topic are 12:22–38 and 14:28–38. In 12:22–38, the flesh is an Aeon that Wisdom (*Sophia*) has emitted. It also received the majesty that is descending "so that the Aeon might enter the one who was reproached, that we might escape the disgrace of the carcass and might be regenerated in the flesh and blood." A rejected Jesus brings spiritual transformation that takes place in the body while it also transcends it. At this point the text has a break, missing several lines. In 13:36 and following verses, a discussion of the Cross takes place, where yet another break in the manuscript occurs that does not allow us to see how the topic is resolved. What we do have in the chapter suggests the Cross lifts up those who embrace it.

There is also a break at the end of 14:28–38 that does not allow the teaching's completion, but these verses say enough so that we can understand what is taught. It reads, "Moreover, when the great Son was sent after his small brothers, he spread abroad the edict of the Father and proclaimed it, opposing the All. And he removed the old bond of debt, the one of condemnation. And this is the edict that was: Those who have made themselves enslaved have become condemned in Adam. They have been [*brought*] from death, have received forgiveness for their sins, and have been redeemed by . . ." At this point, the text breaks. Redemption in this passage achieves life, reconciliation, and forgiveness.

So the *Interpretation of Knowledge* combines an array of views, seeking to bring together the competing factions in the church. Some ideas are present in traditional texts. The wording of removing the debt recalls Colossians 2:14. This is also one new work that mentions forgiveness of sin. It still has elements of dualism, but the passage sits very much in the middle of the spectrum, appealing to virtually every idea across its span. The text ultimately sides with those who teach possession of a superior knowledge, as *Interpretation of Knowledge* 8:6–9:38 shows. Although badly broken up, the manuscript teaches the cosmic creation story we have seen in other new works. It defends teaching that goes beyond the traditional school.

This second-century text attests to the dispute between the traditional and the alternative schools. Their distinct ideas split the church. These ideas were taught before the time of Irenaeus. The *Interpretation of Knowledge* tried to mend the division, but the effort failed.

SUMMARY

Franzmann (1996, 108) nicely summarizes this topic in the new materials while noting that Jesus' major work is as revealer. Seven elements comprise Jesus' work: (1) awakening and calling out of ignorance and forgetfulness; (2) providing enlightenment or causing believers to shine as light; (3) revealing the Father's glory; (4) bringing knowledge, speaking, telling, and revealing the truth and all things and the Father; (5) showing the way; (6) bringing rest or immortality; and (7) moving to union with the revealer. Jesus also liberates by bringing this knowledge and overcoming hostile powers, but his major role is to point the way. His death and ascent make him the pathfinder.

How do traditional materials compare to this list?

STUDY QUESTIONS

1) *What major theme do the alternative materials teach about Jesus' work?*

2) *Which key elements are raised in association with Jesus' work?*

3) *What unusual feature about Jesus' death appears in some of the texts? Reflecting on the Gnostic emphases, what is it about Gnostic teaching that makes this unusual feature not so surprising?*

· THIRTEEN ·

JESUS' DEATH: KNOWLEDGE, SIN, AND SALVATION, PART 2

JESUS' WORK IN THE TRADITIONAL MATERIALS

The relationship of Jesus' work to knowledge and sin is the central issue here. Is Jesus a pointer to the way, or does His work accomplish something more than revealing which direction humanity should go?

In the New Testament
Paul presents a teaching summary in Romans 3:21–26:

> Now apart from the law the righteousness of God (which is attested by the law and prophets) has been disclosed, namely, the righteousness of God through faith in Jesus Christ for all who believe. For there is no distinction; for all have sinned and fall short of the glory of God. But they are justified freely by his grace through the redemption that is in Christ Jesus. God publicly displayed him at his death as the mercy seat accessible through faith. This was to demonstrate his righteousness, because God in his forbearance had passed over the sins previously committed. This was also to demonstrate his righteousness in the present time, so that he would be just and the justifier of the one who lives because of faith. (my translation)

Jesus' work involves what the Law and the Prophets taught, teaching the realization of hope from Israel's God, by dealing with sin and righteousness. All have need of righteousness because all have sinned. Earlier in Romans 3:9, 19–20, Paul said that sin was an issue for both Jew and Greek. Salvation—what Paul speaks of here as justification or being declared righteous by God—is a gift to be received, an act of God's grace. The redemption takes place through Jesus' death, accomplished through His shed blood and His death as a substitution for us. Paul uses the language of sacrifice with its mention of a death at the mercy seat. Faith means believing in this work and produces the justifying salvation that Jesus brings.

Paul appeals to correct knowledge, but unlike the new materials, the object of this knowledge is not our origin or spiritual potential. There is no appeal to a latent divine spark within us. It is rather an acknowledgment of a need because of sin that indwells and corrupts us.

Jesus pays the penalty for sin, and He is the remedy for it. Jesus leads us into a spiritual existence as Romans 8 shows. Being sons of God and being indwelt by God's Spirit are Paul's answer to the painful dilemma in which humanity found itself as a result of sin (Rom. 8:1–17). Part of becoming spiritual for Paul is recognizing how unspiritual we are when we seek God through our own strength and means. Thus, what we need, God completely supplies. Jesus does not point out the way for us to find ourselves; He provides that way as a gift we did not previously possess. Becoming spiritual for Paul, and for other traditional authors, is something very different from what we have seen in most of the new materials.

Second Corinthians 5:18–20 summarizes this way: "All these things are from God who reconciled us to himself through Christ, and who has given us the ministry of reconciliation. In other words, in Christ God was reconciling the world to himself, not counting people's trespasses against them, and he has given us the message of reconciliation. Therefore we are ambassadors for Christ, as though God were making His plea through us. We plead with you on Christ's behalf, 'Be reconciled to God!'" The concept of reconciliation that we saw in the new materials is here. But sin is the main obstacle, not merely ignorance.

Hultgren (1994, 43) notes how a collection of Pauline formulae sayings present the idea that Christ died "for" something, using the Greek term *hyper* (=for). Christ died "for" the ungodly (Rom. 5:6), "for" us (Rom. 5:8; 1 Thess. 5:10), "for" our sins (1 Cor. 15:3), and "for" all (2 Cor. 5:14). Other ideas include that Christ gave Himself "for" me (Gal. 2:20) and Christ became a curse "for" us (Gal. 3:13). God gave Jesus up "for" us all (Rom. 8:32), sent His own Son "concerning sin, he condemned sin" (Rom. 8:3), and sent forth His Son "to redeem those who were under the law, so that we may be adopted as sons" (Gal. 4:4–5).

In another epistle, the summary affirms, "There is one God and one intermediary between God and humanity, Christ Jesus, himself human, who gave himself as a ransom for all, revealing God's purpose at his appointed time" (1 Tim. 2:5–6). The picture of a ransom is of payment made for transgression viewed as a debt.

The Pauline tradition also knows about victory over hostile powers, an idea prominent in the new materials. Colossians 2:13–15 speaks of God making us alive. God accomplished this when we were dead in trespasses and sins and in the uncircumcision of the flesh. God did this, "having forgiven all your transgressions. He has destroyed what was against us, a certificate of indebtedness expressed in decrees opposed to us. He has taken it away by nailing it to the cross. Disarming the rulers and authorities, he has made a public disgrace of them, triumphing over them by the cross." Unlike the new materials, it is the work of Jesus on the cross that makes this victory possible, by dealing with "decrees opposed to us," an allusion to sin and violations of divine law.

Salvation in the traditional materials affirms things we have seen in the new materials as well: reconciliation, victory over the hostile forces, appeals to faith, and the right kind of knowledge. However, other things are not shared. The appeal to knowledge is not primarily about discovering who we are or what we have in ourselves. It is focused on what Jesus provided because of our need. This lack was not in our knowledge but in our being. The deficiency is the capacity to sin and the responsibility we bear to the Creator God as a result.

The book of Hebrews shares this view. In 9:13–14 the author compares Jesus' sacrifice to those in Israel at the temple and says, "If the blood of goats and bulls and the ashes of a young cow sprinkled on those who are defiled consecrated them and provided ritual purity, how much more will the blood of Christ, who through the eternal Spirit offered himself without blemish to God, purify our consciences from dead works to worship the living God." Here Christ's work has a purifying impact, cleansing us from works that cannot save us before God. Responding to Christ's work turns us into worshippers, grateful for the redeeming work of God through Jesus. The closing benediction of the book in 13:20–21 makes the same point: "Now may the God of peace who by the blood of the eternal covenant brought back from the dead the great shepherd of the sheep, our Lord Jesus Christ, equip you with every good thing to do his will, working in us what is pleasing before him through Jesus Christ, to whom be glory forever. Amen." This "eternal covenant" is also called the new covenant in chapters 8–10 where that covenant is developed.

The gospels of Matthew, Mark, and Luke mention this covenant in their summary about Jesus' Last Supper. Paul also discusses covenant in 1 Corinthians 11:23–25. The role of the Supper in the early church is an important topic. Its historical roots possess real clues about the history of the earliest believing communities preserved again in traditional summaries integral to our study.

Paul's Supper discussion is the earliest we possess, written in the fifties. It reads, "I received from the Lord what I also passed on to you, that the Lord Jesus on the night in which he was betrayed took bread, and after he had given thanks he broke it and said, 'This is my body, which is for you. Do this in remembrance of me.' In the same way, he also took the cup after supper, saying, 'This cup is the new covenant in my blood. Do this, every time you drink it, in remembrance of me.'" Jesus' death is a delivering sacrifice, much like the Passover, invoking the picture of Passover protection (Exod. 12) and the forgiveness of sins that the new covenant promises (Jer. 31:31–34).

Luke's Supper account (22:19–20) matches that of Paul. There is some dispute whether these verses originally belonged in Luke because of differences in the manuscript evidence for Luke at this point. The fact that this text so parallels Paul, when a distinct version in Matthew and Mark also existed, speaks to the likelihood the text was a part of original Luke (see Bock 1996, 1721–22, for a detailed defense for the inclusion of 22:19–20).

What of this tradition do Mark and Matthew share? Mark's version of the Supper reads, "While they were eating, he took bread, and after giving thanks he broke it, gave it to them, and said, 'Take it. This is my body.' And after taking the cup and giving thanks, he gave it to them, and they all drank from it. He said to them, 'This is my blood, the blood of the covenant, that is poured out for many'" (14:22–24). Mark's version alludes to the new covenant, without naming it. Jesus' remarks also include imagery from the work of the Suffering Servant in Isaiah 53:10–12. Matthew 26:26–28 parallels Mark.

Important for our discussion is the fact that Mark clearly viewed Jesus' death as a sacrifice for sin. He writes by the sixties at the latest. Thus, the roots of this teaching were tied explicitly to an event in Jesus' earthly ministry from a very early period, from the very earliest sources we possess, including letters and Gospels. This Supper, celebrated as a part of worship in the traditional church, became known as the Eucharist or Thanksgiving meal (the term comes from the Greek *eucharisto,* "give thanks"). This meal is better known as the Lord's Table, one of the sacred elements of worship in today's church.

Acts also discusses Jesus' sacrifice in the only remarks in this book from Paul to church members. The Ephesians' elders at Miletus are to "watch out for yourselves and for all the flock of which the Holy Spirit has made you overseers, to shepherd the church of God that he obtained with the blood of his own Son" (20:28). Here, as in Luke 22, Mark 14, Matthew 26, Hebrews 8–10, and Romans 3, Christ's death is viewed as a sacrifice.

The Johannine tradition also shares this point about death and sin. John 6:22–59 portrays Jesus as the Bread of Life, a sacrifice that gives life. Here His body is compared to bread and His life to blood, that is, food and drink for spiritual sustenance. There also is allusion to the new covenant in this chapter as Jesus speaks of those who partake as being taught of God (6:45), a defining characteristic of the new covenant's presence (Jer. 31:34).

The book of 1 John reinforces the point by considering the person who does not speak about sin. We read in 1:8–10: "If we say we do not bear the guilt of sin, we are deceiving ourselves and the truth is not in us. But if we confess our sins, he is faithful and righteous, forgiving us our sins and cleansing us from all unrighteousness. If we say we have not sinned, we make him a liar and his word is not in us."

Revelation 5 describes the Lamb standing at God's right hand, who is worthy to open the book of the seven seals. He has conquered (5:5) but was slain (5:6). He is the object of heavenly worship as the four living creatures and the twenty-four elders of the heavenly vision bow before Him. One word of praise is, "Worthy is the lamb who was killed to receive power and wealth and wisdom and might and honor and glory and praise!" (5:12).

The first letter of Peter echoes this refrain through two summary texts. In 2:23–25, Peter writes, "When he was maligned, he did not answer back; when he suffered, he threatened no retaliation, but committed himself to God who judges justly. He himself bore our sins in his body on the tree, that we may cease from sinning and live for righteousness. By his wounds you were healed. For you were going astray like sheep but now you have turned back to the shepherd and guardian of your souls." Christ's work treats sin like the work of a doctor and calls those who embrace it to walk in righteousness.

In my translation of 3:17–18, the idea is repeated in a call to imitate His way of living: "It is better to suffer for doing good, if God wills it, than for doing evil. Because Christ also suffered once for sins, the just for the unjust, to bring you to God, by being put to death in the flesh but *also* by being made alive in the spirit." Here we see the contrastive dualism of flesh and spirit that we have noted elsewhere in the recent materials. However, in Peter, this dualism appears in the context of Jesus' real act of suffering, something most of the new materials do not affirm. Earlier we saw how the inclusion of the body as redeemed was a significant part of early Christian teaching. Here's one reason why this teaching of a real death was important. Jesus' suffering is exemplary to His followers, a call to suffer as He did while doing good.

This same point is made in 1 Peter 4:1–2: "Since Christ suffered in the flesh, you also arm yourselves with the same attitude, because the one who has suffered in the flesh has finished with sin, in that he spends the rest of his time on earth concerned about the will of God and not human desires."

Yet for Peter, the Cross and the Resurrection also mean victory over hostile powers. In 1 Peter 3:21–22, Peter discusses baptism and says, "This prefigured baptism, which now saves you—not the washing off of physical dirt but the pledge of a good conscience to God—through the resurrection of Jesus Christ, who went into heaven and is at the right hand of God with angels and authorities and powers subject to him." In this theme of victory over hostile forces, the old and the new materials are one.

All the major strands of the earliest traditional texts declare that Jesus' work is a saving sacrifice for sin, something that most new materials did not affirm. This declaration appears in the doctrinal summaries and in the materials that describe the church's worship, including the Lord's Table. That tradition claims that Jesus passed on this teaching Himself. These practices of worship then have roots that we can show are early, coming from the earliest sources we have. We cannot show such solid connections to the earliest era for the distinctive teachings of the new materials.

The early traditional materials share other ideas with the new materials. Jesus brings proper spiritual knowledge, reconciliation, and victory over hostile forces. However, one great difference exists: in the new materials, the issue is primarily ignorance of spiritual roots, but in the traditional materials, the flaw involves sin and responsibility. Thus, we see a spectrum of positions, but again there is a line within that spectrum that is notable. Jesus' work in being a sacrifice for sin is another difference between the core faith of the traditional church and most of the texts that appealed to special knowledge beyond the tradition.

How does the second century look when it comes to Jesus' work in the traditional materials?

In the Apostolic Fathers

Clement affirms Jesus as a sacrifice for sin in *1 Clement*. In 36:1, he says, "This is the way, dear friends, in which we found our salvation, namely, Jesus Christ, the high priest of our offerings, the Guardian and Helper of our weakness." In 49:6, Clement declares, "In love the Master received us. Because of the love he had for us, Jesus Christ our Lord, in accordance with God's will, gave his blood for us, and his flesh for our flesh, and his life for our lives." Sacrifice is a key to Jesus' work. Chapter 16 cites Isaiah 53 in full. In 16:4, Clement speaks of Jesus, who "bears our sins and suffers pain for our sakes." He declares in 16:7, "The Lord delivered him up for our sins," while verses 13–14 read, "Therefore he will inherit many, and will share the spoils of the strong, because his soul was delivered to death and he was reckoned as one of the transgressors; and he bore the sins of many, and because of their sins he was delivered up."

The author of *2 Clement* does not speak in short, compact sayings about this idea. He expounds it from the start of his work. Relevant parts of 1:1–2:7 read:

> Brothers, we ought to think of Jesus Christ, as we do of God, as "Judge of the living and the dead." And we must not think little of our salvation, for if we think little of him we also hope to obtain little. And those who listen as though it were a little matter are sinning, and we also are sinning, if we do not know from where and by whom and to what place we were called, and how great a suffering Jesus Christ endured for our sake . . . as a father he has called us sons; he saved us when we were perishing. What praise, then, shall we give him, or what repayment in return for what we received?

> . . . For he had mercy upon us and in his compassion he saved us when we had no hope of salvation except that which comes from him, and even though he had seen in us much deception and destruction. For he called us when we did not exist, and out of nothing he willed us into being.
>
> Scripture says, "I have not come to call the righteous, but sinners." He means this: that it is necessary to save those who are perishing. For this is a great and marvelous thing, to support not those things that are standing but those that are falling. So also Christ willed to save what was perishing, and he saved many when he came and called us who were already perishing.

Ignatius also affirms this understanding of Jesus' death. We have already noted the importance of the Lord's Table and its early origin. In his *Letter to the Smyrneans,* Ignatius urges them to shun certain people:

> Now note well those who hold heretical opinions about the grace of Jesus Christ which came to us, note how contrary they are to the mind of God. They have no concern for love, none for the widow, none for the orphan, none for the oppressed, none for the prisoner or the one released, none for the hungry or thirsty. They abstain from Eucharist and prayer. (6:2)

He goes on to connect the Eucharist to Jesus' death for sin, something the opponents deny. This could hardly state the difference between the two views more clearly.

In Polycarp's letter to the Philippians, he is appreciative of their care for those persecuted for their faith. This note of praise appears in 1:1–2:

> I greatly rejoice with you in our Lord Jesus Christ, because you welcomed the representations of the true love and, as was

proper for you, helped on their way those men confined by chains suitable for saints, which are the diadems of those who are truly chosen by God and our Lord; and because your firmly rooted faith, renowned from the earliest times, still perseveres and bears fruit to our Lord Jesus Christ, who endured for our sins, facing even death, "whom God raised up, having loosed the pangs of Hades."

Toward the end of his letter, he exhorts, "Let us, therefore, hold steadfastly and unceasingly to our hope and the guarantee of our righteousness, who is Christ Jesus, 'who bore our sins in his own body upon the tree,' 'who committed no sin, and no deceit was found in his mouth;' instead, for our sakes he endured all things, in order that we might live in him." This citation in 8:1–2 looks to the sacrifice of Jesus as an encouragement to follow in the life He calls believers to have. Polycarp appeals to language already noted from 1 Peter 2:22, 24.

Didache does not mention Jesus' work in detail other than in the context of prayers offered during the Eucharist. With the cup he calls on them to give thanks to the holy vine of David. For the bread, he makes a comparison of broken bread scattered over the mountains and then gathered together to be one. He asks the church to pray to God for the same to be done for the church when it comes into the kingdom (9:1–4). When the meal is finished, thanksgiving should follow for "your holy name which you caused to dwell in our hearts, and for the knowledge and faith and immortality which you made known to us through Jesus your servant" (10:2). Later he speaks of "spiritual food and drink and eternal life" graciously given "through your servant" (10:3). The allusion to the servant in the context of the Eucharist probably looks to sacrifice, as it echoes the pictures of John 6 and of Jesus' teaching at the Last

Supper. However, *Didache* is not as explicit about the point of Jesus' sacrifice as other traditional writers.

When we come to the letter attributed to Barnabas, 5:1 states, "It was for this reason that the Lord endured the deliverance of his flesh to corruption, that we might be cleansed by the forgiveness of sins, that is, by his sprinkled blood." In verse 2, he cites from Isaiah 53:5, 7. In verse 9, he discusses the sinfulness of the called apostles. He makes this point to illustrate what Jesus' work shows, "When he chose his own apostles who were destined to preach his gospel (who were sinful beyond all measure in order that he might demonstrate that 'he did not come to call the righteous, but sinners'), then he revealed himself to be God's Son." The citation quoted in verse 9 is from Luke 5:32, Mark 2:17, and Matthew 9:13, which present these as words spoken by Jesus. In Barnabas 6:11, this work is called a new birth: "Since he renewed us by the forgiveness of sins, he made us men of another type, so that we should have the soul of children, as if he were creating us all over again."

In chapters 7–8, Barnabas rails against those who crucified Jesus, highlighting the picture of the sacrifice of a heifer. He makes an allegory of it in 8:3: "The children who sprinkle are those who preached to us the good news about the forgiveness of sins and the purification of the heart, those to whom he gave the authority to proclaim the gospel; there were twelve of them as a witness to the tribes, because there are twelve tribes of Israel." So this letter also highlights Jesus' work as dealing with sin.

When we come to the *Shepherd*, he is grateful for the revelation of his former sins. In 5:2, he says, "When I reached the place, I fell to my knees and began to pray to the Lord and to glorify his name because he had considered me worthy and had made known to me my former sins."

Mandate 4.3.1, also known as *Shepherd* 31:1–2, presents a controversial discussion of forgiveness:

> "Sir," I said, "I would like to ask a further question." "Speak," he said. "Sir," I said, "I have heard from certain teachers that there is no other repentance beyond that which occurred when we descended into the water and received forgiveness of our previous sins." He said to me, "You have heard correctly, for so it is. For the one who has received forgiveness of sins ought never to sin again, but to live in purity."

The controversy comes when he says later that one who repeatedly sins and asks for forgiveness does not have life. Nonetheless, the *Shepherd* clearly connects life to the forgiveness that Jesus provides.

In a text noted earlier, 59:2–3, there is another explanation of the Son's work: "'Because,' he said, 'God planted the vineyard, that is, he created the people, and turned them over to his Son. And the Son placed angels over them to protect them, and the Son himself cleansed their sins with great labor and enduring much toil, for no one can cultivate a vineyard without toil or labor. So, when he himself had cleansed the sins of the people, he showed them the paths of life, giving them the law which he received from his Father.'"

The final text from the apostolic fathers' period echoes this theme. *Diognetus* 9:2b–4 reads, "He did not hate us, or reject us, or bear a grudge against us; instead he was patient and forbearing; in his mercy he took upon himself our sins; he himself gave up his own Son as a ransom for us, the holy one for the lawless, the guiltless for the guilty, 'the just for the unjust,' the incorruptible for the corruptible, the immortal for the mortal. For what else but his righteousness could have covered our sins?"

The apostolic fathers consistently view Jesus' work as tied to an offering for sin and establishing forgiveness.

In Justin Martyr

Two full texts from *1 Apology* complete our walk through traditional materials before Irenaeus, elaborating the central theme of Jesus' work.

In chapter 50, Justin calls his readers to consider the prophecies of Jesus' suffering: "But that, having become man for our sakes, he endured to suffer and to be dishonored, and that he shall come again with glory, hear the prophecies which relate to this." He then cites Isaiah 53, which refers to the Suffering Servant as an offering for sin. He explains:

> Accordingly, after he was crucified, even all his acquaintances abandoned him, having denied him; and afterwards, when he had risen from the dead and appeared to them, and had taught them to read the prophecies in which all these things were foretold as coming to pass, and when they had seen him ascending into heaven, and had believed, and had received power sent from there by him upon them, and went to every race of men, they taught these things, and were called apostles.

The God of Isaiah rooted the gospel message in promises. The apostles preached that hope. Part of that hope involves the forgiveness of sins.

In chapter 66, Justin gives a full exposition of the importance of the Eucharist. He says in part:

> This food is called among us Εὐχαριστία [the Eucharist], of which no one is allowed to partake but the man who believes that the things which we teach are true, and who has been washed with the washing that is for the remission of sins, and

unto regeneration, and who is so living as Christ has enjoined ...
For the apostles, in the memoirs composed by them, which are
called Gospels, have thus delivered unto us what was enjoined
upon them; that Jesus took bread, and when He had given
thanks, said, "This do in remembrance of Me, this is My body;"
and that, after the same manner, having taken the cup and given
thanks, He said, "This is My blood;" and gave it to them alone.

This text illustrates how the worship of the Lord's Table is
rooted in Jesus' act and apostolic preaching. This link is
recorded in the apostles' "memoirs," Justin's way of referring to
the Gospels. At the teaching's core is the recollection of Jesus'
basic work as a sacrifice for sin.

SUMMARY

The survey of Jesus' work reveals much overlap in language
and expression between traditional and new materials. It also
shows yet another core difference between these two groups.

Overlapping ideas are that Jesus brought true knowledge of
the way to God, that His work defeated forces hostile to God
and humanity, that reconciliation is a result of His work, and
that this work calls the one who believes to walk in a manner
that does not reflect the flesh.

The core difference between the materials emerges from the
doctrinal summaries of the traditional materials and the worship imagery of those earliest communities as reflected in the
Lord's Supper or, what the ancients called, the Eucharist. This
practice originated with Jesus Himself on the very night of His
betrayal. It was passed on to the apostles, who passed on teaching about the rite and what it represents to the church.

Our sources show that this teaching dates to the fifties.
Reaching back as far as Jesus, the teaching is connected with

several people who had ties to the apostles. Later generations understood this link and discussed it as a basis for their faith and understanding. In a real sense, this linkage is the reason that these texts are called the *traditional* view. The term is used not because they are simply old. Nor does it suggest that traditional is always right. Rather, the term reflects the claim that these teachings, at least for the core elements, were passed on from the earliest figures of the faith tied to Jesus' earthly ministry. It was tradition in the sociological sense of that term. This tradition claimed to go back to the beginning, to Jesus. At the least, this is what those who held to the traditional view believed, and we know they believed it very early, long before Irenaeus. In fact, we know that it was something many apostles taught because we have their works affirming it.

One of the core elements is that Jesus Christ came and died for sin—to acquire humanity's salvation through the forgiveness only He could now offer. This is part of the core knowledge of faith. *Every major traditional source of the first two centuries notes this teaching.*

Among those who claimed to be Christians in the first two centuries, there was a wide spectrum of beliefs. Within that spectrum there was, however, a line of demarcation that each side discussed. For one group, Jesus came to inform us of the need to sense the divine spark within us and the victory He achieved over hostile forces that oppose us, something He revealed as a secret to few. For the other group, He came to reveal the defeat of the hostile forces plus one other crucial thing: Jesus came to die for sin, something He told His followers to tell the world. They also celebrated that truth in a rite that would always remind them of what He did for them.

A few of the new works sit somewhere in the middle even as they lean toward the group that emphasized knowledge of the divine spark. However, these works are the exception rather than the norm for the newer materials. This smaller group within the new materials appears to be trying to hold the church together, but the effort failed probably because the emphasis fell on the newer ideas and not on those rooted in what the apostles had taught.

Our tour is complete. It remains only to summarize what the tour shows about alternative Christianities, the new school, and the "missing" gospels.

STUDY QUESTIONS

1) On this theme, what ideas overlap between alternative and traditional texts?

2) What core difference exists between these materials, and what kind of traditional material teaches this difference?

3) How pervasive is this teaching in the traditional material?

4) How far back does such teaching go in the tradition?

• FOURTEEN •

CONCLUSION: THE NEW SCHOOL, THE MISSING GOSPELS, ALTERNATIVE CHRISTIANITIES, AND ORTHODOXY

The recent works from Nag Hammadi are full of fascinating ideas. These so-called *missing gospels* have had a growing impact on Jesus studies and the history of early Christianity. This is only right because these texts possess the teachings of a series of countermovements to traditional Christianity written by those who promoted these views.

No group has worked more tirelessly to promote the significance of these missing gospels than the new school, generated by Walter Bauer. A host of professors teaching religion classes in North American universities write frequently about the topic, some claiming that these important new historical texts require a rewriting of early Christian history. The new school believes it is time for the losers in the great theological debate of the early centuries of the Common Era to be heard and gain their due. This book honors such a request by critically engaging these texts.

Our tour has given you a chance to see these writings up close. Many passages have been cited so that you can appreciate the scope and variety of what was taught. Translations and introductions used for this material are the standards, some of which were written by new school members. The texts are set next to their traditional counterparts from the first two centuries so that the emphases, similarities, and differences are exposed. What do the traditional and the alternative works tell us about history and the new school?

THE CONTRIBUTIONS AND THE LIMITATIONS
OF NEW SCHOOL CLAIMS

The Contributions

Our new sources are worthy of the energy the new school gives them. The new school has made four important contributions to early Christian study:

1. They attest to an alternative expression of Christian claims in the second century that historically affected the emergence of a carefully defined orthodoxy of the third and fourth centuries. The alternatives also reveal a variety of beliefs, most of which were attempts to make Christianity more philosophically acceptable in a Greco-Roman religious environment where gods contended with each other and the dead did not rise.

2. The new school has shown the complexity of the second- and third-century religious environment by highlighting its polemical context. It has examined the church fathers' works in a critical manner and pointed out many places where polemics pushed them to make erroneous claims or associations.

3. It has made us sensitive to the fact that Christianity was expressed with differing levels of diversity in different regions of the world in that time.

4. The new school also has forced historians to wrestle with the question of what the church was like and how Christians

made the case for their identity in the period before the widespread use of what we now call the New Testament. The sense that the church had a recognizable *collection* of sacred books does not clearly emerge until the third and fourth centuries. Many of these texts, such as the key Pauline letters, 1 Peter, 1 John, the four Gospels, and Acts, had influence in the areas where they were sent, *but their work together as a unit influenced the church more and more as the third century arrived.* All of these things are gains for the study of early Christian history.

The Limitations of the New School and the Nature of Early Orthodoxy

The new school, however, suffers from a zeal for the new that has produced distorted claims. These distortions often work from a true historical point but then exaggerate its significance by ignoring other features in the historical equation. There are three major problems in their analyses. The benefits, then, of the new school are limited, and its most extensive claims are not historically sustainable.

Problem 1. The value of the tradition contained in its early writings as evidenced in its small teaching units is ignored or undervalued. Also undervalued is the evidence for the traditional sources still being our best connection to the Christian faith's earliest years. Ironically, by focusing on the issue of the recognition of the Canon and the lateness of recognition for the sacred text, the evidence for traditional views within those texts in these teaching units is largely ignored. This evidence represents more than simply reflecting the presence of one alternative from the early centuries.

Here is how the distortion is produced. From a perspective that emphasizes variety in the early church, the deduction is made that neither side had the right or the ability to claim authority for its views. Earliest Christianity was diverse, and that is what it should have been. No one group had the right to make claims of truth or to throw its theological weight around. One of Pagels's chapter titles in *Beyond Belief* nicely puts it in the form of a question: "God's Word or Human Words?" Here the implication is that all religious ideas are the product of humanity and have equal merit as efforts by creatures to make sense of their existence.

In fact, Pagels tries to blunt the association of the Gospels with the earliest period. She claims that we do not know who wrote the four Gospels. They were merely attributed to apostles, much as the alternative works were (Pagels 2003, 112). Ehrman starts his book (2003, 13–89) with the same point about attributed authorship, calling them forgeries. First- and second-century traditionalists and those of the alternative school made such claims and used such allegedly early texts. It is as if stating the point about forgeries and uncertain authors, which is itself contested, puts an end to the value of pursuing a search for the roots. Never mind that many scholars think we know who wrote all these works or most of them. Above all, the new school does not take stock of the apostolic line of tradition that stood behind most of the first-century works, which is what made them important to the early church.

Pagels is right that scholars debate these points about authorship, but the case that the Gospels are rooted in apostolic connections either directly by authorship or by apostolic association is far greater for the four Gospels than for any of the other alternative gospels, a point the new school often leaves unmentioned. Conservative scholars in general will contend that two of the New Testament gospels come from apostles (Matthew and John) and two from those who were in close association with them (Mark with Peter, Luke with several of them and Paul). Some even tackle the claims of forgery in detail (Baum 2001).

No such potentially plausible claim has ever been made for the alternative texts. The closest one can come involves the more ambiguous text of *Thomas*, but the claim's success depends on a very early date for *Thomas*, which is suspect (Dunn 2003, 161–65). More moderate scholars, like Dunn and Hengel, hold to a more indirect line back to apostolic teaching, through communities that Matthew and John influenced. The result of even such indirect claims is still important historically. Hengel has made this argument in detail, pointing out along the way that the special formula that names a gospel was later imitated by later writers of the apocryphal gospels to give their works an appearance of apostolic claim (Hengel 2000, esp. pp. 48–60; on Mark, Hengel 1985, 65–72). *The Gospels we have in the fourfold collection have a line of connection to the earliest days and figures of the Christian faith that the alternative texts do not possess.* Those associations, whether direct as conservatives claim or more indirect as moderates claim, are stronger for these works while they are nonexistent for the alternative gospels.

The ancient texts reveal this connection. Doctrinal summaries appear in the earliest writings we have. Clement, writing in AD 95, stated the connection this way in chapter 42:

> The apostles received the gospel for us from the Lord Jesus Christ; Jesus the Christ was sent forth from God. So Christ is from God, and the apostles are from Christ. Both, therefore, came of the will of God in good order. Having therefore received their orders and being fully assured by the resurrection of our Lord Jesus Christ and full of faith in the Word of God, they went forth with the firm assurance that the Holy Spirit gives, preaching the good news that the kingdom of God was about to come. (*1 Clement* 42:1–3)

What counted for Clement was that the tradition genuinely reflected Jesus and apostolic teaching.

One could argue that such a claim for an exclusive apostolic connection cannot be made because we have only a limited sample of texts that existed. This point is true enough. So how do we work with this fact?

Given the nature of our textual pool, three options exist:

1. The reason we have no evidence for early diversity is that the early faith actually was not so diverse. Most opponents in the earliest works are troublesome blips on the screen. They did not have any real staying power, nor did they exist in meaningful enough numbers to last. They faded away, never becoming established as credible alternatives. If that were the case, we would see a sudden emergence of alternative texts in the second century, which is really when they emerged. Then the long-held idea that the tradition was first and the alternative came later holds.

2. Any diversity that did exist, if it were really rooted in the early period, would have left traces of its core later as well. My work has assumed this model and has concentrated on the Gnostic movement that obviously was the biggest threat to traditionalists in the second century. Our contention would be that what we have in the alternative perspective of the second century would be close to what existed earlier, if it existed at all. So the examination of later texts can show the tendencies that also may well be hinted at but not fleshed out in the earlier texts we have. However, the flip side of this option is that if the later texts reflect earlier realities, then the differences they show and the subsequent reactions to them as well would have been early, producing the reaction early on as the early texts we have also suggest.

3. Diversity existed, but we do not have any texts that give real evidence for what it was. This could be true, given that our text pool is partial. However, if this is so, then no one can say anything

about this early diversity because it is an argument from silence that cannot be proved or disproved. If this diversity took place and was significant and early, then we need to explain the content of the texts we have. Why is there not more trace of such diversity, given that some of our extant sources are quite early by ancient standards to the founding of the movement?

If there were diversity early and it was as neutral in terms of authority as the new school claims, that neutrality cannot be found in the Nag Hammadi texts, which are often claimed as evidence for this neutral diversity. The teaching of those missing gospels—or better, the ideas reflected in these later texts—produced a negative reaction virtually from the start of our textual record.

I cannot claim to have proved that the traditional view was more widespread or that there were no significant movements that precluded a significant diversity early on. Yet I do think I have shown that this was much less likely than the new school claims. In particular, the Nag Hammadi texts cannot be used as positive evidence of this claim. I can claim historically that these traditional materials possess the best pedigree of any of our early sources.

Problem 2. The new school errs in failing to see that certain ideas in the new texts were important bones of contention virtually from the start. I chose not to appeal to claims of revelation or to highlight the Gospels or the New Testament as sacred text but to examine historical differences in terms of ideas. Our tour has involved an examination of two centuries or more worth of texts from the New Testament as well as others, used and respected on each side of the dispute.

These texts together show important similarities and differences on the key topics we have covered. Those ideas formed the identity of the traditional and the alternative movements. So what existed and emerged in the time before Irenaeus was a spectrum of beliefs. However—and this is the key point—along that spectrum existed points of demarcation, separating the views from each other. Most works of the period reflect this difference in thought. Our tour has shown that these differences rotate around four areas: the view of God, the view of Jesus, the nature of salvation, and Jesus' work. Significant difference in any one of these areas (not necessarily all four of them, as some want to insist before questioning a work) provoked traditionalist reaction. I believe our tour has shown enough unanimity of belief in these four topics among the traditionalists that, for them, these ideas were the core of Christianity.

The core can be viewed as this: There was one Creator God. Jesus was both human and divine; He truly suffered and was raised bodily. He also is worthy to receive worship. Salvation was about liberation from hostile forces, but it also was about sin and forgiveness—the need to fix a flaw in humanity that made each person culpable before the Creator. This salvation was the realization of promises that God made to the world and to Israel through Israel's Law and Prophets. The one person, Jesus Christ, brought this salvation not only by revealing the way to God and making reconciliation but also by providing for that way through His death for sin. Resurrection into a new exalted spiritual life involves salvation of the entire person—spirit, soul, and body. Faith in this work of God through Jesus saves and brings on a spiritual life that will never end. This was the orthodoxy of the earliest tradition. Our tour has shown such teaching was a refrain of early traditionalists.

This belief comes very early in the movement, a point that cannot be doubted. Our historical sources date these ideas to the mid-first century as they contend that they reflect what Jesus taught (Marshall 1976). Evidence that Jesus taught such things is found especially in the community's earliest innovative worship practices. They proclaim Jesus Christ, the Savior, to be worthy of worship. They affirm such worship through the Lord's Supper, hymns, and theological summaries. These elements of worship and the teaching summaries that affirmed them are important historical pieces of evidence for how the core tradition was taught and passed on.

This orthodoxy can also be stated in terms of what was to be excluded and included: (1) God was not to be divided in such a way that He was not the Creator. God was a Creator of all things, and that initial creation was good. (2) A division between Jesus and the Christ in terms of His basic person and work was not acceptable. Orthodoxy was that Jesus as Son of God was sent from God, came truly in the flesh, and truly suffered. (3) Redemption only on a spiritual plane was not the true faith. Salvation included a physical dimension of resurrection and extended into the material creation. (4) Jesus did not come only to point the way to faith, to be a prophet, merely a teacher of religious wisdom, or to be a mere example of religious faith. Rather, His work provided the means to salvation. Jesus was far more than a prophet, which is why He was worshipped and affirmed as sharing glory with God as His Son.

Traditional circles viewed with deep suspicion teaching that faltered on any one of these four points. One could teach without mentioning these issues, but to deviate in any of these four areas would raise questions.

In another work that concentrates on the first century, Arland Hultgren composed a list of six elements that reflected what he calls "normative" Christianity (1994, 86). His first four items parallel ours: (1) The God of Israel can be loved and trusted as the Creator of all that is and as benevolent to humanity. (2) Jesus of Nazareth can be trusted as the One sent by God to reveal God and redeem humanity. (3) In spite of human failure, which would disqualify one from salvation, trust in God's redemptive work in Christ is the way to salvation, which is begun in this life, but completed beyond it. (4) The person saved by faith in God's redemptive work in Christ is expected to care about, indeed, to love others and be worthy of their trust.

Our list focuses on the content of the persons of God and Christ and on Jesus' work with some more detail. Hultgren's ethical emphasis is a part of normative belief, but it is not a distinct element belonging only to the tradition. Many alternative expressions desired to live in a way that honored God at an ethical level.

Hultgren's points five and six treat ethics and community: (5) Those who trust in Jesus as the Revealer of God and Redeemer of humanity are expected to live as disciples in a community whose ethos are congruent with the legacy of His life and teaching; and (6) those who live in communities of faith belong to a fellowship that is larger than that provided by the local community, an extended fellowship. Hultgren's fifth point has merit because of the emphasis in normative groups on how Jesus lived. His sixth highlights the sense of community that the normative church developed in contrast, for the most part, to the alternative movements, but we have not included these elements in our list because we did not work through these topics in detail from both sets of texts as we did the other four themes. Hultgren and I share the point that what became the New Testament was a reflection of such normative beliefs and did not create orthodoxy.

Larry Hurtado, who teaches New Testament at the University of Edinburgh in Scotland, summarizes:

> As a closed collection, the fourfold Gospel also certainly represents a refusal to include the numerous other Jesus books that had begun circulating in the second century. In other words, whatever toleration for diversity was represented by the preference for the fourfold Gospel, it was neither mindless or without

limit. Some Jesus books were obviously unacceptable in proto-orthodox circles; their differences were simply too great. Those, such as *Gospel of Thomas*, that showed disdain for the Old Testament, and/or represented major innovations in belief that departed from what proto-orthodox circles regarded as apostolic tradition (e.g., distinguishing between creator deity and the true God), could not be accommodated. (Hurtado 2003, 584)

Hurtado is saying that proto-orthodoxy existed because a sense of what was orthodox existed. Much of what came to be rejected was already seen as problematic when it went public. Stated positively, Turner in his Oxford lectures says it this way (1954, 27): "The church's grasp on the religious facts was prior to any attempt to work them out into a coherent whole." Our tour has illustrated that it was not just the emergence of the fourfold gospel in the late second century that shows this, but the entire, traditionally oriented material of the first two centuries.

Underneath the entire dispute is a distinct revelatory claim from each side. I have called the "orthodox" or "proto-orthodox" view the "traditional" view. I give it the name "traditional" because of its emphasis on a deposit of teaching laid down and passed on through oral tradition, written text, and worship, often summarized for memory in short bursts of teaching. These elements exist in the writings accepted by these traditional groups. In addition, most of the teaching in the gospel texts used by this group are tied to Jesus in the context of His earthly ministry and present a teaching that is to be proclaimed openly in the world to anyone who will listen.

The alternative texts, for the most part, emphasize a secret teaching, often given by a risen heavenly Jesus that seems designed to trump the claims and ideas of more traditional views. These revelations express themselves in ways that are less countercultural than the traditional message, especially when it comes to sin, resurrection, and the nature of God (and the gods). This view also distanced itself clearly from the God of Israel's promise and from the writings tied to that God as Creator, showing its independent revelatory path. In fact, this distancing from the God of promise is one of the features that made this alternative movement so objectionable to the traditionalists. The central difference between early orthodoxy and other Christian movements surrounded competing views of God, something fundamental to anyone's religious construction of reality. It is no wonder contention arose.

Problem 3. The new school errs historically in claiming that there simply was variety in the first two centuries, with neither side possessing an implicit right to claim authority. The nature of early Christian worship, the inherently closer position of those who wrote from the traditional perspective, and the unity of the core elements indicate a movement with deep roots for the traditionally oriented texts.

Our tour has tried to show these differences in four key areas. A few works sit in between the ends of the spectrum, trying to reflect the alternative view but in a less contrastive way than some of its counterparts. This is where I would place *Thomas* and some of the works by the Valentinian school. They worked in the middle of this spectrum between orthodoxy and alternatives but in ways that show leanings to the alternative approach. This leaning, especially when it came to revelatory questions, explains why eventually they were associated with this side of the spectrum.

Ben Witherington, professor of New Testament at Asbury Theological Seminary, has given a short assessment of the new school. His objections sum up things well (2004, 114–15). (1) The claim that Gnostic Christians existed alongside orthodox Christians at the start of Christianity is "simply false." (2) Gnosticism was "not the first unorthodox belief on the block." The Marcionite heresy likely preceded it (not to mention the Ebionites). (3) "Yet another falsehood that revisionist historians espouse is that there was no core belief system in the first century that could later be called orthodoxy." Showing this falsehood has been a major burden of our tour. Each of our four topics surfaced core teaching. (4) The adoption of the Hebrew Scriptures as canon meant that Gnosticism would have never been recognized as a "legitimate development of the Christian faith." I agree. It is this and the view of the Creator God that were most important in the rejection of Gnosticism.

One question remains: Why does the new school take this tack? Witherington again makes an excellent summation (2004, 119). He speaks of their desire not only to rewrite Christian history but also to remake modern Christianity. He says, "This clarion call needs to be seen for what it is. It's not simply a rejection of the canonizing process and creedal orthodoxy but of the limits of first century Christian diversity in favor of a much broader and more pluralistic model. King calls us to reject our earliest historical sources, the New Testament, as the basis of defining the normative character of the Christian faith. It plays right into our culture's belief that 'the new is true.'" Our study should make it clear that whatever the new school is seeking to do with Christianity, it is neither historically sound nor is it a reflection of what Christianity has been for almost two millennia. As learned as many of these studies are when it comes to helping us with Gnostic sources (and they are excellent pieces of work at that level), they are even more seriously flawed when it comes to describing early Christianity.

CONCLUSION: WHO DESERVES THE MAKEOVER?

Orthodoxy is not the product of third-century theologians. Those theologians certainly developed and honed traditional teaching. They gave flesh to the bones and structure to the basic ideas. However, the core of ideas they worked with and reflected in their confessions can be found in the faith's earliest works. These works embraced what the apostles passed on. The works that we find in the New Testament also testify to this faith. That is why they were recognized as special sources for this teaching, even seen as being inspired by God. Irenaeus was not the creator of orthodoxy; he was created by it. The texts we have surveyed and the debates they reflect show us why someone such as Irenaeus eventually arose. They also explain why Irenaeus called alternative views "ropes of sand," while emphasizing that the church's basic teaching is about "God the Father and the Son" (*Against Heresies* 1.8.1; 1.10.1).

Nag Hammadi has much to teach us about early Christianity, but its value lies more beyond the first century than in it. Philip Jenkins, a professor of history and religious studies at Pennsylvania State University, speaks of new school efforts this way: "At least the ambitious recent attempts to rehabilitate the Gnostics are based on extensive writings of that sect, but Gnostics too can be fitted into the desired historical role only by ignoring a great deal of contrary evidence about the group's attitudes and world-view. In terms of their potential value for reconstructing the earliest Christianity, the ancient heresies are of strictly limited value" (Jenkins 2001, 205).

In other words, the rehabilitation of the Gnostics does not mean the reimaging of Christianity. A comprehensive look at the missing gospels and Gnostic teaching does not make them a light for the twenty-first century, despite the new school's recent claims. To regard them as such is an anachronism of the worst kind, doing immense damage to the Christian faith and to our culture's roots. Such reimaging is a distortion of Gnosticism, the Christian faith, and early Christian history. It deflects attention from our real need to accept responsibility for our actions before a Creator God. It also is a historical disservice to understanding a key faith of the West. Most important, it distorts the claims of a faith that aspires to better the human spirit before God by having humanity enter into a relationship with God in the context of forgiveness, graciously provided through Jesus Christ.

The most important claim of the new school—that the history of Christianity shows Christianity needs redefining—lacks historical grounding. What needs a makeover is not Christianity, but the new school.

STUDY QUESTIONS

1) Name the contributions of the new school.

2) What three problems exist for the new school?

3) What "linage advantage" do the traditional sources have that the alternative sources lack?

4) What did "orthodoxy" affirm in the first two centuries, and what did those early Christians not believe?

5) Is there a spectrum of views in the first two centuries, and which materials reflect a place on the borders between traditional and alternative views?

6) Why were these "borderline" texts eventually rejected by traditionalists?

7) Considered as a historical question, should the history of early Christianity be revised, and why is that question important?

• APPENDIX 1 •

LIST OF EXTANT
TEXTS BEYOND
THE FOUR GOSPELS

The following alphabetical list indexes the newly discovered texts where they are first introduced in our discussion. The Nag Hammadi collection has more works than those cited here, but I have discussed all the gospels found there (Robinson 2000 has a full listing of the fifty-two works).

I did not discuss a few other gospels we know about because they did not contribute to our study or they are so fragmentary that we cannot analyze them. For completeness, I note them now.

Initial reports on the *Gospel of Judas* became public in April, 2006. This gospel is likely from the mid- to late second century because of the description of Creation that reflects developed Gnosticism. This dating emerges from the claim that Sakla, a lesser god, created Adam and Eve and that Judas will emerge as associated with a thirteenth aeon. In fact, the bulk of the gospel details this developed Gnostic cosmology, something the initial publicity on this gospel largely ignored.

Formal date testing on the codex and the manuscript's ink verifies that this is a fourth century manuscript. It is written in Coptic. This is the same work Irenaeus (*Against Heresies*, Book 1, Chapter 31) described as a likely spurious work attributed to Tertullian (*Against All Heresies,* Chapter 2) and Epiphanius (*Panarion,* Section 3, Chapter 38, in the following subsections: 1.5, which cites Irenaeus; and 3.3–6, which gives independent detail along with 4.5–12; 5.1; 6.2; 7.1-6; and 8.1–5). It belongs to the Gnostic sect of the Cainites, who consistently rehabilitated individuals the Bible had rejected, figures such as Cain, the Sodomites, Esau, and Korah. This is a subset of Sethian Gnosticism, a movement that engaged in much reflection on creation and the status of aeons or light emanations from God. This newly released manuscript seeks to rehabilitate Judas.

This gospel has Jesus reportedly tell Judas to go do what he will do in order to fulfill God's will. It has Jesus note that Judas will be hated for generations but will rule over all who reject him one day. It characterizes Judas as Jesus' favorite, most trusted disciple. Judas understands that the One who sent Jesus is indescribable in words, a view comparable to what is said of Thomas's understanding of Jesus in the *Gospel of Thomas,* saying 13. Judas's betrayal is an inevitable act of God's plan for which the world should be grateful as his act frees Jesus' spirit but not his body to ascend. The gospel stands the normal view of Judas on its head.

According to Epiphanius, some Gnostic Cainites believed that Judas sought to betray Jesus because Judas knew that Jesus' death would destroy the other cosmic rulers, and by doing so, according to their movement, "Judas performed a good work for our salvation." In this way, Judas should be commended because release for Jesus and cosmic victory took place. Epiphanius rejects this explanation in emphatic terms and goes on to say that Judas's act was from ignorance, envy, and greed of the denial of God.

There is nothing historical in the *Gospel of Judas.* If Judas's act were so positive and Jesus had really commended him, then it cannot explain Judas's reaction to his own act in Matthew 27: 3–5 when he returned the blood money and committed suicide nor in Acts 1:18, which recounts his ignominious death. It also cannot explain how the entire earliest Christian tradition makes it clear that Peter had a major role among the disciples, that John was the beloved disciple, and that Judas receives no mention as a primary disciple anywhere else in the tradition. The *Gospel of Judas* teaches us about a second-century Gnostic group on the fringe of the Christian movement, adding detail to our understanding of the diversity of second-century Christianity. Anyone claiming it addresses the first century or attests to diversity is going beyond what the evidence of this gospel shows. For a brief overview on the contents of the *Gospel of Judas*, please visit www.thomasnelson.com/missinggospels.

Infancy gospels, including the *Protoevangelium of James*, the *Infancy Gospel of Thomas*, and the *Gospel of Pseudo-Matthew*, mostly add events to Jesus' infancy and childhood. They also often seek to elevate Mary's role or explain Jesus' power as a youth. Their goal is to exalt Jesus. These works range from the late second to sixth century. As such they do not impact the discussion of alternative Christianities in the early period but reflect the pious reflections of later generations.

We did not treat fragments of the gospels we possess (Klauck 2003, 22–35). These include *Papyrus Egerton 2*, *Papyrus Oxyrhynchus* 840, the *Strasbourg Coptic Papyrus*, the "Unknown Berlin Gospel," and a highly disputed "Secret Gospel of Mark." There is doubt about whether this last work is an ancient gospel at all. These works are too short in length to analyze.

Another gospel we did not discuss was the *Gospel of Nicodemus*, a work of piety that is a passion gospel and is also called the *Acts of Pilate*. Justin referred to tradition it reflects (*1 Apology* 21.24). Klauck (2003, 90–91) dates it to the early fourth century, too late for our study.

The *Epistula Apostolorum* is a mid-second-century document involving a series of questions and answers in the form of a letter to the apostles. It is a work of traditional piety as well, defending a physical Jesus and a material resurrection (Klauck 2003, 152–59).

This leaves three Jewish-Christian gospels, which are attested to and cited by church fathers but otherwise are unknown (Klauck 2003, 36–54). They are the *Gospel of the Hebrews* (cited by Clement of Alexandria and Origen), the *Gospel of the Nazareans* (noted by Eusebius), and the *Gospel of the Ebionites* (noted by Epiphanius). The *Gospel of the Hebrews* was regarded as a work of tradition but not as canon. *Nazareans* has a variant version of the parable of the talents. Other pieces noted by church fathers, like Jerome, are sometimes tied to this gospel. It possibly comes from the mid-second century and is another piece of traditional piety. *Ebionites* seems to have been an attempt at a gospel harmony that lacked an infancy account and genealogies. Its treatment of Jesus' baptism has adoptionistic and docetic views that made it questionable to later writers. These materials are so fragmentary that not much can be made of them.

ALPHABETICAL LIST OF EXTANT TEXTS

• APPENDIX 2 •

LIST OF KEY TEXTS IN THE APOSTOLIC FATHERS

This lists the key passages on our four themes. All these works belong to the late first or early second century. The page numbers for the texts noted in the main treatment of our themes are included in this list.

1 Clement

7:2–5 (importance of tradition)

16:4–7 (citation of Isaiah 53 on Jesus' death) 191

16:13–14 (Jesus' work and death) 191

19:2–3 (God as Creator) 89

20:11–12 (God as Creator) 89

26:3 (resurrection and the flesh) 157

27:4 (God as Creator) 89

32:4 (how Jesus saves)

33:2–4 (God as Creator) 89, 90

36:1–2 (salvation) 121, 191

37:5 (the image and example of the body as a picture of the church)

42:1–4 (the roots of tradition) 204

47:1–2 (Paul's connection to the gospel)

BIBLIOGRAPHY

The indispensable bibliographical tools for serious students of Gnosticism in general, and of the Nag Hammadi texts in particular, are David M. Scholer's *Nag Hammadi Bibliography 1948–1969* (Leiden: Brill, 1971); his *Nag Hammadi Bibliography 1970–1994* (Leiden: Brill, 1997); and his annual supplements in *Novum Testamentum*.

Altendorf, Hans-Dietrich. 1969. "Zum Stichwort: Rechtgläbigkeit und Ketzerei im ältesten Christentum," *Zeitschrift für Kirchengeschichte* 80: 61–74.

Bauer, Walter. 1964. *Orthodoxy and Heresy in Earliest Christianity*. The New Testament Library. 1971 translation of the 1964 German 2nd edition. Ed. Robert A. Kraft and Gerhard Krodel. London: SCM Press.

Baum, Armin Daniel. 2001. *Pseudepigraphie und literarische Fälschung im frühen Christentum*. Wissenschaftliche Untersuchungen zum Neuen Testament 2. Reihe 138. Tübingen: Mohr Siebeck.

Beyschlag, Karlmann. 1974. *Simon Magus und die christliche Gnosis*. Wissenschaftliche Untersuchungen zum Neuen Testament 16. Tübingen: Mohr Siebeck.

Bock, Darrell L. 1996. *Luke 9:51–24:53*. Baker Exegetical Commentary on the New Testament 3b. Grand Rapids: Baker.

———. 2002. *Studying the Historical Jesus: A Guide to Methods and Sources*. Grand Rapids: Baker.

———. 2002b. *Jesus According to Scripture: Restoring the Portrait from the Gospels*. Grand Rapids: Baker.

————. 2004. *Breaking the Da Vinci Code: Answers to the Questions Everyone's Asking.* Nashville: Thomas Nelson.

Brown, Raymond. 1994. *The Death of the Messiah.* 2 vols. New York: Doubleday.

Colpe, Carsten. 1961. *Die religionsgeschichtliche Schule: Darstellung und Kritik ihres Bildes vom gnostischen Erlösungsmythus.* Forschungen zur Religion und Literatur des Alten und Neuen Testaments 78. Göttingen: Vandenhoeck & Ruprecht.

Coxe, A. Cleveland, ed. 1867. *The Ante-Nicene Fathers: Translations of the Writings of the Fathers Down to A.D. 325.* Vol. 1. Ed. Alexander Roberts and James Donaldson. 1974 reprint of 1886 edition. Grand Rapids: Eerdmans.

Davids, Adelbert. 1973. "Irrtum und Häresie. I Clem.—Ignatius von Antiochen—Justinus." *Kairos* 15:165–87.

Desjardins, Michael. 1991. "Bauer and Beyond: On Recent Scholarly Discussions of *Hairesis* in the Early Christian Era." *Second Century* 8:65–82.

Dunn, James D. G. 2003. *Jesus Remembered.* Vol. 1 of *Christianity in the Making.* Grand Rapids: Eerdmans.

Ehrman, Bart D. 2003. *Lost Christianities: The Battles for Scripture and the Faiths We Never Knew.* Oxford: Oxford University Press.

Fitzmyer, Joseph A. 1981, 1985. *The Gospel According to Luke.* 2 vols. Anchor Bible. Garden City, NY: Doubleday.

Franzmann, Majella. 1996. *Jesus in the Nag Hammadi Writings.* London: T & T Clark.

Grant, Robert M. 1970. *Augustus to Constantine: The Rise and Triumph of Christianity in the Roman World.* Reprint, Louisville: John Knox Westminster, 2004.

Haenchen, Ernst, Martin Krause, Werner Foerster, Kurt Rudolf, Jes Peter Asmussen, and Alexander Böhlig. 1997. *Die Gnosis: Zeugnisse der Kirchenvüater, Koptische und mandaische Quellen, Der Manichäismus.* 3 vols. Düsseldorf: Artemis and Winkler. (Orig. pub. 1943–44.)

Harnack, Adolf. 1893. *History of Dogma.* Vol. 1. 3rd ed. Trans. Neil Buchanan. Reprint, Eugene, OR: Wipf and Stock, 1997.

————. 1908. "Rezension über: Wilhelm Bousset, *Hauptproblem der Gnosis.*" *Theologische Literaturzeitung,* pp. 10–13.

Harrington, D. J. 1980. "The Reception of Walter Bauer's *Orthodoxy and Heresy in Early Christianity.*" *Harvard Theological Review* 73:289–98.

Hedrick, Charles W. 1989–90. "Thomas and the Synoptics: Aiming at a Consensus." *Second Century* 7:39–56.

Hedrick, Charles W., and Paul W. Mirecki. 1999. *Gospel of the Savior: A New Ancient Gospel.* California Classical Library. Santa Rosa, CA: Polebridge Press.

Hengel, Martin. 1985. *Studies in the Gospel of Mark.* Philadelphia: Fortress.

———. 1997. "Der Ursprünge der Gnosis und das Urchristentum." In *Evangelium, Schriftauslegung, Kirche: Festschrift für Peter Stuhlmacher zum 65. Geburtstag,* 190–223. Göttingen: Vandenhoeck & Ruprecht.

———. 2000. *The Four Gospels and the One Gospel of Jesus Christ.* Harrisburg, PA: Trinity Press International.

———. 2001. "Das Begräbnis Jesu bei Paulus und die leibliche Auferstehung aus dem Grabe." In *Auferstehung–Resurrection,* 119–83. Eds. Friedrich Avemarie and Hermann Lichtenberger. Wissenschaftliche Untersuchungen zum Neuen Testament 135. Tübingen: Mohr Siebeck.

Henry, Patrick G. 1992. "Why Is Contemporary Scholarship So Enamored of Ancient Heretics?" *Epiphany* 12:63–67.

Hilgenfeld, Adolf. 1884. *Die Ketzergeschichte des Urchristentums.* Reprint, Darmstadt: Wissenschaftliche Buchgesellschaft, 1966.

Hoffman, Daniel L. 1995. *The Status of Women and Gnosticism in Irenaeus and Tertullian.* Studies in Women and Religion 36. Lewiston, NY: Edwin Mellen Press.

Holmes, Michael, ed. 1999. *The Apostolic Fathers: Greek Texts and Translations.* Grand Rapids: Baker.

Hultgren, Arland J. 1994. *The Rise of Normative Christianity.* Minneapolis: Fortress.

Hultgren, Arland J., and Steven Haggmark. 1996. *The Earliest Christian Heretics: Readings from Their Opponents.* Minneapolis: Fortress.

Hurtado, Larry. 2003. *Lord Jesus Christ: Devotion to Jesus in Earliest Christianity.* Grand Rapids: Eerdmans.

James, M. R. 1924. *The Apocryphal New Testament.* Oxford: Clarendon.

Jenkins, Philip. 2001. *The Hidden Gospels: How the Search for Jesus Lost Its Way.* Oxford: Oxford University Press.

Kelly, J. N. D. 1978. *Early Christian Doctrines.* 5th ed. San Francisco: HarperSanFrancisco.

King, Karen L. 2003a. *What Is Gnosticism?* Cambridge, MA: Harvard University Press.

————. 2003b. *The Gospel of Mary Magdala: Jesus and the First Woman Apostle.* Santa Rosa, CA: Polebridge Press.

Klauck, Hans-Josef. 2000. *The Religious Context of Early Christianity: A Guide to Greco-Roman Religions.* Studies of the New Testament and Its World. Trans. Brian McNeil. Edinburgh: T & T Clark.

————. 2003. *Apocryphal Gospels: An Introduction.* Trans. Brian McNeil. London: T & T Clark.

Koester, Helmut. 1965. "ΓΝΩΜΑΙ ΔΙΑΦΟΡΟΙ: The Origin and Nature of Diversification in the History of Early Christianity." *Harvard Theological Review* 58:279–318.

————. 1990. *Ancient Christian Gospels: Their History and Development.* Philadelphia: Trinity Press International.

Lampe, Peter. 1989. *Die Stadtrömischen Christen in den ersten beiden Jahrhunderten.* Wissenschaftlichen Untersuchungen zum Neuen Testament 2.18. Tübingen: Mohr Siebeck.

Langerbeck, Hermann. 1967. *Aufsätze zur Gnosis.* Ed. Hermann Dörries. Göttingen: Vandenhoeck & Ruprecht.

Lapham, Fred. 2003. *An Introduction to the New Testament Apocrypha.* London: T & T Clark.

Layton, Bentley. 1995. "Prolegomena to the Study of Ancient Gnosticism." In *The Social World of the First Christians: Essays in Honor of Wayne A. Meeks,* 334–50. Ed. L. Michael White and O. Larry Yarbrough. Minneapolis: Fortress.

Logan, Alastair H. B. 1996. *Gnostic Truth and Christian Heresy: A Study of the History of Gnosticism.* Edinburgh: T & T Clark.

Löhr, Winrich A. 1996. *Basilides und seine Schule: Eine Studie zur Theologie- und Kirchengeschichte des zweitens Jahrhunderts.* Wissenschaftliche Untersuchungen zum Neuen Testament 83. Tübingen: Mohr Siebeck.

Markschies, Christoph. 2003. *Gnosis: An Introduction.* Trans. John Bowden. London: T & T Clark.

Marshall, I. H. 1976. "Orthodoxy and Heresy in Earliest Christianity." *Themelios* 2:5–14.

McCue, James F. 1979. "Orthodoxy and Heresy: Walter Bauer and the Valentinians." *Vigiliae Christianae* 33:118–30.

McVey, Kathleen. 1981. "Gnosticism, Feminism, and Elaine Pagels." *Theology Today* 37:498–501.

Meyer, Marvin. 2003. *Secret Gospels: Essays on Thomas and the Secret Gospel of Mark.* Harrisburg, PA: Trinity Press International.

Mitros, Joseph F. 1968. "The Norm of Faith in the Patristic Age." *Theological Studies* 29:444–71.

National Geographic. 2006. *Gospel of Judas.* Washington, DC: National Geographic Society.

Nilsson, M. P. 1960. *Opuscula Selecta: Linguis Anglica, Francogallica, Germanica Conscripta.* Vol. 3. Lund: C W K Gleerup.

Nordsieck, Reinhard. 2004. *Das Thomas-Evangelium: Einleitung—Zur Frage des historischen Jesus—Kommentierung aller 114 Logein.* 2nd ed. Neukirchen-Vluyn: Neukirchener.

Norris, Frederick W. 1976. "Ignatius, Polycarp, and 1 Clement: Walter Bauer Reconsidered." *Vigiliae Christianae* 30:23–44.

Pagels, Elaine. 1974. "Conflicting Versions of Valentinian Eschatology: Irenaeus' Treatise Vs. the Excerpts from Theodotus." *Harvard Theological Review* 67:35–53.

———. 1979. *The Gnostic Gospels.* New York: Random House.

———. 2003. *Beyond Belief: The Secret Gospel of Thomas.* New York: Random House.

Pearson, B. A., ed. 1990. "Introduction." In *Gnosticism, Judaism, and Egyptian Christianity,* 1–9. Studies in Antiquity and Christianity. Minneapolis: Fortress.

Pearson, Birger A. 2004. *Gnosticism and Christianity in Roman and Coptic Egypt.* Studies in Antiquity and Christianity. London: T & T Clark.

Pearson, Birger A., and James E. Goehring, eds. 1986. *The Roots of Egyptian Christianity.* Studies in Antiquity and Christianity. Philadelphia: Fortress.

Pelikan, Jaroslav. 1971. *The Christian Tradition: A History of the Development of Doctrine: The Emergence of the Catholic Tradition (100–600).* Chicago: University of Chicago Press.

Perrin, Nicolas. 2002. *Thomas and Tatian: The Relationship Between the Gospel of Thomas and the Diatessaron.* Academia Biblica 5. Leiden: Brill.

Petrément, Simone. 1984. *A Separate God: The Origins and Teachings of Gnosticism.* Trans. Carole Harrison. 1990 translation of the 1984 edition. San Francisco: HarperSanFrancisco.

Prümm, Karl. 1972. *Gnosis an der Wurzel des Christentums? Grundlagenkritik an der Entmythologisierung.* Müller: Salzburg.

Rebell, Walter. 1992. *Neutestamentliche Apokryphon und Apostolische Väter.* Munich: Chr. Kaiser.

Roberts, Colin H. 1977. *Manuscripts, Society, and Belief in Early Christian Egypt.* London: Oxford University Press.

Robinson, James M. 1982. "Jesus from Easter to Valentinus (or to the Apostles' Creed)." *Journal of Biblical Literature* 101:5–37.

———, ed. 1990. *The Nag Hammadi Library in English.* 3rd ed. San Francisco: Harper & Row.

———, ed. 2000. *The Coptic Gnostic Library: A Complete Edition of the Nag Hammadi Codices.* 5 vols. Leiden: Brill. (Orig. pub. 1975–95, a 14-vol. ed.)

Robinson, James M., and Helmut Koester. 1971. *Trajectories Through Early Christianity.* Philadelphia: Fortress.

Robinson, Thomas A. 1988. *The Bauer Thesis Examined: The Geography of Heresy in the Early Christian Church.* Studies in the Bible and Early Christianity 11. Lewiston, NY: Edwin Mellen.

Rudolph, Kurt, ed. 1975. *Gnosis und Gnostizismus.* Wege der Forschung, Band CCLXII. Darmstadt: Wissenschaftliche Buchgesellschaft.

———. 1983. *Gnosis: The Nature and History of Gnosticism.* Trans. Robert McLachlan Wilson. Edinburgh: T & T Clark.

Segal, Alan F. 1977. *Two Powers in Heaven: Early Rabbinic Reports About Christianity and Gnosticism.* Reprint, Leiden: Brill, 2002.

Smith, Carl, II. 2004. *No Longer Jews: The Search for Gnostic Origins.* Peabody, MA: Hendrickson.

Snodgrass, Klyne. 1989–90. "The Gospel of Thomas: A Secondary Gospel." *Second Century* 7:19–38.

Stewart, Zeph, ed. 1972. *Arthur Darby Nock: Essays on Religion and the Ancient World.* 2 vols. Oxford: Clarendon Press.

Taylor, Vincent. 1966. *The Gospel According to St. Mark: The Greek Text with Introduction, Notes, and Indexes.* 2nd ed. London: Macmillan.

Turner, H. E. W. 1954. *The Pattern of Christian Truth: A Study of the Relations Between Orthodoxy and Heresy in the Early Church.* Bampton Lectures 1954. London: Mowbray.

White, L. Michael. 2004. *From Jesus to Christianity: How Four Generations of Visionaries & Storytellers Created the New Testament and Christian Faith.* San Francisco: HarperSanFrancisco.

Wilken, Robert L. 1981. "Diversity and Unity in Early Christianity." *Second Century* 1:101–10.

Williams, Michael A. 1996. *Rethinking "Gnosticism": An Argument for Dismantling a Dubious Category.* Princeton, NJ: Princeton University Press.

Wilson, R. McL. 1968. *Gnosis and the New Testament.* Oxford: Basil Blackwell.

Wisse, Frederik. 1971. "The Nag Hammadi Library and the Heresiologists." *Vigiliae Christianae* 25:205–33.

Witherington, Ben, III. 2004. *The Gospel Code: Novel Claims About Jesus, Mary Magdalene, and Da Vinci.* Downers Grove, IL: InterVarsity Press.

Wright, N. T. 2003. *The Resurrection of the Son of God: Christian Origins and the Question of God.* Vol. 3. Minneapolis: Fortress.

Yamauchi, Edwin M. 1983. *Pre-Christian Gnosticism: A Survey of the Proposed Evidences.* 2nd ed. Reprint, Eugene, OR: Wipf and Stock, 2003.

———. 1997. "The Issue of Pre-Christian Gnosticism Reviewed in the Light of the Nag Hammadi Texts." In *The Nag Hammadi Library After Fifty Years: Proceedings of the 1995 Society of Biblical Literature Commemoration,* 72–88. Ed. John D. Turner and Anne McGuire. Leiden: Brill.